THE ADVISOR'S GUIDE TO
Money Psychology

Taking the fear out of financial decision-making

BY OLIVIA MELLAN
WITH SHERRY CHRISTIE

IA
INVESTMENT
ADVISOR
PRESS

Shrewsbury, New Jersey

THE ADVISOR'S GUIDE TO MONEY PSYCHOLOGY. Copyright © 2002 by Olivia Mellan & Associates. All rights reserved. No part of this book may be used or reproduced in any manner whatsoever withour written permission, except in the case of brief quotations embodied in critical articles and reviews. For information, write Investment Advisor Press, 3 Revmont Drive, Shrewsbury, NJ 07702.

Book design: Jeff Brown and Dorothy O'Connor Jones

Printed in the United States of America.

ISBN 1-878604-42-2

Investment Advisor Press books may be published for educational, business, or sales promotional use. For information, write Investment Advisor Press, 3 Revmont Drive, Shrewsbury, NJ 07702.

To my husband Michael, my first and foremost money mentor; my son Aniel, whose relationship with money is starting out a lot better than mine did; and all the therapeutic financial advisors who began as colleagues and ended up as friends.
— *Olivia Mellan*

To Harry, who always understands; and Carey, sine qua non.
— *Sherry Christie*

Contents

ACKNOWLEDGMENTS vii
INTRODUCTION ix

SECTION 1–YOUR CLIENTS

BUILDING RELATIONSHIPS 3
   Getting Off on the Right Foot 6
   Learning to Listen 14
   Encouraging Change 20
   Moving Clients to Action 26
   Dealing with Difficult Clients 32
   Restless Relationships 44

DEALING WITH DIFFERENCES 49
   Money Personalities 51
   Caveat Gender 69
   Coming from Different Places 83

FAMILY MATTERS 89
   Couples Conflict 91
   Children of All Ages 103
   Issues of Aging 119
   Family Business 128

STRESS AND TRAUMA .135
   9/11 137
   Sudden Wealth 146
   Financial Loss 154
   Personal Loss 166

SECTION II–MORE THAN MONEY 171
    Intrinsic Values 175
    Charitable Giving 180
    Walking Your Talk 188

SECTION III–YOUR PRACTICE 197
    Coping with Change 201
    Preventing Burnout 209
    Relationships with Colleagues 217
    Getting Support 229

AFTERWORD 237
ADDITIONAL RESOURCES 239

Acknowledgments

It's always hard to know where to start in thanking the folks who support me in my work and in my life; those who inspire me and help me keep evolving both personally and professionally.

Thanks to all the therapeutic financial planners and advisors who have made me feel partnered in my work with individuals and couples and in my speaker career. To John Cammack, and others at Alexandra Armstrong Associates, who brought my message to other planners in the early 1980's. Special thanks to Bob Clark, who believed strongly enough in the importance of money psychology for financial professionals to invite me to write for *Fee Advisor* and *Investment Advisor*. Deep appreciation to Peg Downey, and to Dave Drucker, Susan Freed, Candi Kaplan, Mary Malgoire, and Dick Vodra for their expertise, support and ultimately, for their friendship. Thanks, as well, to Bob Veres, whose prophetic voice inspires my creativity and keeps me laughing at his sharp wit while I'm learning from his view of trends and changes in the planning profession.

To other believers in the therapeutic value of exploring folks' relationship to money: Victoria Collins, Arlene Matthews, Judy Barber, Marty Carter, Anne Slepian and Christopher Mogil, and other kindred spirits who remind me that I'm not alone in my principles and my commitment to help individuals and couples reach what I call money harmony.

I appreciate the wonderful women I met when I was traveling across the country giving speeches to women about money and empowerment: Eileen Michaels, Barbara Stanny, Karen Sheridan, Deborah Owens, Pamela Ayo Yetunde, Karen Ramsey, Sue Vanderlinden and Joan Coullahan. Daria Dolan, meanwhile, is partnering with me in my work around women and money, and Margo Geller has joined with me to spread the word about the possibilities of integrating counseling skills into the offices of financial advisors.

Thanks to all the financial planning organizations, banks, insurance companies, and stockbrokers who affirmed the principles and techniques of money psychology and invited me to present to their staff and clients. And of course, thanks to all the clients who remind me why I still continue do this work in money coaching and money therapy.

To the wonderful folks at Walker & Company: George Gibson, Jackie Johnson, and all who cheered me on when I wrote *Money Harmony*, *Overcoming Overspending*, and *Money Shy to Money Sure* for them, and who encouraged me to widen my focus to financial advisors and their clients in writing this book for Investment Advisor Press.

I couldn't feel more appreciative about my fabulous editor, Jamie Green, and William Glasgall, *Investment Advisor's* editorial director. Working with them both has been a total pleasure, and I count my blessings for their warmth and support. Since 1996, my "work marriage" with my personal editor and co-author, Sherry Christie, has been a partnership which I continue to marvel about in contemplating the richness and effortlessness of our collaboration. Enhancing my understanding of psychology with her knowledge of money and investing, she often amazes me by translating my thoughts more clearly than I can myself.

Since I write a fair amount about the importance of cultivating your own sources of support and nourishment, I feel so grateful to my own network of nurturing, the members of the Washington Therapy Guild, my "work family" with whom I've shared my therapist work life since the mid-1970s. I feel gratitude, as well, to my close friends, who help me "walk my talk" and remind me of the precious value of heart connections. And finally, thanks to my own supportive family: my husband, Michael Shapiro, a model of rationality around money matters and my "guru of rest;" my loving son, Aniel, who's more frugal than his mom ever was; and my sons Scott and Bennett, who continue to brighten my life as we all evolve toward money harmony—and other kinds of harmony as well.

Introduction

Have you ever presented a client with a comprehensive financial plan that you believe suits his needs perfectly, only to have him leave your office to "think about it" – and never get back to you?

How many times has a couple turned their consultation with you into a heated argument about whom to leave their money to, whether to pay for their kids' college education, or when and where to retire?

And how did you handle that normally sensible client who came into a big windfall, and suddenly developed wildly off-the-wall ideas about what to do with the money?

Most financial advisors are trained in rational skills such as asset allocation and risk management, not in dealing with client resistance or resolving marital squabbles. But unless you can connect with the emotional issues influencing your clients, many of them will never fully benefit from your financial expertise and decision-making skills.

I believe that a better understanding of money psychology can help you connect with all your clients on a deeper level. For years, in fact, I've encouraged financial advisors to become "therapeutic educators." The "educator" part of this term means helping clients learn how sensible financial planning can enable them to meet their life goals, while giving them enough information about investing and money management so that they can become full partners in decision-making and recognize whether you are serving them well. The "therapeutic" part enriches this role by combining it with an understanding of your clients' fears, anxieties, past traumas, and other life experiences that influence their decision-making.

As a therapeutic educator, you'll need to practice skills that counselors and therapists learn: to listen with compassion and empathy, and to build bridges between a client's irrational places and your greater objectivity that lead to better decisions. The rewards are great: not just in improved client rapport, retention, and referrals, but in the satisfaction of helping people achieve their most deeply felt hopes and dreams.

In *The Advisor's Guide to Money Psychology*, we'll explore a number of areas that will make it easier for you to understand your clients' deeper needs and desires – and your own as well. I'll answer questions like these:

- Why are so many people irrational about money?

- What steps in establishing a client relationship will promote good rapport and connection?
- How can you become more effective at listening, encouraging change, and motivating clients to make decisions?
- How do you know when to simply listen, when to urge clients to confront their own resistances, and when to suggest action steps?
- How can you deal more productively with particularly difficult clients?
- How can you quickly identify a client's money personality type to make your advice more effective?
- How can you use an understanding of your own money type(s) to build your ideal practice?
- What real differences between genders should you be aware of? How can you bridge the gulf between men and women with opposing views?
- How can you use Mellan's Law of Couples Polarization to help couples align their desires and goals?
- How can you help clients resolve painful generational conflicts?
- What do you need to know in handling stress in your clients' lives, and in your own? How can you promote healing from financial or personal losses?
- What does it take to build a practice that fulfills your needs, gives you support from knowledgeable colleagues, and helps prevent burnout?
- How can you build clients' loyalty by understanding their values and working sensitively with their emotional and spiritual yearnings?
- Finally, why is "walking your talk" important to enhance your own sense of purpose and meaning – and what do you need to do to get there?

I've been helping financial professionals take the fear out of their clients' decision-making for many years. When I opened my Washington, D.C., private practice in the 1970s, I specialized initially in women's issues, then in couples counseling, and finally in conflict resolution and business therapy. But in 1982, a colleague of mine, Michael Goldberg, made a simple observation that completely changed my focus. As we were discussing topics for a series of public workshops, he said, "You know, we should do them about money."

This struck me like a thunderbolt. For many people, money is indeed the last taboo. In everyday family life, it's often harder to talk about financial matters than sex or childhood trauma. When my clients' feelings about money came up in therapy sessions, it often felt as if ghosts of family members were sitting around the room. Some of these ghosts were my clients' and some were my own, but no one talked about who they were or what messages they were imparting to us.

These insights led to the first Money Harmony workshop in late 1982. Our primary message was that everyone has a lifelong relationship with money, much like a relationship with a person, that is either in balance or out of balance. If one's moneylife is out of balance, having more money will not solve the problem. People who are spenders will simply spend more, worriers will worry more, hoarders will stash more under a figurative mattress, and "money monks" will feel guiltier because they believe that money corrupts. In short, amassing more money can actually worsen the situation unless you achieve what we called "money harmony:" a relationship that is rational and balanced, where money is merely a tool to accomplish some of life's goals.

An article in The Washington Post led to magazine and radio interviews, and my first appearance on Oprah. Michael, who was not a therapist, soon moved on to other interests, but I found that creating a "safe space" to deal with and resolve money conflicts made a powerful difference to many of my clients. Pressing the "trigger" of money, and helping them explore their complicated relationships with it, offered opportunities for deep spiritual and emotional healing that led to greater self-esteem, inner security, and serenity. Before I knew it, money harmony work had taken over half of my therapy practice and two-thirds of my professional life.

Among those who attended one of the first Money Harmony workshops was financial planner John Cammack (then with Alexandra Armstrong Associates, now with T. Rowe Price). John found the workshop's messages tremendously useful. He told me, "Every financial professional should know about this, and use it to make their own work more effective with clients." His enthusiasm led to an invitation for me to speak at the International Association for Financial Planning national conference in New York City and subsequently at many other conferences – the beginning of fruitful relationships with many financial professionals like you.

Bob Clark, then editor of *Investment Advisor*, was another dedicated believer in the importance of financial advisors learning about money psychology. In 1995, he suggested that I write a monthly column on that topic for *IA*.

Now, seven years and nearly 100 "Psychology of Advice" columns later, we've come so far that there's even concern in some quarters about whether advisors (particularly those who do life planning) are crossing into the hazardous terrain of therapists, pastoral counselors, and other spiritual advisors. I feel strongly that you don't need to take on this task by yourself. If you fear opening wounds that you can't heal, team up with experienced helping professionals – a therapist, perhaps, or a priest, rabbi, or minister.

One of the few disappointments in my 20 years of money psychology work is that the financial planning industry has not incorporated therapeutic training more actively into their education and certification process. It seems clear to me that unless advisors learn some of these so-called softer skills, all the financial knowledge in the world will not enable them to truly connect with their clients and create relationships that stand the test of time.

Someday, a financial advisor's training will include in its core curriculum an understanding of money personality types, couples polarization patterns, and listening and empathy skills – knowledge that can help advisors guide their clients to act more wisely and productively. I eagerly look forward to that day, and hope that by applying the insights and tools you'll find in this book, you will help bring this goal that much closer.

SECTION 1

Your Clients

Building Relationships

I f you want to build strong client relationships, I believe the most important skill to cultivate isn't scientific asset allocation or an understanding of the equity risk premium—it's *listening*. Learn to listen to your clients' needs and concerns without judging them or imposing your own script on their agendas.

In this section of the book, you'll discover how empathetic listening skills can help you attract and retain clients, in conjunction with these ten tools and techniques of money psychology:

1. Asking the right questions. The most important first question is, of course, "Why are you here?" When you and the client both know the answer, it can lead to clearer expectations on both sides.

With some clients, you may have to read between the lines to find out the reasons for a consultation. Are they seeking reassurance for actions they've already taken? Hoping to find out whether they can retire earlier? Looking for an authority figure to help them control their spending, or get them moving on a financial plan?

Another key question is "Where do you want to be?" Encourage new clients to make a list of time-sensitive goals several times during the first month of the relationship. Goals that persist are ones they can trust to be more than momentary fantasies.

A third question I'd be sure to ask is "What kind of experiences have you had with other financial professionals?" This can help you identify challenges that may lie ahead. For example, clients who have been burned by untrustworthy advisors may carry their trauma and suspicion into your relationship. If so, you can lessen this distrust by addressing their concerns fully, openly, and patiently.

On the other hand, clients who used to work with a deeply trusted advisor may be hoping you will be an exact replica of him or her. In this case, see if you can blend some of the good qualities of this past working relationship into your own style, to help ease the client's transition into a new relationship with you.

A fourth useful question is "Tell me about your strengths and weaknesses when it comes to money." If clients struggle to come up with things they feel good about, begin by supporting their positive steps—such as consulting you. Clients who find it harder to list their weaknesses may be in denial to some extent, a tip-off that your role may involve helping them confront and resolve difficult issues.

2. Be sensitive to clients' money personality types. These initial questions will indicate whether a client tends to be a spender or a hoarder/saver, a worrier or an avoider, a risk taker or a risk avoider. You'll also be able to tell whether he or she obsesses about amassing more and more money, or believes that too much money corrupts (the view of "money monks"). With client couples, you'll see whether one is a "money merger," and the other a "money separatist." By understanding your clients' money types, you'll know where to focus your attention and how to speak sensitively to each client's needs. The Money Personalities chapter will suggest some ways to deal with style-related issues.

3. Know your own money type to understand your biases. Learning about your own money personality will help you determine which clients you most enjoy working with. If you're a hoarder, for instance, do you feel impatient with overspenders, or do you like to work with them because they're so different from you? If you're a recovering overspender, are you contemptuous of spenders who are not yet on the right track, or do you have the necessary compassion to help them? Self-awareness questions like these are useful in determining how to attract the types of clients you work best with and enjoy the most.

4. Practice timing and patience instead of rushing clients into action. As I mentioned earlier, it's essential to put your own agenda aside, listen to your clients, and empathize with them before trying to move them toward a decision. If you try to hurry them forward before their fears and concerns have been heard, you'll lose them.

5. Work with clients' emotional blocks and irrationalities. The most effective technique is generally to "go with the flow" instead of tackling a sensitive issue head-on. The best analogy comes from aikido and other martial arts, where instead of meeting a blow directly, you "embrace" the fist and dance with it until you can move it in the direction you want it to go.

For example, if a client has inherited unsuitable investments from a parent, don't slam head-first into the issue by criticizing the parent's judgment or the client's reluctance to sell the investments. Instead, try to enter their mindset and shape your argument to support their underlying needs and feelings. For example, you might say, "Your father obviously wanted to be sure his money would be here for you after his death. Considering the world he grew up in, it's understandable that he didn't feel comfortable trusting this legacy to the stock market. But things have changed a great deal since he was young, and you might consider what he would want you to do with it now...."

6. Defuse loaded issues. A corollary to working with clients' resistance is to defuse highly charged issues such as past money traumas, sudden wealth, sudden loss, gender conflicts, and negative family messages about money, success, work, and so on. Try to identify each client's "hot spots" so you can work with them more effectively.

7. Help clients learn more about money to enhance their self-image. Your task, as I see it, is to empower your clients to make better money decisions, not to serve as a surrogate parent or rescuer. Even though a savior's halo may feel good at the outset, it often blows up, toppling you from your pedestal and leaving you not just unappreciated but under attack.

As a therapeutic educator, you need to create a safe space so your clients can ask questions and learn from your expertise without feeling stupid or disrespected. The more knowledgeable they become, the more responsibility they will take for decision-making. Then, if and when their portfolio takes a downturn, they won't blame you for leading them astray but will solicit your help in turning things around again.

8. Know your own strengths and weaknesses. To offset criticism from clients who focus only on your flaws, acknowledge your strong points to yourself. Learn to build on these strengths in your work, and try to minimize the impact of your weaknesses. Ongoing help from supportive mentors or colleagues, as well as further training or reading, may be invaluable in helping you make your personal qualities more effective. Work on attracting and retaining the kind of clients you really enjoy dealing with.

9. Know when to refer clients to other professionals for help and support. Keep an up-to-date list of therapists, couples counselors, grief groups, Alzheimer support groups, and other referral sources, so you'll know where to refer a client whose issues are just too complex for you to handle.

One of the signs that referral may be appropriate is that you keep thinking about a particular client on weekends, or worry about him or her when you can't get to sleep. Your goal should be to develop client relationships that are balanced and forward-moving, so that when you leave the office you can re-energize yourself by fully focusing on your personal life, your health, and your sources of nurturing and creativity.

10. Build trust. I believe this priceless quality depends on three things. First, your clients know you're really concerned about their general well-being, not just doing a job. Second, they know you listen. Maybe you play back to them what they said or use other listening techniques; maybe you don't, but you definitely make sure they feel heard. Last, they know what to expect from you, starting with an explanation in the very first session of the way you propose to work with them. This clarity will help prevent misunderstandings, disappointments, and conflicts later on.

Caring and patience, empathetic listening and feedback, honesty and openness—these Golden Rule guidelines will help you build trust and solidity in your client relationships that enables them to stand the test of time.

BUILDING RELATIONSHIPS

Getting Off on the Right Foot

Starting out properly with new clients is crucial in building good relationships. In some cases, it may take a lot of sensitive listening to begin bridging the gap between what they say they want and what they may really need. Focus on their stated goals, and work patiently on gaining their trust until the time is right to help them broaden their horizons. Above all, take care not to push your agenda on them too soon or treat their anxieties and actions too lightly, or your expertise may be squandered before they're willing to benefit from it.

Once Burned....

My newest client seemed very guarded and uneasy at our first meeting. When I asked about his investment history, it came out that he had entrusted close to $100,000 to his wife's uncle for "can't-miss" stocks that imploded. I don't blame him for being somewhat gun-shy now, but how can I get him to trust me?

First, ask him about this past investment trauma. Probe for as many details as he is comfortable sharing (and you are comfortable taking time to hear). Allow him to vent his shock and fear. Empathize with how violated he must have felt when his trust was betrayed.

To move him slowly toward greater confidence, tell him about your own experience, your philosophy, your staff's training, and so on. Emphasize the professional differences between you and your wife's uncle, and encourage him to ask you questions about yourself and the way you work.

Once reassured that he's not in for a repeat performance, he may gradually begin to trust you and separate you from the investment "expert" who victimized him in the past.

Should a "New Kid" Contradict Trusted Advisors?

A new client of mine, an older man with a successful small business, recently told me his tax attorney has advised him to convert his traditional IRA to a Roth IRA. His accountant agreed. But after doing projections based on our interview, it seems to me that their estimates of his rate of return and retirement tax bracket are unrealistically high. Contrary to everything he's been hearing, a Roth conversion may not be a good choice for him. What's the best way to handle this delicate situation? The two "experts" are old family friends, and I'm the new kid on the block.

Consider asking your client's permission to communicate with his attorney and accountant. Then introduce yourself to them, and try to clarify what prompted them to recommend this course of action. Depending on how receptive they seem to be, you may want to share your own views with them. If they take issue with your opinion, assure them that you'll address their viewpoint as well as your own when you make your recommendation.

In your presentation to your client, discuss the "convert/don't convert" options with him in a fair, objective way that doesn't reflect badly on his other advisors' judgment. Once he understands the more complicated picture, it will be easier for him to make an appropriate decision. Whatever his choice, I believe he'll appreciate the fact that you didn't just go along with the conventional wisdom, but took time to research the matter more carefully with his best interests in mind.

Easing into Trust

My new client announced right off the bat that he just wants me to help make his portfolio grow; he's not at all interested in involving me in other aspects of his life. I'm convinced that if we take time to review his goals, dreams, and values, I could do a much better job of advising him. But when I suggested this in the first session, I almost lost him. What should I do?

A crucial part of good relationship-building is knowing when to push what you believe is the right agenda, and when to step back and go with the client's stated needs.

In this case, it's best to step back from your own agenda (it's always a good idea to enter a relationship with an open mind, anyway) and focus on giving your client what he wants. Once he begins to appreciate your expertise and has more confidence in you, you can gently suggest that he may benefit even more if you work together to plan where he will go from here. But save this proposal for later, once rapport has been solidly established.

How Far Should I Push a New Client?

A divorcee recently brought in a shopping bag full of maturing CDs which she wants to use to buy real estate or invest in a friend's business. I strongly feel she should put this money in an investment portfolio, but she's extremely averse to market risk. Can I educate her about intelligent risk-taking without seeming pushy or patronizing?

Yes, you can—but it will take both compassion and patience.

As a first step, you need to bond with this woman by exploring why she's so resistant to investing in stocks. What old messages are controlling her? How valid are they?

If you're truly sympathetic to her fears and not too impatient about rushing her through them, there's a good chance she will come to trust your recommendations. Encourage her to postpone investing in property or a business (which have risks of their own), while you coach her on asset allocation and other tools to reduce market risk. In the meantime, you might suggest an interim portfolio solution, such as Treasuries or a short-term bond fund. Just don't try to push her into action before her feelings and fears are aired fully, or she may bolt.

Being sensitive to a client's fears and worries is never patronizing when it is infused with real empathy. The more you can tune into her long-term needs and goals as you teach her about the financial markets, the more likely you are to help her take appropriate action with her money.

How Do You Gently Burst a Bubble?

In trying to plan for the future with a new client, I've discovered a big disconnect between her dreams and her life and values today. For example, she now rents a modest apartment, but her vision of retirement is to live in a custom home in an exclusive neighborhood and continue to travel, study, and go on spiritual retreats. She'll need at least $500,000 for the lifestyle she has in mind, but so far she's saved only $50,000. I'm a numbers guy. Without demoralizing her, how can I explain that her dreams may be unattainable?

I agree that it wouldn't be right to encourage her self-delusions. The key here is to be gentle and uncritical in exploring the discrepancy between her present lifestyle and her future goals. To help her think more objectively about this gap, ask her questions—not in a critical, challenging tone but in a curious, slightly puzzled way that invites clarification.

Suggest that she revisit her goals several times over two or three weeks, to see if they stay the same or change with her moods. If it's evident that she really does want a more lavish lifestyle, she needs to begin building her portfolio now, with whatever discipline that requires. Caution her about the tradeoffs—for example, she may not be able to afford long-term care insurance and may need to cut back on travel.

This can be an awkward conversation. If you're timid about helping this client to "get real," you might consider explaining that you probably aren't the best advisor for her, and refer her to a colleague who is empathetic and has stronger people skills.

As an advisor, you can help clients make sure their goals are in harmony with their values by examining what they want to achieve in light of their deeply held beliefs. But not everyone is ready for this kind of deep probing, and it's not your responsibility to force it down an unwilling client's throat.

Gracefully Saying, "Oops"

While I was taking a shower one morning, it occurred to me out of the blue that I'd misfigured part of a new client's financial statement. Unfortunately, I'd already put the darn thing in the mail, so I had to call and apologize. The client said it was okay, but judging by the tone of his voice, I doubt that I made a very good impression. What's the best way to handle a situation like this in the future?

First of all, I hope you're lucky enough from now on to catch any mistakes before they leave the office. (Maybe more showers would help?) In case you're not, I would do exactly what you did: contact the client immediately and apologize for the inaccuracy. If this has never happened to you before, I'd encourage you to mention that, too, so your client understands that you view this as a fluke.

To emphasize your commitment to prompt, accurate service, it's a good idea to send him the amended statement by messenger or overnight courier. Better yet, tell him you want to hand-carry it to his office or home so you can discuss it with him. Your traveling to him will underline your willingness to go the extra mile to serve him well. In addition, seeing him face to face will give you an opportunity to sound out and resolve any uncertainties he may have about you as a result of your goof.

During this meeting, don't dwell on your mistake—but don't pretend it never happened, either. I would suggest you begin with a comment that acknowledges your error but puts it in the past (for example, "I'm glad to know I caught this error before it could mislead you"). Allow the client to air his reaction, and then move on to discuss the statement as you normally would. Be sure to take the incorrect version with you when you leave and put it in your files, with a note describing how you handled the computational error.

This sterling service should go a long way toward persuading your client that you sincerely value his continued goodwill. Further, I think he will appreciate the swiftness with which you moved to correct the error, and realize that your honesty and professionalism make you someone he would like to continue working with.

The Buck Stops Here

In working up a financial plan for a client couple, a young planner I recently hired made several unrealistic assumptions. The result is that the couple believes their retirement portfolio should grow to well over $1 million when it's likely to be much less. I blame myself for giving this new hire too much latitude—but the key question now is how to salvage a valued client relationship.

With an error of this magnitude, I strongly recommend a face-to-face meeting. Invite your clients in for a consultation (at no charge to them, needless to say), explaining that you feel it's in their best interests to discuss the assumptions underlying their plan.

If the planner who made these errors will be continuing with your firm, he or she should also participate in the meeting. If you can honestly do so, present the issue as a difference of style and outlook, and ask the couple for their opinions about risk and return. When you amend the plan later they may value it even more, since it contains more direct input from them.

On the other hand, if the assumptions in the plan are really egregious (such as a 40% annual rate of return over the next 20 years), you may have to bite the bullet and say that a mistake was made. If you try to whitewash the error, you'll only increase the sense of distrust and insecurity this couple will feel upon learning that their retirement is much shakier financially than they thought.

If your clients are really upset, don't go overboard in putting all the blame on your employee. Whether or not you should have double-checked the work, they expect you to share the responsibility since you hired the planner in the first place.

The best thing you can do to make amends is to advise how they can make up the shortfall in their portfolio, so their retirement will be adequately funded. If you handle this well, you may be able to salvage the client relationship.

It may mollify this couple to be given the option of working directly with you in the future. If your workload just doesn't permit this, see if they would be willing to switch to a senior member of your staff instead. Or if you feel their confidence in you is seriously wavering, you might offer to refer them elsewhere. By showing how important their trust is to you, this may paradoxically reassure them that they'd do well to keep working with you.

Confronting Your Blind Spots

When I met with a new client several months ago, I forgot to ask whether she might need to be financially responsible for her parents in the future. (I may have blocked out this routine question because I'm currently dealing with my own father's lengthy illness.) From something a mutual acquaintance mentioned the other day, I'm now aware that she has a widowed mother who is not financially well off. This new information may well invalidate the plan I prepared for her. How should I handle this mistake? Should I level with her about the stress I'm under, to explain why I didn't ask her this important question?

Do you feel you can discuss your omission without bringing up why you got foggy about this issue? If not, I think it's okay to explain briefly about your father, as long as you're comfortable sharing this personal information and your client doesn't mind seeing you briefly step off your professional pedestal.

My own preference is to be as open about myself as the client is comfortable with, which I think facilitates trust and candor on both sides. However, you do have to be sensitive to the personality of the individual you're dealing with, as well as to your own comfort level.

As to rectifying your error, I would suggest telling this client that you realize your earlier discussion omitted an issue which could have a major impact on her financial plan. If she asks why you neglected to inquire about her parents before, it may give you an opener to disclose your personal problem in as brief and matter-of-fact a manner as possible. While you don't want to burden her with your feelings about your ailing father, your explanation that this may have affected your thinking will undoubtedly make sense to her.

If she has some compassion and empathy, there's a good chance she will continue to trust you and your expertise. This is all the more likely, I believe, if you promptly and professionally amend her plan to incorporate the missing information.

Egg on My Face

I've been trying to win the business of a client whose family has dealt with the same financial advisor for decades. After his first visit, I drew up a preliminary plan which the client then showed to this family advisor. The advisor pointed out mistakes that stemmed from my incomplete understanding of the conflicts in a business my client shares with his brother. Because the client didn't fill me in on this emotional subtext, I feel we share responsibility for the errors. What to do now?

If the client has come to you for some objective reason (for example, he's a retired Navy commander and you specialize in working with former military officers), you might consider calling the family advisor to introduce yourself, as long as the client is comfortable with this. Emphasizing that you both want the client to succeed, try to see what more you can find out about the issues and undercurrents in the family business. Even if the advisor is rude, condescending, or hurt that you are taking over his domain, the effort won't have cost you anything except a few minutes of unpleasant interaction.

In any event, you'll want to meet with your new client pronto to discuss how your lack of knowledge about the complexities of the family business led you to the wrong recommendations. I agree that you don't deserve all the blame for this. Try to find an empathetic way of saying to your client, "You probably found it hard to talk about this, but you didn't let me know that you and your brother were having such a hard time working together. Can we talk a little more about what that might mean for you financially?"

Though it's important to accept responsibility for your own imperfections, it's also crucial to forgive yourself for your shortcomings and stress-related lapses. Be willing to gently lay accountability back on your client if he or she has not been willing to fully disclose all the emotional overtones of a complex situation. Both internally and in your client relationships, it's vital for personal honesty to go hand in hand with personal forgiveness when you confront your errors and take action to correct them.

Biting Off More Than You Can Chew

A prospective client informed me that he needs an advisor who can organize and advise him on many aspects of his life—non-financial as well as financial. My background is in portfolio management, but I told him I was willing to learn new skills in order to get his business. However, the more research I do, the more I realize that I may have gotten in over my head. How should I handle this?

First, be honest with yourself. Do you want to expand into this new client's area of need because it really interests you, or is it just another potential source of revenue?

If you're not deep-down-passionate about helping clients in a holistic way, you might do better to focus on honing your expertise in your own specialized niche. To meet your client's other needs, put together a team of top specialists—estate planners, retirement planners, elder care experts, and so on—to address these complex subjects. This will allow you to pursue excellence in an area you do care deeply about, while positioning yourself as the conductor of your client's financial orchestra.

However, if you're truly interested in becoming a life planner whose responsibilities would encompass wider concerns like these, be aware that changing your professional focus will take time and effort—it's a process of evolution, not revolution. You can begin this journey by getting together with your team of experts and learning as much as you can from them. As your knowledge grows, you'll be able to advise clients more confidently about life planning issues and alternatives.

Unfunny Bunny

I have a client whose nonstop talking has been driving me crazy. Recently, I cracked a joke comparing her to the battery-powered bunny that keeps going and going and going. I hoped that by calling attention to her behavior in a humorous way, I might make her more aware of it and prompt her to stop. Instead, she now talks more incessantly than ever, and seems insulted by my every remark. What should I do now?

It's always risky to use humor to convey a message about behavior that's driving you nuts. Unless the recipient is very self-aware and has enough self-esteem not to feel threatened by your criticism, humor could sting enough to shut her down—or, by making her even more uncentered, intensify the behavior you dislike.

In your position, I would apologize for the hurtful remark. Explain that you were actually trying to avoid hurting her feelings, and confess that you would love it if she would slow down and breathe deeply so the two of you can discuss things in a calmer, more focused way. Suggest that you could be of greater assistance to her if you had more opportunities to address her questions and concerns.

I would also ask her if there's something about the meetings with you that makes her feel compelled to fill all the spaces in your conversation. By exploring this issue, you may not only help heal the rift, but gain some insight into what is fueling her behavior.

I Kid You Not

One of my newish clients is very nervous about the stock market, apparently as a result of past family experiences. After a few sessions, I thought our relationship was good enough to try getting him to lighten up. However, after my joking comment that his current situation and our economic climate aren't dire enough to make him want to jump out of a window, he spaced out and didn't listen to a word I was saying. What should I have done? And what do I do now?

When someone is as traumatized by the past as your client evidently was, lightness may be inappropriate for a long time.

In fact, you might forgo humor with this client entirely—unless he leads the way by being willing to joke about himself. Even then, I'd proceed carefully. People who are willing to mock their own attitudes about money and life may not be nearly as ready to hear you do the same.

As to what you could have done, I would first have discussed with him what actually happened to his family and the extent of their fears about the stock market, and empathized with him about what a painful emotional legacy he has inherited. Only after exploring this fully with you, probably over several sessions, would he have felt you understood him well enough to touch on the topic in a light, familiar way. He might then have been willing to accept your comment, relax, and agree to invest his money more aggressively to meet his goals.

Taking Action

To help ensure that relationships get off to a good start, listen and read between the lines to find out why new clients have really come to see you, and take time to develop real rapport. Ask about their past experience with other professionals to discover what emotional charge, if any, they are bringing into the relationship. The better you understand their situation, the easier it will be for you to treat them with respect and sympathy. Insensitivity to a client's inner pain and anxiety is a major reason why relationships get off on the wrong foot.

In particular, be wary of using humor with a client whom you don't know well. First ask yourself if you're hoping to help the client learn something that might aid him or her in making decisions. Are you trying to create a closer bond and more empathy between the two of you? Or is it a veiled attempt to vent some hostility, instead of sharing your feelings more straightforwardly? By examining your own motives along with the client's vulnerabilities and openness (or lack thereof), you'll know better when to joke about something, and when to deliver the message more directly and seriously.

BUILDING RELATIONSHIPS

Learning to Listen

Many of us live on the run—racing around from dawn to dark, talking on cell-phones while we drive, reading e-mails while we answer phone calls, and mentally reviewing all the other items on our to-do lists while trying to wrap up each client meeting as efficiently as possible.

In a culture that rewards fast action and doesn't value time spent in reflection and stillness, it's a challenge to make the time to listen until your clients feel safe enough to think rationally and take action. To slow down your internal clock, it may help to practice meditation, yoga, or Tai Chi, to go on long walks, sail, golf, garden, or otherwise slow down and smell the roses.

What's more, while you're learning to listen to your clients more deeply, empathetically, and respectfully, you'll probably find you're listening to yourself that way, too. This is truly time well spent.

Mirror, Mirror

A young widow whose husband was killed in a car crash has consulted me for financial planning help. But when we get together, all she wants to talk about are her emotions—her grief, fears, and so on. I'm pretty logical, not a touchy-feely type. How can I give her the financial advice she came for?

People feel jarred when they are given advice before they are through sharing their thoughts and feelings. My reading of this situation is that your client knows you have not listened fully to her, and therefore she is not ready to move on to accept your guidance.

To become a better listener, consider a simple but powerful "mirroring" technique taught by psychotherapist and author Harville Hendrix. Step one is simply to mirror what the other person has just said. Don't paraphrase it, just repeat it in a sympathetic, nonjudgmental tone of voice.

For example, if your client says, "I feel like I've been run over by a Mack truck," you would just say something like "Since your husband died so unexpectedly, you feel like you've been run over by a Mack truck." Then ask, "Did I hear you right?" and "Is there more?" If playing back her comments this way feels too artificial, you might wait until she's shared several thoughts and feelings and play back all of them, as closely as you remember them.

People tend to feel safe when they are respectfully heard. So I invite you to risk mirroring back what your clients are saying, then asking them, "Did I get it?" and "Is there more?" and see what happens.

Mirroring is the first part of an empathetic listening process that can be a powerful tool for healing. Read on to learn about other aspects of this method for bonding with clients and others in your life.

Validating Clients' Emotions

Several of my clients still seem so traumatized by the market's plunge that they're hesitant to make any portfolio decisions. I'm not having much luck calming them and reassuring them that I know what they feel. How can I get through to them?

You may not be "getting through" to them because they feel they haven't gotten through to you yet. I would begin by mirroring whatever they say to you about their emotional state. (See previous question.)

When you believe you have heard them fully, try validating their feelings by saying something like "That makes sense to me, considering what happened to you last year." If you feel you can't say, "That makes sense" because you believe they are reacting irrationally, keep asking them to help you understand. For example, you might say, "Can you tell me more about what happened to you and your money during the worst of times?" As they share more of their emotions and experiences, you may finally be able to tell them that their outlook makes sense in view of its context.

Helping clients feel heard and then validated builds a strong bond of trust between you and them. And once they feel heard "as they wish to be heard," they will be much better disposed to take action with their portfolio.

Mirroring, Validation, Empathy

I'm trying to work with a couple who are intensely angry and upset with one another about their different estate planning wishes. The wife wants to leave most of their wealth to their two children. The husband says that leaving the kids so much money will spoil them. He insists that most of their assets should go to an institution that nurtured him as a child. How can I help them resolve this dilemma?

I believe the key to success may be to make sure both parties feel you have listened to and fully heard them.

In working with this couple, I would tell them that you'll take a few minutes to hear them one at a time, until each spouse feels completely understood. The first step is to listen and mirror what each person says, carefully and respectfully. Once you repeat what that person has said, summarize everything and ask whether you heard them right. If the client says, "Yes, that's it exactly," then go to the next step. If not, ask, "Is there anything more?" Then play that new part back.

Right after the client agrees that you have heard correctly, validate what he or she has said. For the wife, this might mean saying something like "That makes sense, considering that you feel leaving a legacy for your kids is an important way of expressing your love." In the husband's case, you might say, "That makes sense, since you fear that giving too much money to your kids wouldn't be good for them, and you feel so grateful to this institution for giving you the tools to succeed in the world."

Now take the third step: making your respectful listening more empathetic. For instance, you might say to these conflicted clients, "I imagine you may be feeling a little sad, kind of hurt, and maybe even lonely at the gulf between your priorities." Ask whether that accurately describes their feelings. If they say, "No, I'm not feeling sad, I'm feeling angry," you can mirror that back to them, too.

Once you have mirrored each spouse's views with truly compassionate listening, they may well feel you have created a respectful and safe space that allows them to reach a win-win compromise. They may even be able to sit down with their kids, or write them a letter, explaining that the decision to leave some of the money to them and the rest to the cherished institution is a choice that both parents believe in.

Listen and Learn

I frequently give financial seminars to new investors. Generally, I'm very entertaining and lively, and have funny visuals. When I talk, no one leaves. But in recent months, I feel I'm not connecting with my audience. What should I do?

In these trying times, many speakers feel challenged to connect in new and deeper ways. We and our audiences are fighting anxieties that come from losing a sense of safety in the world (however illusory it may have been).

I suggest varying your presentation to build in many more learning modes that involve the audience and help them feel you are truly listening to their concerns about the future. Many people learn best through lectures, others through visuals. Still others prefer to talk in small groups about their personal insights and realizations, while some learn via kinesthetic "experiencing of the material in their bodies" through role-playing and similar techniques.

One simple practice is to ask questions that evoke audience response, and write down the exact words of participants' answers. People feel respected and heard when their words are mirrored and put into print for everyone else to see. You might also add an exercise where the audience breaks into groups of two or three people to talk about your learning points. Then reconvene all the participants to share what the individual groups have discovered or discussed. Build rapport by jotting down their words on the whiteboard or flip chart, verbatim if at all possible,. (Some people will feel corrected or invalidated if you change their words.)

Good luck in deepening your connection to your audience—and to yourself as well!

Hearing But Not Listening

I've always prided myself on listening carefully to my clients' goals and feelings. But lately, several clients in a row have failed to act on my recommendations for no good reason. What gives?

If they are all balking "for no good reason," it suggests to me that you have not really heard their deepest concerns and fears. Try practicing the mirroring technique I've explained above, playing back everything they say quite literally. Be sure to ask, "Is there more?" and wait patiently for the answer. You might even ask, "Is there an underlying concern or fear I've overlooked?"

In your body language, tone of voice, and facial expression, be careful not to communicate any desire to move along too quickly to closure and action. If you seem impatient, your clients will pick up on this and not feel safe enough to tell you all of what is going on. And until they do, they won't be ready to act on any of your recommendations, no matter how intelligent or appropriate.

Getting Past Old Messages

An acquaintance I keep running into at Rotary seems like an excellent prospect for my services—he's a senior executive whose last child just graduated from college. But when I casually brought up the stock market's performance to him, he said his family has only invested in real estate ever since an uncle went bankrupt in stocks in the '30s. I have an idea I can talk diversification until I'm blue in the face and never get to the root of this aversion of his. Any tips?

For every three or four people who have done very well in the bull market of the '90s, there's probably at least one holdout like this man, who was too intimidated by old family horror stories to venture any money on stocks. A surprising number of people are still influenced by family tales of financial tragedy during the Great Crash and the Depression. In this case, it sounds like your Rotary acquaintance feels he would be breaking with hallowed tradition by investing in the stock market, a real taboo in his family.

To help him move from the past into the present, I would suggest that the next time you get together with him (perhaps over lunch or a drink), you begin by taking some time to empathize with him about the effects of his family's past financial trauma. Allow him to air his fears about loss and poverty. Once you've validated these scars from decades past, you can gently point out some of the major differences between then and now. If he seems to respond well to this approach, you might invite him to visit you to discuss his financial concerns in more detail.

No matter how good your coaching is, his old fears are likely to revive during market setbacks. Respect and respond patiently to them, instead of plowing on obliviously to execute the next phase of your investment plan. If you're willing to take the time to listen to your client, you can help him learn to overcome the early programming that now limits his financial opportunities.

Restoring Trust

I've been talking with a couple whose former broker embezzled more than $80,000 from their account. Though he has been caught and is awaiting trial, they feel burned by the entire system. How can I help restore their trust?

People who come to you traumatized by dealings with dishonest professionals are like wounded children. They need to be healed before they can move, and they'll need your help to walk again before they can run.

So when you meet with them, take time to explore their hurt feelings. Listen to them as patiently as you can, and empathize with their shock, betrayal, and moral outrage. Then gradually differentiate yourself and your business methods from the way they were treated by their broker. Share information about your background, your experience, and your communication practices. Consider providing references from other clients or colleagues. You might also offer them a short-term agreement that would limit their risk if they don't feel comfortable with you.

Just remember that whether or not you deserve their distrust, it may flare up and be projected onto you. If you are patient in listening to their fears and feelings and reassuring them of your desire to serve their interests rather than your own, you may find you've earned the trust of two loyal and grateful clients.

Can I Be Held Liable for Listening?

I've always focused on tuning in to clients' values and needs in order to build stronger relationships with them. One of my colleagues says that by listening to my clients' feelings and giving them "therapeutic" homework assignments, I'm practicing therapy without a license. We chuckled over this, but then I started to worry. Is this really something to be concerned about?

I'm no lawyer, but my basic feeling is that if both you and your clients are comfortable with the relationships you've established, then you are providing an invaluable service to them and should continue to do so.

However, if you find you've begun worrying about them on weekends and losing sleep over the emotional issues you're helping them grapple with, you're in over your head. If so, consider referring them to therapists or counselors so you're not shouldering the burden of their psychological problems. (Some planners bring a therapist into client meetings, a team approach that I expect to become more prevalent in the future.)

But for heaven's sake, don't beat yourself up for being perceived as acting like a therapist. In fact, I'd consider this a high compliment. It probably means you're particularly well attuned to your clients' concerns.

Remember, you're not alone in your concerns. If you look around, you can always find balanced, nurturing colleagues willing to share the burden with you and help you think of creative ways to lessen your anxieties.

How'm I Doing?

After being cautioned about not talking down to my clients (men as well as women), I'm confused about whether I'm communicating well enough to build strong relationships with them. How can I get a good reading on this?

How about asking for feedback on how well they feel you hear them?

You could discuss this issue face to face with clients you know will be candid. But many others won't—so consider instead preparing a short questionnaire that all your clients can fill out and return to you anonymously.

Look at this as an opportunity to ask a variety of questions about your style. Find out if your clients feel you talk down to them, talk over their heads, push them to action before they're ready, let them procrastinate too much, force more risk on them than they're comfortable with, and so on. Or do they feel your approach and your timing are absolutely on target? By reviewing their written responses, you'll be able to spot patterns that will give you a better idea of your strengths and weaknesses.

This direct approach may make you feel uncomfortably vulnerable. But if you take on this task in the spirit of learning, I believe it can yield information that will help you fine-tune your listening skills and build even better client relationships.

Taking Action

These days, our beliefs in people's basic honesty and integrity, and in the value of our institutions and economic system, have been shaken. Take time to identify sources of faith, hope, and healing in your personal life, and anchor yourself in that positive place so you can take the necessary time to help clients heal from their own disillusionments and losses. By listening fully to their pain, anxiety, and disappointments and mirroring, validating, and empathizing with their feelings, you can finally urge them forward, helping them move beyond financial security to true serenity.

BUILDING RELATIONSHIPS
Encouraging Change

"She's a born worrier."

"He's a spendthrift—always has been, always will be!"

Most clients just do what comes naturally. But if they're acting against their own best interests, they may need to practice what isn't natural to them. For example, a major life-altering event (positive or negative) may call for a different money personality to develop or emerge. You can help clients learn to change by encouraging them to "practice the nonhabitual." Also described as "being where they ain't," this transformative principle is at the core of my money harmony work with individuals and couples over the last 20 years.

Here are some situations in which it could be wise for clients, colleagues, or even you yourself to change your coloring.

Gather Ye Roses

After reviewing a new client's financial situation, I realized she might well be broke within ten years. Recently widowed, she spends lavishly on her divorced daughter and grandchildren, paying for an expensive car, a trip to Europe, private schools, etc. When I advised her that she needed to be more frugal for the sake of her own financial security, she said life is short, and it's more important to make her family happy. How can I get through to her on this?

This is a common scenario for a certain kind of overspender. Giving—even overgiving—to their loved ones gives many women profound pleasure, helping them feel connected at the deepest level.

First, I would empathize with this client's need for connection to her remaining family after having lost her spouse—one of the most painful disconnections of all. Then, explain to her that the greatest gift she can give her daughter and grandchildren is to show her love for them in a way that doesn't threaten her own security.

Also point out to her (if you haven't already done so) that if she neglects to take care of herself, she may well become a financial burden on them later in life—which would not be a loving or giving thing to do. You might add that if she keeps indulging her grandchildren, they may grow up to be overspenders, incapable of managing money wisely.

To care for herself better, this addicted overgiver needs to practice the non-habitual in two ways. First, work with her to devise a spending plan to cut back what she spends on her family. (Stopping outright would be an intolerably "cold turkey" solution for her.) Second, help her think of creative ways to give to her family that don't compromise her own financial future.

If she's concerned that her daughter won't understand her changed behavior, you might suggest that all three of you get together. After explaining the situation gently, you can invite the daughter to help brainstorm ideas for family activities or treats that won't put so much stress on her mother's limited resources.

Dow Mania

A woman recently dragged her husband in to see me, complaining that his obsession with the stock market has been causing him to miss meals, lose sleep, and blow up at the kids over trivial matters. The last straw, she said, was when he took his family on a vacation and spent most of the time watching market news on TV in their motel room. He fumes about day-to-day dips, even though all his investments are for long-term goals. How can I help him get back into balance?

First of all, it's important to glean whether he's aware that he has a problem and needs to change. Listen to his perspective sympathetically, so he doesn't feel you've automatically allied yourself with his wife.

I imagine you've already showed him a comparison of short-term and long-term stock market volatility. If he understands the irrationality of getting upset about daily fluctuations and is willing to try moderating his habits, suggest that he take a three-day "vacation" from the market. Tell him you'll check in with him at that point to see how everything's going, and how his life feels in general.

If he resists "doing what doesn't come naturally," you'll need to work a little harder. He has to see, in some way, the price and perils of his addictive behavior. Appeal to his desire to have a good relationship with his wife, children, and others he comes into contact with. You might even ask him whether having more than enough money outweighs a quality relationship with his wife and great relationships with his kids. Help him think of ways to feel good about himself at less cost to himself and his intimates.

If he agrees to abide by a three-day respite from market news, you might suggest that he eventually expand this period to a week, or maybe even a month. This will allow him to recoup his energy, assess his portfolio from a calmer, less frantic place, and reevaluate the balance in his life from that same viewpoint.

Not Enough Money to Invest

I've suggested that my client let me invest a percentage of her substantial salary for her. So far, however, all she's given me is her last yearly bonus, complaining that she doesn't have any other money to spare. Yet she spends hundreds of dollars every week taking friends to lunch, collecting cute tchotchkes (each costing "almost nothing"), and buying gifts for others. How can I help her get her priorities straight?

This client is prone to what behavioral finance experts call "errors in mental accounting." Considering her salary to be spendable income, she obviously feels no qualms about spending it all. Bonuses and other windfalls, not being part of her regular paycheck, are mentally designated for saving and investing.

While applauding her decision to invest her bonus (which is, after all, much better than doing nothing), you can help her upgrade her accounting standards. She needs to understand that although her money may come out of different faucets, it all flows into the same pool of lifetime income. No matter where it comes from (salary, bonus, inheritance, etc.), some portion needs to be invested regularly for her future financial security. Automatic payroll deductions are by far the easiest way to ensure that this will happen.

However, be prepared for this client to resist any reduction in her disposable income if she has become addicted to overspending. Many spenders in denial piddle away enormous amounts of money on small things; but because no single choice looks lavish or unreasonable, they tell themselves that they are fine and that their spending is under control.

To make your client more conscious of how much she spends, suggest that she keep track of every expense, even the smallest, in a notebook carried with her at all times. If she adds to each recorded purchase a brief note of how she feels about it (e.g., "I needed this!" or "I felt lonely and thought I needed a treat"), she'll become more aware of her spending patterns and motivations. Help her recommit to her long-range goals and dreams (perhaps keeping a visual reminder in her wallet of what they are), so she can resist the urge to dribble away all her money on short-term, impulsive purchases.

An understanding of behavioral finance and its findings can help you free clients from this kind of self-defeating behavior. If you'd like to know more, see the Bibliography for some good references.

Serial Avoider

My 60-ish client has just parted from her second husband, and she wants me to be Number 3 (at least from the financial standpoint). She's never been involved in managing her money—one reason why Husband #1 was able to lose their savings in bad investments while #2 gambled away thousands of dollars on sports events. Being "no spring chicken," she says it's too late for her to start learning about financial matters. I'm not really comfortable letting her give me total responsibility, but isn't the customer always right?

While applauding your instincts, I must cluck disapprovingly at your client's belief. In addressing women's money conferences, I am reminded that women are never too old to change and adapt—and that nothing is better for their sense of self-respect and self-esteem. Women of all ages tell their stories at these conferences, including many older women who went to college late in life, got graduate degrees, learned about investing, overcame hardships, and found other ways to keep learning and growing.

In this particular situation, you might agree to automate some financial functions for your client, so you can be sure she continues moving toward her goals. However, I would gently insist on helping her educate herself little by little about money and investing, so she can eventually take a hand in making decisions about her assets.

Be specific about what you think she should learn. You might give her small tasks at the outset, such as balancing her checkbook. Also, try providing interesting financial articles or brochures, and asking her to discuss this material with you after she's read it. These assignments can help you track her progress.

Remind her that if anything happens to you, she might be left at the mercy of someone who is less trustworthy than you are. It's important that she learn enough about money matters to be sure her interests are well served by the money expert(s) she works with.

Adapting to the Unexpected

My client's 22-year-old son was recently in a serious car accident. Badly hurt, he has had to move back home and will need extensive ongoing therapy and possible surgeries. I've recommended that my client, who has always been an aggressive investor with a sizable margin loan balance, reposition his assets to better meet this financial challenge. However, he doesn't appreciate the need to begin investing more conservatively and is resisting changing his ways. How can I help him see that this shift makes good sense?

First, you need to understand that this change isn't as simple and logical for your client as it may seem to you. Risk-takers don't just love the thrills and chills that can lead to peak experiences; they actively hate alternatives that feel too safe. Low-risk choices bore them, depress them, even make them claustrophobic.

Like a diehard lottery player, your client may be fueled by thrilling fantasies of instant life transformation through instant wealth. Coming down to earth from this fantasy realm is never fun. In fact, it's often quite grueling.

Knowing this, you may need to take a little time to harmonize with his mindset. For example, you might say something like this: "I know this will feel uncomfortable to you, maybe even painful at first. But by moving to more conservative investments, you'll be able to take care of your son's and your family's needs with assurance."

Then step back to hear his reservations about making this change. If need be, remind him of the downside of risk (risk-takers never like to think of this part). If you're patient and firm, there's a good chance he will eventually move toward your sensible recommendations.

Father Knows Best

Whenever my middle-aged client comes to see me for financial advice, she brings her father. I feel uncomfortable with this since her best interest is not always the same as her father's, but she seems unable to cut the cord. Even when she does visit me by herself, she's quick to phone him to bring him up to date, and he calls back to make sure he understands and approves of what I've recommended. I suppose I should just keep my mouth shut and go along, but it doesn't feel right to me. What do you suggest?

I would invite this client to meet with you for a one-on-one discussion of how you can work together more effectively. Ask her gently if she is concerned that something bad will happen if she begins to make financial decisions on her own. If so, encourage her to tell you what those fears may be.

By learning about her anxieties, you may be able to address them rationally and help her overcome them. Explain some of the ways in which she and her father might have divergent self-interests, and be guided by her reactions.

This woman probably could benefit from seeing a therapist to help her individuate and become more healthily independent. While you can't provide this psychological counseling yourself, you can suggest ways she might educate herself financially. After all, her father won't be around forever, and if she doesn't wean herself away from his influence now, she'll be devastated and helpless once he's gone. So I'd encourage you to persevere, if you have the patience, to help empower this client to stand on her own two feet.

Unconventional Wisdom

So many new clients I see these days are convinced of truisms they've picked up here and there, like "We're married, so of course we want this account in both our names" or "Of course I'll retire at 65." Butting heads with conventional wisdom like this isn't a great way to start a relationship of trust. How can I tactfully help clients see that these "rules of life" may not necessarily apply to them?

You might point out that "truisms" are only generally true; they shouldn't be adopted unless they happen to be true in your clients' specific situation.

The issue of joint accounts is a good example. I often find that husbands lobby for putting all the money together, while wives secretly or not-so-secretly wish for money of their own. Keeping some money separate helps women protect their own separateness, countering their tendency to "overmerge" in a relationship. The high divorce rate, coupled with the post-divorce decline in the average woman's standard of living, also argues strongly that women need separate money to safeguard their security. That's one reason why I often recommend that newlywed couples merge only enough money to cover joint expenses and savings, while keeping the rest separate, at least until they know more about each other's money personality, history, strengths, and weaknesses.

Estate planning implications aside, you may want to use these arguments to debunk the truism that married couples should "of course" merge all their money. The real truth, I think, is that couples should manage their money in the way that best meets their individual needs.

The same holds true with the axiom about retiring at 65. These days, 65 is just another birthday—and not a very significant one to people who won't qualify for full Social Security benefits until age 66 or 67. Some folks will prefer to (and be able to) retire at 55 or 60; others may want to start gearing down in their 60s instead of stopping work completely. In reminding clients of the many options open to them, you'll need to probe beyond the "retire at 65" truism to see what they really want to do. Their own needs (and of course their financial preparedness) should determine their retirement timetable—not conventional wisdom.

Taking Action

When people change chronic, ingrained patterns that have been leading to dysfunctional behavior, they experience new choices, flexibility, creativity, and more intimacy in their relationships. In short, tremendous good can come from "doing what doesn't come naturally" (in moderation, of course).

In encouraging clients to change their old behavior, take care to communicate in an empathetic, respectful way. Remember that many of them will resist taking new actions, even if the change will ultimately feel good and lead to better results.

When you succeed in helping these clients progress from irrational reaction (or inaction) to wiser behavior, your relationship with them will also benefit. Instead of needing you to be their emotional nurse or policeman, they'll be free to partner with you more fully in creating a financial plan of action that will serve them well as they travel through life.

BUILDING RELATIONSHIPS

Moving Clients to Action

You made a wonderful presentation, replete with solid logic and clear action steps. The client said it was great.

Then nothing happened.

When clients are reluctant to act on a recommendation, set goals, or change bad habits, getting them off the dime sometimes requires creative thinking. But an idea that works like a charm with one person can backfire with the next. How do you know when (and how) to push, when it's better to back off for good, and when to bide your time and revisit the issue later? These case studies may help.

Where There's Life, There's Hope

How can I persuade my client to sell last year's losers? Even though he can use the tax write-off (he bought them at high prices before we started working together), he insists they'll climb back to nosebleed heights any day now.

When bad things happen, many of us persist in hoping and believing that they'll get better. This is fortunate for the survival of the human race, but it leads many investors to cling to a particular stock or mutual fund long after it has gone into the tank.

Since you don't hold out a lot of hope for these particular investments, the key to changing your client's behavior is figuring out why he won't go along with the opinion he's paying you for.

Risk-averse clients often hesitate to sell investments because what they own (good or bad) feels safer than buying something they're less familiar with. In other words, better the devil you know than the one you don't. If fears of this sort are paralyzing your client, try to explore them empathetically with him.

On the other hand, he may be suffering from the common malady of overconfidence in his own judgment. Most of us would like to believe that our investment choices, like the children of Lake Wobegon, are all above average. So even though he may rationally understand that there's no good reason to hold onto these investments, his self-esteem could prevent him from admitting that he made a mistake in the first place. Selling a "loser" may seem so personally humiliating that he would rather just hold on, close his eyes, and pray for a miracle.

After you find out the reason for his reluctance to sell, try to frame your suggested action in suitable terms. For example, if he's afraid of selling familiar old X and buying scary new Y, work on acclimating him to Y—its market, management, fundamentals, performance, and so on.

If he's reluctant to admit that he goofed in buying X to begin with, reassure him that at that time there were reasons why it was a sensible investment. However, things have changed since then, and now there are other reasons why it makes sense to sell (if only to free up money to invest in more likely winners).

With calm persistence, you have a good chance of persuading this client to join the ranks of investors who know when to hold 'em and when to fold 'em.

You Can Lead a Duck to Water...

Since I started working with this couple about six months ago, they've taken to the stock market like ducks to water. But it seems as though the more they learn, the harder it is for them to buy anything. Now that they know how big a difference stocks can make in their portfolio, why are they content to do nothing? And how can I get them moving?

These clients are almost certainly paralyzed by information overload. Never before has it been possible for ordinary investors to know so much so quickly, or to act or react in so many different ways.

This data glut can heighten people's fear of making mistakes, which is often linked to a perfectionist view of themselves. If your client couple have misidentified success with stocks as an indicator of their own self-worth, you may need to help them see that it ain't necessarily so.

Gently lead them away from overresearching and overanalyzing. Praise them for the excellent work they've done so far, and let them know that you recognize how much more they know now than when they began. Reassure them that they can make a fair amount of stock-picking "mistakes" and still have their portfolio do fine overall. And as they strive to become better investors, their most valuable lessons will come from these inevitable missteps.

Where you can really add value is in helping them separate the useless chaff from the information they need to build an appropriate portfolio. Point out that it isn't really investment behavior that will determine their success, but investor behavior—in other words, whether or not they get going.

This coaching may ease their investment paralysis, allowing you to outline a plan of action that moves them forward before they lose much more time.

Keep Off the Estate

My client badly needs better estate planning. His attorney, an old family friend, has developed a plan that I can see does not suit his needs. The problem is that my client is consulting me for retirement planning, and doesn't want me to address estate issues. He feels it's better to compartmentalize his advisors, instead of having all his eggs in one basket. Do you have any suggestions?

Before taking any action on this estate planning matter, make sure you have given your client what he asked for: a solid, workable retirement plan. Once you are confident that he trusts your expertise in this area, you can point out that the retirement plan should tie in with his estate planning goals. This would be the time to tactfully explain the weaknesses you see in his current estate plan, and suggest that you could fine-tune it so the two plans work together more effectively.

If he remains adamant about compartmentalizing the pieces of his financial life, you might recommend that he consult an estate planner you respect. This would resolve his "eggs in one basket" concern, while allowing you to make sure the two plans are well integrated.

However, he may feel obliged to stick with the attorney who drew up the original estate plan. If so, ask if you may contact the attorney to discuss how the two plans could mesh together better. But tread lightly, so your client doesn't feel you're horning in where you were not invited..

No Dreams

I think it's important to know a client's emotional needs and dreams before developing a financial plan. But one young professional just keeps saying that all he wants is to make lots of money over the next fifteen years. When I probe for more details, he clams up. How can I get him to be more open with me?

It's not unusual for men (and some women, too) to have trouble expressing their feelings, needs, and desires. Some people don't know what they want until they fail to get it, which can be a real tragedy when there's no time to regain lost ground.

So don't give up. Think of new ways to find out your client's fears, as well as his dreams or fantasies and unexplored areas of interest. While asking him questions, you might also suggest examples of other people's desires and fears, to see if he identifies with them.

To help him relax, consider telling him how you've been able to help other clients make their dreams come true and resolve their fears. If he's still blocked in spelling out his true goals as specifically as you'd like, why not give him a multiple-choice list of possible goals and fears, or positive and negative outcomes, and ask him to check the ones that resonate with him? (Give him the option of filling in entries of his own that might fit him more precisely.)

Keep pushing—but don't be pushy. You'll need patience, sensitivity, and fortitude when it comes to this crucial step in the planning process.

When Women Clients Pass the Buck

Throughout my professional life, I've been dedicated to educating other women about financial matters. But no matter how hard I work to coach them, many of my career-women clients ask to turn the decision-making over to me, saying they just don't have time to read prospectuses, reports, statements, and so on. I'm honored that they trust me to make choices that suit their objectives, but I really want them to partner me in making good decisions. Should I make a pest of myself by pushing them to stay involved?

Many women were raised to believe that with luck, somebody else would take care of this money thing for them. This old message is deeply ingrained and dies very slowly, regardless of conscious attempts to be liberated and independent. Liberation is a non-issue, of course, for some women who would rather feel secure and taken care of than self-sufficient. Many of us (maybe most of us) are a paradoxical combination of these two yearnings.

To handle your clients' similarly paradoxical mix of competence in the workplace and personal dependence on you, you need to be mindful of their general stress level. At the same time, whenever they slow down enough to listen (and it may be hard to find this window of opportunity with some of them), look for openings to gently suggest that they become more knowledgeable about specific aspects of good money management.

Remind them that you may not always be around, and suggest how much more secure they'll feel if they know enough to monitor whether any financial expert is truly meeting their needs. Consider meting out assignments in bite-sized pieces, and don't have rigid time expectations of how fast these tasks get done.

You might also consider helping your clients become more knowledgeable and self-reliant by referring them to a good resource guide. You'll find some recommended titles in the Additional Resources section, including my own book, *Money Shy to Money Sure: A Woman's Road Map to Financial Well-Being*.

Time Is of the Essence

My client, a recent divorcée, needs to reallocate her portfolio to correspond with her new circumstances. In fact, she's dangerously overweighted in investments that are very risky for her. I know it's not a good idea to push traumatized clients into making radical changes—but if I delay, she could justifiably blame me later for any financial losses. What's the best way to approach this?

I'd explain the situation to her just as you outlined it here. Tell her you fully understand that, for her psychological health, now is not the best time for further major changes. You might help her think out ways to stabilize her life situation as quickly as she can, if you're comfortable doing this.

But you also need to explain the risks if she doesn't make the changes in her portfolio that you advise. After you make your recommendations to her, give her the power to decide when to act on them. If she fails to act, and tries to blame you later, be sure you've recorded your notes of this conversation to refresh her memory.

Take care, though, not to go overboard in prophesying gloom and doom if she doesn't leap to make changes. The last thing she needs right now is more catastrophizing—she's probably feeling that her financial security is threatened enough as it is. You can help her by trying to create a non-panicky atmosphere for her to consider her choices. Reassure her realistically (assuming her situation is not yet disastrous) so she'll be calm enough to take the right steps to secure her financial future.

Defusing Trauma

A brother and sister in their 50s have asked me to advise them on investing their father's life insurance benefit. Unfortunately, their idea of investing is CDs and savings accounts. They know their father lost a lot of money during the Crash of 1987, and they're terrified of the stock market. The sister's hands literally shook when I mentioned buying some blue-chip stocks. But this is their only retirement nest egg—I can't in good conscience tell them it's okay to be so fearful of taking any risk. How can I best help them?

Listen patiently to their tales of woe about this awful (but fortunately rare) event. After empathizing with them about the effect of this market crash on their family, educate them on some of the ways good financial experts like you have reduced market risk for your clients.

Diversification, dollar-cost averaging, buying and holding over longer periods: I'm sure you have all the tools you need to communicate these important concepts. But be sure to take time to ask how they feel about what you're saying, and encourage them to express their fears, concerns, and questions. If you rush through the process without addressing their inherited trauma, you risk scaring them into financial paralysis. Once you've made time and space for them to air their anxiety, there's a better chance of persuading them to make more balanced decisions about their money.

1040, Good Buddy

My client has a successful law practice which he's slowly building, but he hasn't filed an income tax return since 1994. Although I've known for years that he was a procrastinator and a clutterbug, I just found out about this serious lapse. I'm floored! He doesn't have any major financial problems, so I'm sure he's not deliberately evading taxes. What might be going on here, and how can I help him?

Even though you've known this client a long time, it's not surprising that he's only just admitting his tax avoidance to you. Many men tend to feel humiliated and ashamed to admit incompetence and difficulty—especially if they're supposed to be highly competent professionals.

This attorney's procrastination with taxes may arise partly from failing to plan ahead. Without enough money to meet all his needs, he may be borrowing from Peter to pay Paul, and putting off whatever he can in the hope that he can pay for it tomorrow. Or on a deeper level, he may have fallen into a pattern of shooting himself in the foot whenever things start to come together for him. This self-sabotage is sometimes a residual effect of growing up with the idea that one is incompetent, not good enough, or a loser (the legacy, perhaps, of overcritical parents).

In short, I think you may be dealing with a much more emotionally loaded problem than simple disorganization and procrastination—a problem that most likely has its roots in the distant past. Your client's inability to create order in his life may well indicate a state of inner chaos that requires longer-term therapeutic intervention. Consider referring him to a therapist or counselor who specializes in working with self-sabotaging clients.

In the meantime, if he's willing to work with you and you're comfortable with the idea, you could volunteer to help him restore enough order in his finances to file his back taxes. Or if you don't want the task, perhaps you know an accountant with good people skills who would be willing to help him get his tax life organized. In any event, he (or his tax lawyer) should call the IRS, 'fess up, and work out a payment plan ASAP, before they pounce on him with truly punitive penalties for tax evasion.

Taking Action

When you try to get hesitant clients to act, you'll need to rely on your sensitivity to their total situation to know when to listen and wait, when to empathize, and when to push. Take it slowly, and remember that you can't get someone to act wisely until they're able to get past their fully-aired emotions and are clear on their goals. Determine how open your clients really are to changing their deeply ingrained attitudes or behavior. And take into account such emotionally charged issues as divorce, the death of loved ones, illness, an unexpected inheritance, or any other traumatic life-change.

In these situations, a little communication goes a long way. If you also practice patience, sensitivity, and compassion, I suspect you'll be rewarded with loyal clients who remember how you supported them at a time when they were feeling unsure of themselves, and needed your guidance to take the next step.

BUILDING RELATIONSHIPS

Dealing with Difficult Clients

You probably consider yourself to be, on the whole, a fairly reasonable person. But I'm sure there are times when clients make you see red to the point where you risk compromising your professional demeanor. In other words, you feel like swearing, throwing something, or jumping up and punching them in the nose.

Well, we all have days—and clients—like that. Here are some suggestions on how to handle incendiary situations that really yank your chain.

Serf's Up

After 12 years in business, I consider myself a seasoned advisor, but I'm having a hard time dealing with a wealthy new client. This man, a lawyer in private practice, told me he came to me only because he doesn't have time in his busy and successful life to manage his portfolio, and he expects me to follow his instructions closely. As a woman, I feel angry and demeaned by this arrogance. If we're ever going to work together, he needs to understand that I have valuable knowledge to offer. How can I communicate this without being overwhelmed by my own resentment?

People who act like know-it-alls are often overcompensating for not feeling good enough about themselves, perhaps because they were put down regularly by a parent or other strong influence in childhood.

You may feel more compassionate towards your client and be able to approach him more openly and pleasantly if you imagine that beneath his facade, he's actually feeling anxious and needs to puff himself up to counter old insecurities. Remember, too, that many men are conditioned to hide vulnerabilities and feelings of incompetence with a veneer of false confidence.

To get your client to consider your ideas, it won't work to confront him with both guns blazing. Don't put down his judgment or try to overwhelm him with your superior expertise. ("Mr. Smith, I ran a style analysis on this large-cap fund you think is so wonderful, and guess what? It's really an emerging-growth fund that could cost you your shirt!") Instead, try to get in under his radar by starting with a compliment: "I think it's an excellent idea to do what we can to weatherize your portfolio, and this large-cap fund seems like a solid choice." Then, segue into suggesting a course of action that lets him stay in control: "As I'm sure you know, style drift is becoming a concern for many knowledgeable investors. I have access to tools that can help you make sure this choice is still the best one for your portfolio objectives. If you agree, I think running this analysis would be a smart defensive move." When you review the results of the analysis with him later, you'll both be on the same side instead of on opposite sides, so you should find it easier to guide him toward appropriate action.

In the meantime, remind yourself to not take his arrogant tone and manner personally, and remember that you *are* in fact the expert here. Take a little time to sort out whether you're reacting so strongly because important men in your own family didn't acknowledge your competence. If so, try to separate that family history from your present situation. This understanding may give you the necessary detachment to be patient with what may be a survival technique for your client—the defense of arrogance.

Moody Blues

A client I know well, and like, has been edgy about small things that never used to bother him. Yesterday, he blew up at my assistant and left her in tears. I'm angry about this and wonder how best to handle it. What do you suggest?

I think you can help both your client and your assistant reestablish perspective and balance. First, call the client (or even better, meet with him) to see how he's doing. At the right moment, ask what happened that made him so upset with your assistant. Encourage him to reflect on it more calmly. Explore his own stresses with him, and see if the two of you can think of things that might relax him more. If he regrets the blowup, suggest that he call or write your assistant to apologize.

Then meet with your assistant. While sympathizing with her hurt feelings, help her understand the stresses that fueled the client's unfair overreaction. If he said anything conciliatory to you, let her know. You might tactfully explore whether anything in your assistant's life is making her more sensitive than usual.

In any case, try to soothe her and make sure she understands that what happened was not her fault. When under pressure, some of us just do not behave like our normal rational selves. Though sad, this is inevitable while we try to find our way back to a more serene place.

Steamed Over a Surprise Tax Bill

A client called me recently, furious and incredulous that he owes capital gains tax on a mutual fund that lost money last year. I've tried to explain this apparent paradox to other clients in the same situation, with mixed results. Is there a good way to respond to him that will calm him down?

Instead of rushing in with a rational explanation of why this has happened, take time to sympathize with his feelings. Remind him that he's far from alone in being frustrated. If you too were caught in this tax trap, you might mention it.

Once your client feels he has been fully heard, his anger is likely to cool a bit. Then you may find him more willing to listen to your explanation of how funds that lose money can have taxable gains.

This serves as a good reminder to keep educating clients about risk before they feel its painful effects. If you forewarn them of what may happen and how they may feel about it, it helps them develop what I call "witness consciousness" of their emotional reactions during an actual event. The result is that when they call you in the midst of a market downturn, they're more apt to say, "Remind me of what you said in that seminar about market fluctuations" instead of "How could you do this to me?"

Whoa, Boy!

A client of mine is extremely prone to acting on impulse. Only a few weeks after losing most of the money he'd invested in stock recommended by a health-club buddy, he called to say he wanted to get in on an IPO touted in an online discussion group. How can I make him see the light about investing more sensibly?

Sometimes preventing a client from acting can be as hard as encouraging others to move ahead. In this case, the herd instinct is at work... or, to be more precise, the desire to join a small "in the know" herd in hopes of being out in front of the rest of the herd.

People who are willing to risk money on hot tips are generally fueled by fantasies of instant wealth, success, and one-upmanship. From the gold fever of the 'Forty-Niners to the click-and win allure of day-trading, Americans have always been convinced they can bring our society's rags-to-riches mythology to life.

To complicate matters, your client may also be fond of taking big risks. In love with the thrill of the ride and the intensity of its peak, he's apt to ignore the danger of basing decisions on scanty information from questionable sources.

I'd suggest pointing out to him that being ahead of the herd isn't so smart if it means he's the first one to plunge off a cliff. Recount other people's tales of woe (I'm sure you have a good supply) about losing money and self-respect with an ill-advised investment that had seemed to promise effortless riches.

To help your client veer away from this risky behavior, recommend saner choices to him. Encourage him to recommit to his long-range goals by taking action that might seem a lot less exciting in the moment, but will serve him much better over the long haul.

Is There a Therapist in the House?

I find myself wondering so often where a client is coming from (i.e., what could be motivating his irrational outlook) that I'm thinking about asking a psychologist or therapist to consult with me regularly. Is this a good idea? And if so, how would I find someone who fits the bill?

More and more financial advisors are telling me they've begun consulting with a mental health counselor, psychologist, or social worker to whom they refer clients before or during their planning work. Some planners are even beginning to have counselors sit in with them from the outset—a great idea, if the chemistry is right between both professionals. In fact, this partnership has the potential to be a marriage made in heaven. The therapist can lighten the heavy emotional burden which may be distorting your clients' attitude toward money, and you can then do your good work with these now-saner folks.

To find a suitable therapist (assuming you don't already know someone recommended by a colleague), I would suggest interviewing two or three potential partners to find out how at ease they really are with the subject of money. While money is often a cover for other issues such as love, power, dependency, and so on, the therapist needs to be comfortable enough in dealing with money itself to know whether it's appropriate to deflect clients' money talk into those other areas. Many therapists are so unaware of their own money issues that they'll wrongly redirect the client's focus because of their own particular anxieties and blind spots.

To tell which therapists have enough money harmony in their own lives and learn how they feel about dealing with money issues, be sure to interview them in person and observe how emotionally charged the atmosphere is (or isn't) when you talk about money with them.

As a group, therapists tend to be highly anxious and conflicted about money. But I enjoy doing workshops and training sessions with them because once they get a handle on this, they quickly learn to evolve toward better balance in their own lives. With some careful research, you shouldn't have any trouble finding a therapist who can join you in helping your least harmonious clients move toward greater money harmony.

Tired of Troublesome Clients

I have a few really terrific clients who have been with me for years and are a joy to work with. How can I transform other frustrating, hard-to-please clients into similar models of harmony and loyalty?

I'd start tackling this tall order by reevaluating your relationships with your difficult clients. What's working? What isn't working? Are you the right kind of advisor for them? Get their take on the situation, too. If it doesn't appear that things will improve between you, consider referring them elsewhere to make room for clients who truly appreciate your services. Even if you've worked with some of these stress-producing clients for a long time, it's worthwhile letting go if the end result will be more enjoyment and fulfillment in your worklife.

At the same time, ask your most satisfied clients what they appreciate about working with you. Is it your financial knowhow, your understanding of their needs, your responsiveness? Figure out ways to extend these strengths to others. For example, if financial savvy is your forte, showcase it in a newsletter or newspaper "advertorials" to draw more new clients.

Also, ask yourself whether the clients you most enjoy share any common qualities, or perhaps a common profession. This in turn may suggest a niche that you can focus on to populate your practice with a more simpatico clientele.

Last, ask your happiest clients for referrals. This doesn't need to be heavy-handed. You might, for example, write to thank each of them for their loyalty over the years, and let them know that you would be glad to see if you can help any like-minded friends or associates they might send your way. By opening their minds to this possibility, you might further expand your practice in the direction you want it to go.

Won't Take a Hint

I've tried every polite way I can think of to get an impossibly cantankerous client to leave for greener pastures, but he won't take the hint. It's gotten to the point where talking to him elevates my blood pressure to dangerous levels. My conscience won't let me just dump him flat, but I've got to find a way to farm him out to someone else before I blow a gasket. Ideas?

I think you should tell the truth, or at least a part of it. Inform this client that you need to refer him to another advisor because you're having some health problems.

Keep it professional —i.e., don't tell him what a pain in the neck he is. There may be a tactful way of coaching him to change his behavior with the new planner, but I wouldn't be too optimistic. Cantankerous folks, especially if advanced in age, are generally too set in their prickly ways to change. It may be a better idea to accentuate the positive by emphasizing to your client that he deserves an advisor who's more accessible and helpful than you are currently able to be.

Offer to help him get situated with a new advisor, if you know someone with lots of patience who's trying to build a practice. Give him space to express feelings of loss at the breaking up of your relationship (he may think working with you is terrific, even if you can't say the same), and wish him godspeed. "Doctor's orders," you can say regretfully but firmly.

If you stick to your guns, the blood-pressure spikes caused by your crotchety client may be a thing of the past within a week or two. You'll be a lot happier and he'll go away thinking you're a wonderful person with his best interests at heart.

Snidely Backlash?

I do life planning for a very wealthy couple. The husband enjoys making snide comments to his wife in my presence—how clueless she is about money, how she couldn't raise the chil-

dren without him, etc. He thinks it's funny to joke about having to "keep her in line." As a woman, I'd like to ditch this obnoxious client, but where will that leave her?

How much do his macho putdowns really seem to upset his wife? Maybe this insecure man secretly has a heart of gold. In this case, you might simply find a way to squelch his questionable humor without infuriating or humiliating him. (Ask your colleagues for ideas.)

You always have the option of referring this couple to another planner who is less irritated by his personality. But if you keep working with them and the putdowns continue or escalate, the couple may be in real marital distress. If so, it could be appropriate to refer them for counseling. But make sure the wife is truly bothered by her husband's disparaging remarks before you suggest any kind of help. In other words, put aside what you think would be best for them, and follow their lead on where they want to go. Your job is to help them reach their goals, after all—not to serve as a marriage counselor.

Dueling Spenders

Moments after we met for the first time, a client couple launched into a vicious verbal battle in my office. He accused her of spending so much on designer clothes that they never had enough money to invest, and she fired back something about a Porsche he'd bought without consulting her. I was so uncomfortable that I had them reschedule for another time, but now I'm wondering if this is a warning not to deal with them at all. If they start fighting again, is there any way to begin a more productive dialogue?

Unfortunately, the way a couple relates to each other in the first session is often a tip-off to how difficult they'll be as clients. As a colleague in my field once said, "It's not how much the partners differ that determines the amount of marital discord; it's how they handle these differences."

Often, spouses who exhibit a lack of good will and respect toward their partners are secretly trying to suck you into their war zone as an advocate for their own views. So if the verbal sparring is vicious and nasty, you might reasonably conclude that working with them will be difficult at best. This leaves you several options:

1. Tactfully refer them to a good couples therapist who's not afraid to tackle money issues. They probably should do some work with this therapist before consulting you. (In some cases, they may choose to undertake counseling and planning at the same time.)

2. Refer them to a colleague who doesn't mind dealing with extremely contentious clients.

3. Take them on, but accept that your role will be to confront them on their individual issues (in this case, they may both be overspenders) and to try to get them on the same page with their goals and dreams.

If you decide on this third option, you might begin by asking each of them to make a list of goals for themselves as individuals and for their family. (Advise them to write this list at least twice, to discover which items come up repeatedly.) When they bring their final lists to the next session with you, you'll be able to see how much commonality there is and determine some mutually agreed-upon goals.

Second, suggest that each of them track every penny of spending for a month, writing down in a small notebook not only what they spent, but how they felt about each purchase ("excited," "so-so," "a waste!"). With each purchase over a certain amount, ask them to calculate how many before-tax hours they must work to replace that money. Invite them to reflect on areas where they may be spending impulsively or excessively.

If they're willing to do this work, you may be able to get them over the hump of their chronic money disharmony to become "good-enough" clients. If not, remember that there are always polite ways to pass them on to others who may be able to help them (or try, anyway!).

Don't feel too bad if you find that your work with vituperative couples turns out badly or ends in deadlock. As hard as you try, you can't help everyone.

Back in the Lecture Hall

My new client is a college professor (now the chairman of the business department) whom I met while teaching there several years ago. Though he knows very little about investing, his manner and tone with me are always authoritative and pontificating. In spite of my years of experience as a planner, his attitude makes me feel flustered and incompetent, as though I'm back in the faculty room being lectured. How should I deal with this?

This is a tough one, because working with him tends to put you back in past history—both in your former profession and probably in your own childhood, when you dealt with authority figures who made you feel insecure. Perhaps presenting some of your expert judgments and analyses formally to him with flip charts, on a whiteboard, or in a carefully prepared printout would make you feel more like *you* are the person in authority here. Be firm but tactful—remember, you're the teacher, and it's your classroom.

If you still have a hard time overcoming your sense of being intimidated, visualize your client as a naive but opinionated college freshman whom you want to educate. If this doesn't work, you could always try imagining him naked.

Avoid the temptation to exaggerate your own experience or expertise. Just share what you do know that will be of value to him. You might be able to create more of a positive bond by emphasizing your mutual ties to the university life you've both experienced. Once he feels more at ease, he may be much less apt to put on professorial airs when talking to you. Good luck in working out this delicate situation!

Passive Aggression

I've worked on commission ever since I started out five years ago, and I don't plan to change as long as the majority of my clients continue to prefer it. One of my newer clients has started to drop snide references to the fact that my buy and sell recommendations must be guided by the payment schedule on my new car. I've always prided myself on my personal and professional integrity, and I'm tired of pretending that I find this funny. Although I'd hate to lose his business, I'm afraid I'll blow my top if he doesn't quit it. How can I handle this without losing my cool?

If his challenge to your integrity triggers your rage so much that you're losing the capacity to talk to him calmly, I suggest you take the bull by the horns and let him know how offended you are.

Write him a letter clearly detailing your professional training, experience, and any peer or client recognition your abilities have earned. I would encourage you to state your commitment to integrity in all aspects of your business. You might even offer some references—names of other clients who have found your services to be valuable and your objectivity irreproachable. Remind him that you've made it clear from the outset that you are compensated on commission. Last, you may want to suggest that if he just isn't comfortable with this kind of arrangement, he is at liberty to find a financial advisor who uses a different method of compensation.

In the meantime, try not to take his snide attacks personally. It may well be that this client is the sort who looks for any opportunity to be "one up" by putting others on the defensive. Alternatively, he may be convinced that everyone else has it in for him in one way or another, and your commission structure merely serves to strengthen his feelings of victimization.

The more secure you are in your own integrity, the easier it should be to respond to this aggravating client with equanimity instead of wanting to deck him. With luck, he'll soon realize he can neither browbeat you or recruit you to join in his game of "poor me."

The Green-Eyed Monster

I was initially pleased to start working with a new client with whom I have several friends and acquaintances in common. However, since he knows I belong to our local country club, he takes every opportunity to remind me how much better off I am than he is. I don't mean to downplay his struggle to escape his blue-collar background, but I'm angry at his constant sniping at my own economic status. Am I overreacting?

No, I don't think so. And I believe the solution may come from learning why he is so bitter and envious of your financial success.

If you aren't too angry to talk to him calmly, turn the tables on him with a little compassion. Ask him more about his upbringing. Did he grow up with wealthy people all around him who could afford things he was denied?

If you too have had to struggle to get where you are today, you may want to share your own story with him. On the other hand, if you've always had money, it could help to consult some wealthy friends who have dealt successfully with people like your client. They may have a better perspective on the envy and anger that's often directed at those who are born with the proverbial silver spoon in their mouths.

In any event, it may help quench your anger to know that your financial success is probably one of the reasons why your client sought you out—even though he may also begrudge you that blessing.

Biting the Hand

Until recently, my client did quite well following my advice. But then, despite my reservations, he got greedy, borrowed a lot on margin to expand his holdings, and took a big hit when the market dropped. He blames me for allowing him to get overextended, and is threatening to file a complaint against me. I'm upset and irate. After all we'd been through together, I guess I took his continued trust and goodwill for granted. Unfortunately, it's only my word against his that I advised him to rein in his borrowing. Can this client relationship be salvaged?

Unless your client really doesn't understand the nature of market risk (i.e., the fact that an investor's life is not just a continued series of "ups"), there's a possibility that other things are happening right now to make him more anxious about money. I would suggest that the two of you revisit his financial plan and see if his goals and concerns have changed. You might share a story or two with him about other (anonymous) clients who took a hit in the past, but by staying the course later recouped their losses and went on to greater success.

In other words, try to calm him down. Remind him that if you'd known for sure that the market would drop, you certainly would have been firmer in your advice against borrowing on margin. However, neither you nor any other financial advisor is omniscient (a fact that obviously frustrates him now). Tell him you feel confident that he employed you to be his advisor, not his parent—so when he chose not to follow your advice, you quite appropriately stepped back to let him take action he was determined to take.

You don't say whether your client signed an agreement that any dispute would be settled through arbitration, but I hope he did. If worse comes to worst, arbitration is likely to be less expensive and adversarial than litigation. It's a hard way to learn the lesson that you should always keep notes on your conversations with clients.

Meanwhile, if his hostility continues unabated, you may want to refer him to another advisor. But I wouldn't jump to that conclusion until you've first tried getting to the bottom of his anger and anxiety.

Crossing the Line

Knowing I've been actively seeking new business, a friend referred a client to me who's a real macho type. This man's first remark to me was "If you're as smart as you are pretty, I'm sure we'll do just fine together!" Though I've never been less than businesslike with him, he tends to talk to me patronizingly and compliment me on various aspects of my appearance. This may be a lost cause—but before I walk away from this piece of business, I'd like to know if there's a way to work it out that I haven't considered. Any ideas?

You may have been too low-key with this client, not wishing to reject your friend's kind referral. But for your own peace of mind, I think you need to lay your displeasure on the line.

At the very beginning of your next meeting with this man, broach the subject politely but firmly. Tell him you feel his comments to you are not appropriate for this professional relationship. Ask him directly if he has any doubts about working with a financial advisor who is a woman. If so, he may need a reminder about your training and expertise. If he insists that he doesn't doubt your qualifications, you may want to ask if he finds it too distracting to work with a woman. This may embarrass him into correcting his inappropriate behavior.

Should he volunteer another patronizing or awkward remark later on, don't let him get away with it. Without missing a beat, say something like, "We've discussed the inappropriateness of comments like that. Are you sure you're willing to keep this relationship completely professional?"

No matter how eager you are for your practice to grow, dealing with clients who anger or humiliate you will undermine the energy you can direct toward your work. In other words, it's not worth it to let yourself be harassed and condescended to by a client. The price in lost energy and self-esteem will make it harder to project yourself positively as you seek to build your business.

Buy and Hold...Hold...Hold

The corporate executive I'm working with, a good-humored Dr. Jekyll during the portfolio-building phase, suddenly turned into an irrational Mr. Hyde when I recommended dumping a poorly performing stock with a dim earnings outlook. Insisting that his loss isn't a loss until he sells, he's dragging his feet on taking action. I still believe he should get rid of this clunker, but how can I help him see the light?

Welcome to the club! Many other planners share your frustration in trying to persuade reluctant clients to unload unpromising investments.

It's possible, of course, that your Jekyll-and-Hyde client is blinkered by a belief in buying-and-holding at all costs. But if you've already determined that this isn't the case, he may view selling this stock as an admission that he goofed in choosing it. And like many men, he may feel humiliated at the thought of acknowledging a mistake.

Men aren't alone in being unwilling to admit errors, of course. But as any woman who has ridden with a lost male driver can testify, some people of the XY persuasion can be quite stubborn about throwing in the towel.

I think the key is to help your client separate this investment from his self-esteem. It's very likely, after all, that this stock had promise when he bought it, but circumstances beyond his or your control (a new manager? drought in the Midwest? a decline in the euro?) have changed the picture. Remind him that if it were possible to be infallible, professional money managers would never be beaten by the *Wall Street Journal* dartboard. Anything you can do to cushion his pride will help him feel less like a "failure," and more willing to consider selling his clunker.

When Hand-Holding Turns to Clinging

I'm working with a valued client whose life is coming apart: while trying to care for her elderly mother, she's also been drawn into her daughter's messy divorce. Although I understand that this makes her act irritable and short-tempered, I don't know how to handle her constant calls asking me to do this or that personal financial chore for her. I really don't have the time, and her demands are making me just as grouchy as she is. How can I get this relationship back on an even keel?

I think you need to talk with her as soon as possible about all the stresses in her life. Empathize with how difficult and overwhelming her situation is right now, and ask if she is getting enough support in the rest of her life.

If she feels she's all alone in carrying these burdens, you might try steering her to a therapist, a support group for people caring for elderly parents, or a good friend she can talk things over with. Ask her what kind of help she wants and/or expects from you. Then, tell her honestly which of her expectations you are willing to meet, and which ones are out of your comfort zone.

If she insists on the kind of hand-holding you're just not willing to do (even temporarily), you have the option of sending her to someone else who can provide this service. But I'd urge you to try to work it out if at all possible. This woman is already dealing with several major losses (actual or imminent), and being rejected by you could hurt her far more than you expect. If you offer her a sympathetic ear and some concrete suggestions for help, support, and comfort, she may scale back her demands on you and help you get back to the courteous and amicable relationship you had before.

Tax Aversion

I'm wondering about the unusual behavior of a client I've just begun to work with. He told me he's almost certainly been overpaying his taxes for years, but he didn't want to let an accountant figure them for him. This is especially odd since he comes from a family of CPAs (although I gather he had a rather unpleasant upbringing). I'm thinking there may be more to this than meets the eye. What's your opinion?

There's a strong possibility that your client is being controlled in his adult life by some childhood trauma. Your description of his avoidance behavior suggests that his inner "child" is in control and running the show.

If his fear or avoidance of accountants is a result of painful early experiences with his family, he should seek counseling. Perhaps you could suggest that he see a psychotherapist to discuss this debilitating block. One possibility is to look for a therapist trained in EMDR (Eye Movement Desensitization and Reprocessing), a therapeutic technique being used more and more to resolve some childhood traumas fairly quickly. This early damage can paralyze clients unless they are courageous enough to seek help and tackle the block directly.

On the practical side, try referring him to a tax preparer who is not a CPA. This may lessen his resistance to moving ahead with filing his taxes.

Taking Action

Whenever difficult clients are making you irritable, it's useful to step back and ask yourself several probing questions. First, what could be going on with them to cause their abrasiveness? (It's a good idea to ask them about this fairly directly, if you can manage to be both polite and kind.) But also, what's going on with you? What's the deeper issue that has triggered your anger or sent you reeling? Often, reflection will lead you to recognize an exaggerated emotional charge in your own response, which may shrink or even disappear completely when you understand why you're feeling so hurt, injured, or angry.

Anger is a defense. Underneath it, there's always a deeper emotion: fear, hurt, sadness, loss, or feelings of being powerless and out of control. If you can identify these deeper feeling or feelings in yourself and in your clients, you'll be on the road toward reestablishing a more rational and even-tempered relationship with them.

BUILDING RELATIONSHIPS
Restless Relationships

Has the honeymoon turned ho-hum? Before familiarity has a chance to breed contempt, it usually breeds boredom. The result, unfortunately, can be too-high turnover among longtime clients—with a consequently dire impact on your revenues.

When you have clients who don't seem to love you like they used to do, first run a monotony check on yourself. If the client's discontent simply reflects your own lack of zest for your job, that's a big problem you need to address separately.

But at times, even the most motivated advisor may have clients who pace restlessly by the fence, convincing themselves that the grass is greener on the other side. Here are some ways to handle the problem.

Livening Up a Humdrum Relationship

A long-term client left a message on my voice mail telling me he needs a change to "liven up his portfolio." He's decided to seek a new advisor when he returns from a two-week trip abroad, which gives me some time to plan my response. How can I get him to reconsider?

Clearly, he's telling you that the relationship between you has gone stale. Do you agree? If so, your first priority should be to think of ways to liven it up (and perhaps add spark to your practice in general). Should you communicate with this client more often? Suggest that he become more adventurous with part of his portfolio? Make your get-togethers more open and informal? Ask your colleagues for their input, too.

As soon as he returns from his trip, ask if he'll get together with you to resolve your relationship in a positive way. If he hesitates, tell him you won't try to talk him out of leaving. Acknowledge that you understand he feels dissatisfied with the relationship and his portfolio, and mention that his comments have inspired you to think about changing some of the ways you work.

When you get together with him, be candid with him about the changes you are considering, and ask him to be equally open in explaining what he is looking for. Let him know the reasons why you value him as a client. You might also restate his goals as you understand them, and explore whether changes in this area are prompting his restlessness.

Above all, don't pressure him or plead with him to stay. Be prepared to accept that *que sera, sera*. If he decides to stay, great; if not, so be it. The less desperate you feel, the more creative you can be in communicating your new ideas and perspectives to him.

Sharper Than a Serpent's Tooth

After helping a client build a high-six-figure portfolio from scratch, I've just been told that he wants to turn part of it over to an independent money manager recommended by a friend. I'm trying to take this calmly, but I feel angry and frustrated. Is there a way to persuade this ingrate not to split up his assets, or should I just tell him to get lost?

First of all, take some time to get a grip on your feelings of being hurt and threatened. After all, your client didn't say he wanted to leave you outright. Perhaps he just revels in the excitement of newness and change.

As a first step, respectfully probe his desire for a new source of investment expertise. What's motivating him to tinker with your relationship? Is he bored with the work you've done for him? Does the recommendation to try this money manager come as a "hot tip" whose appeal is more emotional than logical? Once you understand his motivation, you can talk to him more knowledgeably about whether something needs to change in your working relationship.

In the event that he still insists on parceling out assets to the other manager, consider meeting this professional to see if the two of you can cooperate rather than compete. If you can work together in some complementary way, this creative challenge may lend spice to your own worklife.

After all is said and done, I would counsel you not to take your client's decision too personally. No matter how fabulously you've worked with and for him, he may simply want something different. That certainly isn't your fault. If exploring other options doesn't work, you may just have to let him go.

Not Her Father's Financial Advisor

I more or less inherited a client I'll call Susan, after having been her late parents' advisor for over a decade. Although we've worked well together for a year, Susan has confided to my assistant that she's thinking of finding an advisor "more attuned to her own needs." This bothers me, since I've consistently treated her as an individual, not as a clone of her parents. Any ideas to help me keep this client?

Susan's desire to get out of her parents' shadow is certainly understandable. But if you believe you can serve her well, you owe it to yourself (and her) to communicate this.

I'd start by empathizing with her need for financial autonomy. After giving her a few moments to absorb this, you might suggest beginning a new relationship free of old habits and traditions. For example, offer her new ways of working together that reflect her own unique goals and personality. Emphasize the differences between these approaches and the ways you once worked with her parents.

This may reassure her that she can stay with you without being pigeonholed as her parents' daughter.

If she is still unsatisfied with the relationship, consider teaming up with a colleague to give her some fresh perspectives. For example, perhaps one of the other planners in your firm is a tax expert or a retirement-planning specialist who could supplement your own areas of strength. As a last resort, you might refer her completely to a partner in your business or a trusted colleague at another firm.

By taking an active role in steering your client to the right solution, you improve the chances that she will appreciate your willingness to meet her needs, and eventually send more business your way.

Fuddy-Duddy

My longtime client seems to think I'm behind the times on such matters as portfolio theory, risk, and sector exposure. For example, he recently got the idea to try recouping recent losses by loading up on the shakiest kind of high-yield bonds. When I recommended against the risk, he called me an old fuddy-duddy and threatened to leave. (We're about the same age, actually.) What's gotten into this formerly loyal client, and how should I handle him?

I'm guessing that you've already talked until you're blue in the face about the importance of diversification, the volatility and credit risk entailed in junk bond investing, and so on, without making a dent in your client's determination.

My advice would be to start at the other end by finding out why he wants to move in this direction. Listen as empathetically as you can to his desires and preferences, without getting defensive or pontificating about your own opinions. Has his financial situation changed so drastically that he believes it's necessary to take big chances to restore his fortunes? Does he feel left out of an exciting market sector? Is he bored with his prudent portfolio, and eager for the thrill of venturing onto thin ice? Does he find your relationship tedious and humdrum?

In this respectful discussion, look for a middle ground. For example, would you endorse his taking more risk with a small percentage of his assets? Remind him tactfully of his long-term goals, and the results he has enjoyed so far with your guidance.

If this dialogue doesn't change your client's view of you as an old stick-in-the-mud, it may be best to split up. Knowing when to hold and when to fold a client relationship is a difficult but necessary part of your job. In this case, a colleague may be able to meet this client's need for adventure without jeopardizing his financial security.

Declaration of Independence

I've had a good working relationship with an entrepreneur client for more than three years. Recently, she told me she's thinking of taking over her own portfolio management. I honor her desire for more independence, but how can I keep the door open to our continuing to work together?

The way you asked the question shows you have empathy for this client's desire to take full charge of her money life. Why not invite her to a special conference (or maybe lunch) to brainstorm ways she can take on more control while checking in with you periodically for tune-ups? She may feel comforted by a slower weaning-away process that allows her to continue benefiting from your wisdom and your services, as opposed to jumping straight into deep water to see whether she sinks or swims.

The more helpful you are in educating her, the more she will appreciate your role in her life. If she does eventually decide to go it alone, her gratitude for your training and support will probably make her a great source of referrals. I've often found that clients who leave my therapy practice send others to me as a parting "gift" or vote of confidence.

Taking Action

In general, alarm bells should go off when a client wants to jump the fence for greener pastures. Sometimes the reasons may be beyond your control. But quite often, it happens because you haven't understood their needs, or have been unable or unwilling to meet them.

Take time to evaluate these clients' yearnings and discontents to see if you need to revitalize your ways of working, or hone your skills in some area. Let them know you understand their feelings and needs, and see if you can make changes leading to a renewed sense of connection.

If you try your hardest and a client still wants to move on, accept this decision as gracefully as you can. By letting go of people you just can't please, you'll make space for other clients who can nourish your spirit as you nurture their financial well-being.

Dealing with Differences

You know that wonderful feeling when you meet someone who thinks or expresses things just the way you do? You feel completely understood, as if your own experience is being validated and supported.

Much more often, relationships with a partner, colleagues, or clients are colored by major differences in perception, language, and attitude. Looked at in the best light, these differences can complement your own strengths, and even compensate for your blind spots. They will enrich your experience of life and broaden your horizons—if you allow them to. But all too frequently, dealing with people who think or act differently makes us feel lonely and threatened. In order to validate our own perspective on things, we try to argue them out of theirs.

This section will help you learn how to deal with these differences. You'll be encouraged to identify your own biases, so you can recognize and work with viewpoints that are different from your own. You'll find out how to use language with sensitivity to these differences, helping you build stronger connections to clients and colleagues—and as a side benefit, to your family and friends as well.

The first area of difference is in money personalities. Most people are a combination of money personality types, usually with one type predominating. Hoarders, for whom money equals security, love to save and are reluctant to spend on purchases that give them immediate gratification. They are often found in relationships with spenders. Money worriers tend to partner with money avoiders; risk takers (usually men) frequently associate with risk avoiders (usually women); and money monks, who think that money is dirty and might corrupt them, often form relationships with money amassers, who believe that the one who dies with the most assets wins.

It's evident from these pairings that opposites really do attract, in "work marriages" as well as intimate relationships. In fact, even if both members start out with the same money orientation, they tend to become polarized over time. For example, two spenders who hate to budget or save will fight each other for the "super-spender" position. The "loser" will gradually become more of a hoarder. Eventually, both of them will lock into these polarizations and will probably begin attacking each other for their differences.

I'll show you the different universes inhabited by hoarders and spenders, risk takers and risk avoiders, and money monks and amassers, and help you learn how to guide clients towards what I call "money harmony": less polarized stances that yield more flexibility and creativity, as well as more intimacy for couples.

Gender is another important area of difference. Even though the old messages about men's and women's traditional roles with money are slowly fading away, our social conditioning still emphasizes gender distinctions that create different levels of self-confidence, different fears, and different expectations. These differences show up in the ways couples make money decisions, plan charitable gifts, choose financial advisors, assign blame and credit for investment performance, and deal with power and decision-making.

Indeed, many male/female relationships sometimes seem like an uneasy alliance of two disparate cultures separated by a gulf of misunderstanding, anger, and hurt. Understanding these differences will help you coach clients of both genders to tolerate each other's complementary divergences, and learn to meet in the middle more often. You'll also discover how to deal more effectively with individuals or couples who reverse the typical gender patterns.

Last, you're sure to encounter religious and cultural viewpoints based on different values and leading to different priorities. While a complete analysis of these differences is beyond the scope of this book, I hope to prepare you to handle them when they crop up with the full force of cultural and family traditions behind them.

The more fully you understand these differences and their psychological underpinnings, the more easily you will be able to connect with a widely diverse group of clients. You won't have to struggle to be patient and compassionate; you'll know when it's appropriate to empathize, when to gently educate, and when to confront obstacles to wise decision-making. Most important of all, understanding and respecting these differences will allow you to integrate them creatively into a plan that helps your clients reach their deeply held goals.

DEALING WITH DIFFERENCES
Money Personalities

We all have a money personality—an attitude toward money usually shaped by our upbringing. Some people mirror the personality of a parent or another major influence, while others react by adopting a personality that's 180 degrees the opposite.

Much of the time, money personalities are expressed in unexceptional behavior. But extreme situations—an extreme spender, hoarder, or risk-taker, for example—may indicate a financial addiction that leads to feelings of depression, anxiety, and being out of control.

When you encounter clients with strong money personalities, here are some ways you may be able to help them resolve their conflicts and fears—and then achieve their hopes and dreams with a financial plan that blends sensible choices with their fundamental nature.

MIXED DOUBLES

To Merge or Not to Merge?

An engaged couple asked me whether they should merge all their money when they marry, given the difference in their money styles. He's a spender, she's a saver; he's an avoider, she's a worrier; he takes investment risks, she's pretty risk-averse; he's a dreamer, and she's a planner. They want to know what they can do to harmonize these differences (and between the lines, they're probably asking me whether they should even get married). Where do I start?

Start by teaching them Mellan's Law: "If opposites don't attract right off the bat—and they usually do—they'll end up in opposite places eventually." In other words, oppositional behavior of the kind you described is extremely common and should not be cause for undue alarm. Working out these differences will take open, honest communication, a lot of good will, an ability to be vulnerable and gentle with the other, and a willingness to acknowledge the positive aspects of their mate's money style.

To help them both move toward the middle, give them homework assignments to "be where they ain't." For a hoarder, this means buying something that provides immediate gratification. A spender should practice saving; a planner should write out her wildest dreams and fantasies; a dreamer should create a step-by-step plan to reach a financial goal, and so on. Having done this, they should reward themselves for their new behavior in a way that doesn't undermine their progress (e.g., spenders shouldn't spend, and hoarders shouldn't stash more under a figurative mattress).

As for combining their money, the first thing I caution marrying couples who are just beginning to know each other deeply is this: Do not merge everything, and do not merge too quickly. All couples have intimacy fears and defenses, and overmerging can be dangerous when you don't know exactly what you're getting into.

Instead, suggest that they make a list of monthly household expenses (including savings and an emergency fund), to be paid out of an account to which they'll contribute proportionately to their income and/or assets. The rest of their money should to be kept separate for now. (Many women will feel relieved at this—they often need and want money of their own to feel they haven't lost their individuality.) If a couple would rather not merge anything, that's fine, too. Solutions unique to both individuals' needs are better than "one size fits all" approaches.

If your clients have good will toward each other, communicate openly, and are willing to work on their own imperfections, the differences in their money personalities should not create marital discord. What's important is how they handle these differences—how capable they are of understanding where each other lives.

Not Playing Favorites

What do you do when the goals of one member of a couple seem much more valid than the other's? I'm thinking of a couple I've begun working with—she wants to save, while his goals are a custom-built home, a high-speed cigarette boat, etc. My advice about increasing their investment portfolio will undoubtedly appear weighted in favor of the wife, and I'm concerned that if the husband feels unsupported, they won't act on my advice. Not only will they lose out, but they may tell other prospective clients that working with me was a waste of time.

The most delicate aspect of working with couples is finding a way to sit midway between them, so you can help each build a bridge to the other that will be based on respect and appreciation of their differences, as opposed to contempt for the other's blind spots and defects.

Considering that you're there to help the couple invest their money and get it to grow, this task of building bridges is difficult when you deal with a spender, who lives in the world of short-term pleasures and immediate gratification. You're right in assuming that you won't be able to reach the husband if you weigh in with a validation of his wife's position.

To begin establishing a foundation for harmony, you need to start slowly, teaching both of them that each one's money personality has positive and negative aspects. Many hoarders (who usually worry about money) secretly admire spenders' ability to enjoy money right now, give generously to themselves and others, and live a less worried, more spontaneous life. On the other hand, spenders (who are typically money avoiders) tend to admire their partners' ability to not only delay gratification but also plan, prioritize, and work toward long-term goals. However, neither will normally confess to this secret admiration for fear of reinforcing the other's bad habits.

After discussing the generic pros and cons of both financial extremes, you can encourage your clients to consider how they might move their own money mode closer to a middle ground and toward each other. You may be able to validate some of the spender's choices (for example, a luxury home could be an excellent investment), or at least empathize with his desires. You can also validate the hoarder-worrier's desire to hold onto money and, if she's really an amasser, her desire to see her money grow.

At the same time, be sure to caution each of them about their blind spots. For example, hoarders, worriers, or amassers may be so focused on making sure they have enough money that they ignore such crucial aspects of life as quality time with their family, restful vacations, and downtime with friends. Similarly, spender-avoiders can at times feel out of control— a sensation which erodes self-esteem, and may lead in turn to feelings of resignation and hopelessness about ever reaching longer-term goals.

If one or both partners are permanently locked into the blame game, you may not succeed in helping them agree. But if there's at least a modicum of self-reflection and goodwill on the part of both partners, this harmonizing work can eventually result in fruitful decision-making.

Just remember, no one likes to feel like the screw-up in a relationship. Even if one partner's money behavior seems considerably more bizarre, you'll almost always find areas where the other's irrationality dominates. In my couples therapy work, I've discovered that 99% of the time, the two partners are evenly paired in terms of nuttiness and imbalances. In other words, it's usually a good match—for better and/or for worse.

Defusing Disagreements

A couple came into my office for some advice about tax management. Within 10 minutes, they were fighting about whether he was "anal" about money, whether she overspent, whether he wanted too much documentation on minor purchases, and whether she was "burying her head in the sand" about money. How can I defuse this situation so I can begin to help them?

Remind your clients that at stressful times like tax season, couples tend to polarize into survival mode in which they attack each other for their differences, instead of appreciating how these same traits complement each other.

In this classic dyad, the husband appears to be a worrier, while the wife is a money avoider (at least in relation to him). He is a hoarder and she is a spender (again, relatively speaking). This double whammy of a hoarder/worrier married to a spender/avoider is the most common kind of marriage. In fact, even if they started out with similar approaches to money, some polarization would inevitably occur. If they were both worriers, for example, the less extreme worrier would inevitably turn into an avoider to escape all that intense worrying.

Knowing this, see if you can get your client couple to agree to gentle, respectful communication during this stressful time—no blaming, no attacks, no angry demands. Encourage them to restrict themselves to patient, rational requests and responses, to offset their tendency to snipe at each other. If their oral conversations are too acrimonious, suggest that they communicate through respectful written notes or e-mail.

As the next action step, ask them to review their tax planning tasks with you and brainstorm ways to achieve them more efficiently. If you wish, you can take the lead by giving each of them a list of things to do to complete tax filing this year and improve their tax management in the future.

Can Couples Reconcile about Risk?

I wish I had a dollar for every client couple I've dealt with who are divided over risk. It seems he's always willing to take risks while she wants to avoid them, and the tension and distrust in my office gets so thick you could cut it with a knife. I've just been through this again with new clients in their 50s. Isn't there an easy way to get the two of them on the same page?

A reporter once asked me if I thought men's brains might be genetically programmed to predispose them toward racing high-powered cars and taking high-powered financial risks—some gene or hormone that women are missing. Not being a geneticist or endocrinologist, all I know from my own personal and professional experience is that there are differences of social conditioning which explain men's greater comfort with financial risk, and women's uneasiness with it.

To begin with, many men are raised to believe that they'll be good at handling money and investing, while women are more likely to be taught that if they're lucky, their husband will take care of it for them. (The latter view is changing, but more slowly than most of us would like to believe.) On average, men also earn 133% as much as women do, so they're more apt to be confident that they can replace any lost savings. Furthermore, today's tsunami-high rate of divorce leaves a tidewrack of newly poorer women in its wake, while ex-husbands usually end up wealthier.

Thus, it's no wonder your clients have polarized worldviews. To complicate matters further, risk takers and risk avoiders live in totally different worlds. What's hell for the husband may be heaven for the wife, and vice versa. In particular, playing it safe probably feels constraining and claustrophobic to your male client, while risk-taking feels liberating and exciting. For your female client, taking financial risks may feel as suicidal as diving off a cliff, while keeping her money locked up makes her feel secure.

You mentioned "getting this couple on the same page," and that's literally where I'd begin—by asking them to generate a list of goals to review with you. They should go through this process individually at first, identifying short-term, intermediate-term, and long-term goals, and probably making several lists at different times to discover which goals tend to recur.

Then suggest that they share this final list with each other (at home or in your office, whichever works best), and come to a consensus about prioritizing goals they both agree on, as well as goals that may mean more to one person than to the other. Some negotiation will be involved here, some compromise, and most likely the deferral of certain goals. As they work through which items on the list will have top priority, ask each of them to choose one goal that moves toward the style of the other. For example, your risk-taker might buy into a goal of short-term financial security by agreeing to keep six months' living expenses in a safe place. Meanwhile, the risk-avoider might agree to a goal of vacation travel every year, financed by putting some of their money in a potentially riskier but higher-yielding investment.

Emphasize to them that it's natural to feel uncomfortable and disoriented in moving toward each other's way of thinking, and remember to be a sympathetic listener if they "freak out" temporarily in adjusting to these uncomfortable new money modes.

But in stretching toward each other this way, they may end up with new flexibility, intimacy, and more sensible financial choices. In fact, I've seen couples who go through this exercise reap the rewards of mutuality and shared goals as they move into their prime years.

Remember, risk takers and risk avoiders really do live in different universes—and depending on which place you yourself inhabit, you may have to stretch to understand a client whose attitude is a world apart from your own. But by making this effort and earning your clients' trust, you can guide them out of their patterned rigidities toward a more sensible middle ground, where creative new choices will be possible.

Equal and Opposite Addictions

While a client couple were here for their first session, they started sniping at each other when I asked where their discretionary money goes. He accused her of spending a fortune on an extravagant collection of designer dolls. She promptly fired back that someone who spent all his time working couldn't blame her for enjoying such an innocent pastime. How can I defuse this hostile atmosphere so we can work together?

Many couples are locked into negative power struggles where two kinds of addictive behavior vie for center stage. The wife's expensive doll-collecting hobby may be prompted (at least in part) by her husband's workaholism, exacerbated by feelings of loneliness or emptiness arising out of his emotional inaccessibility. In different ways, they're both avoiding facing themselves and dealing with their fear of intimacy.

It might be appropriate for you to suggest that they see a couples counselor about her overspending and his overworking. (If you keep a list of good therapists available, along with stories about couples whose relationship improved through similar intervention, you may help motivate dueling clients like these two.)

Again, I would recommend that they start the process of moving toward the middle by writing down (at first separately, then together) their goals for the near future and the longer term. If you can get them to agree on some of these goals, they may be able to begin moving together in small but significant ways toward what I call money harmony.

SPENDERS AND HOARDERS

The Long Arm of the Past

My client knows she needs to live more within her means, but I can't seem to make a dent in her spending binges. She has to have the newest clothes, cars, home furnishings, electronics, everything. I suspect that as one of many children in a low-income family, she may have grown up feeling deprived. She once told me that whenever she asked for money, her father would either refuse or insist that she account for every penny of the last sum he'd given her. Is there any way to help a woman who's reached her 40s with so much emotional baggage?

As a recovering overspender myself, I know you'll have your work cut out for you with this client. The best way to begin, I believe, is by honoring her past. Acknowledge sympathetically how hard it must have been to keep feeling that she never had enough money to buy the things she wanted. You might also share stories of other people you know who labored under similar burdens, but eventually were able to move from buying whatever they desired to setting limits on their spending and (here's the important point) learning to reward themselves in other ways.

Overspenders will almost always experience what I call an "inner tantrum" when they have to say no to themselves about immediate gratification. Teach your client to be prepared for this reaction, and help her find ways to reward herself that will lead to a real feeling of security and contentment. Some suggestions: visits to free museums, lunch with a friend at a reasonable restaurant, a spiritually oriented activity, community service, even the pleasure of investing (i.e., spending on her future).

To help reinforce her new behavior, consider suggesting homework assignments based on saving or investing. It may help her control her impulse to go on spending sprees if she selects a picture that represents the goal she's saving for and carries it in her wallet next to her credit cards. Urge her to write down how it feels to be changing her old ingrained spending habits, and to reward herself (not by overspending!) for sticking to her commitment.

You'll need an extra reserve of patience and perseverance to help this client, since progress (if any) will probably come in the form of two steps forward and one step back. Relapses are common. The important thing is to keep reminding your client that she has charge of her money now, not her father, and that it's up to her to stick with the program.

Solving a Faraway Spending Problem

My client's daughter, who lives several hundred miles away, is constantly begging her mother to bail her out of financial crises. The daughter has at last admitted that she may have a spending problem, and is willing to seek help. Where should my client direct her to go?

Today's far-flung families (often further separated by multiple marriages) complicate this increasingly common problem. Because financially responsible clients are more likely now to live too far away to directly help a family member with spending problems, the need for a network of support resources is increasing.

If your client's daughter lives in or near a big city, the first step I'd recommend is that she look for local Debtors Anonymous groups to participate in at least once a week. I would specify "groups" in the plural, not "group," because it's best for new attendees to check out several meetings in their area to see which one(s) they feel most comfortable attending.

Second, your client should urge her daughter to look for a therapist who works with addictions and is comfortable talking about money. It's the "money" part of this prerequisite that may be tricky, because many therapists are so uneasy dealing with money issues that they immediately deflect these discussions into other areas. The daughter really needs someone who is at ease dealing with money problems while exploring the deeper meaning of her overspending. If you're willing to phone some therapists to discuss their experience with clients like yours and find out how they would work with this type of situation, it could be of great assistance to your client and her daughter.

There are some good self-help guides available (see the Additional Resources for suggestions). However, books alone won't do the job; overspenders need therapeutic help and emotional reinforcement to stay on track. In my experience, a combination of counseling and support groups like Debtors Anonymous has proved to be the best method of treatment.

Spending for Solace

A woman of about 70, whom I'll call Betty, was recently referred by a friend who is a longtime client of mine. According to my client, Betty moved to a condo in this area a few years ago after her husband died. She has few other friends here, however, and spends quite a bit of her time shopping for new designer-label clothing and high-end home furnishings. My client is concerned that all this spending may mean Betty will outlive the money she was left by her husband. As I plan for my first meeting with Betty, how can I help her stop her unnecessary spending?

This woman is probably still in shock about the death of her spouse and the change from her old life, and loath to face the loneliness of her new situation. By endlessly shopping, dressing herself well, and filling her home with beautiful objects, she's trying to fill a gaping emotional hole with activities and "things." Trying to keep up with Joneses she doesn't even know, and impress neighbors she hasn't even met, may also be an attempt to create a grand life she always wanted but could never afford (or wasn't allowed to indulge in while her husband held the purse strings).

Betty sounds in dire need of friends, family, and grief counseling or other good therapeutic intervention. Is there a support group for widows and widowers in your area that you could recommend to her? I think you also ought to enlist the aid of her friend in gently confronting her about her excessive spending. Setting up a visit with you is a wonderfully loving way the friend is trying to reach her lonely pal.

Before your first consultation with Betty, you might want to call her to break the ice. Tell her you've worked with other women in her situation, and have been able to help give them financial security and peace of mind—true serenity. I see Betty as a frenetic woman who probably craves serenity on many levels, and might respond well to this compassionate reaching out on your part.

Piggy Bank Blues

This is a new one for me! My spendaholic client told me that when she was about four years old, she eagerly saved every spare nickel and dime in a piggy bank her grandparents had given her. One day her mother came into her bedroom needing money for something, broke the bank, and took her money. She never replaced the savings, and never even understood why her little girl was so upset. My client now says that every time she has money saved, she feels impelled to spend it as soon as possible, frittering it away on meaningless little purchases or indulging her own three kids. Does this make sense to you, and if so, can I help her?

Unfortunately, this story makes all kinds of sense. People can be paralyzed well into adulthood by an early childhood trauma, even one caused by an event that we rationally "understand" once we're grown up.

You need to be as compassionate as possible with your client about this awful event—that cheated four-year-old is still alive, well, and actively raging inside her today. Once you give her some of the understanding she never got from her parent, she may be willing to accept your suggestions about small actions she can take to begin accumulating money.

Encourage her to focus on her goals—the good things in life that savings can bring her down the road—and reassure her that you're there to help her reach those goals. If you're deeply committed to this task, she'll feel it and know that you're not like her mother, who thoughtlessly helped herself to her child's painstakingly accumulated money, without ever replacing it or acknowledging the feelings of violation and catastrophe that ensued.

Assure her that you'll be her advocate to make sure no one in any way violates her new savings. At least initially, you may want to recommend investment vehicles that are both safe and relatively illiquid, such as long-term CDs or individual Treasury bonds. This will help her resist any temptation to spend the money. Investing in mutual funds or stocks which lose value may cause her to re-experience some of her old trauma. However, by discussing this possibility with her in advance, you can help her feel that she is in control of her money and financial decision-making no matter what happens.

When you're dealing with messages or emotional wounds that originated in the past, be exceedingly patient and gentle in suggesting sensible financial choices. The more time you take to acknowledge and reassure the hurt or damaged child that may live within the adult sitting in your office, the better your chances will be of getting these clients to follow through on your good advice and guidance.

The Difficulty of Deferring Gratification

A client of mine wants to use the proceeds from a recent sale of stock to add to his collection of antique firearms. Based on past experience with his spending habits, I know that if he does this, the probability of his having enough money to pay the next quarter's estimated taxes is virtually nil. How can I convince him to save the money for Uncle Sam?

Take care not to attack him for his spending tendencies, or to get judgmental about his financial choices. In fact, you might begin by affirming his desire to enjoy his money and spend it on a personal passion.

Then gently (perhaps even with light humor) remind him that spending this money now means that he will probably be scrambling to pay taxes in a state of high stress and even panic. Remind him that one of the reasons he hired you was to help him decrease tension in his life, so he could enjoy his money instead of worrying about it.

Once you have communicated all this in the right tone free of condemnation or contempt, you may be able to jolly him back to his senses. If he is totally in denial about the likelihood of an estimated tax shortfall, you might try a few cautionary tales about other taxpayers who have dug themselves into terrible holes with similar behavior. Once the meter starts running on interest and penalties, his debt to the IRS will mount every day.

If he still doesn't agree to apply the sale proceeds to current taxes, see if he will consider putting aside part of this money. Anything you can do to interrupt his tendency towards impulsive spending and financial imbalance would be providing him a great service.

Helping a Hoarder Have More Fun

A client has asked for my help in persuading her husband to be less miserly with his money, "so we can take a few nice vacations together before we die." A colleague at another firm tells me she once advised a super-hoarder client to use some of his money for a two-week vacation in Paris, and even handed him the plane ticket. I'd like to try this with my clients, but it feels presumptuous. What do you think?

You're right to be cautious. While this controversial tactic might be very successful, it could equally well blow up in your face.

Before attempting it, I would want to know the answers to some key questions:

1. How much is your "miserly" client willing to relax his attitude and move toward a more balanced state of mind?
2. How tired is he of living a life marked by sacrifice and delayed gratification?
3. Would a trip to Paris (or something similar) really be a pleasure for him, or would it feel so extravagant that he wouldn't enjoy himself at all?

If you talk this over with the wife in advance, she may be able to clue you about whether to try this tack with her husband. Be aware, though, that if he's become an extreme hoarder, she's likely to have become his opposite: a spender who loves to spend money on immediate pleasure.

With her approval, you might meet with the husband alone to sound him out about the possibility of a pleasure trip before you take any concrete action. In any case, you need to be sensitive to the needs of both in order to build a bridge between them. Bonne chance!

Improving the Social Life of a Scrooge

My client, a 75-year-old former oncologist widowed several years ago, has a seven-figure portfolio but acts as though he's one step from the poorhouse. He refuses to spend any money on himself, makes lady friends pay for their own meals, and worries constantly about the stock market. When a widow he's been seeing suggested that they go Dutch treat on a Caribbean cruise, he told her he needed to save all his money for a rainy day. I think he'd be happier enjoying some of his wealth instead of just hoarding it, but how can I help him see that he has more than enough?

It's never comfortable for a hoarder to become more of a spender, especially not at first. You can expect your client to feel guilty and self-indulgent, as if he's wasting his money.

A planner I met at a recent conference found an effective way to persuade a similar client: he ran the numbers and showed the client that there was enough money to last him comfortably to age 120. "You could see him visibly relax once he saw this in black and white," the planner reported. "I printed out the summary in large print and handed it to him to take home."

Consider trying this dollars-and-cents solution to persuade your frugal client that penury isn't right around the corner. If it works, encourage him to set aside a sum of money every year for his own enjoyment (perhaps including a cruise with a companion).

Your concern does you credit. By stepping out of his bank vault to smell the roses, your client will eventually feel more relaxed about life in general, and perhaps experience more closeness with his family and friends.

Split Personality

Talking to a new client of mine is like being in a war zone. She ricochets back and forth between worrying incessantly about losing her money, and wanting to put it in high-risk investments in hopes of getting rich quick. She also bounces between impulsive spending sprees and long periods of fearful hoarding. Is there any hope that she'll ever pull herself together?

Although you may feel as if you've accidentally wandered into *The Three Faces of Eve*, polarization patterns can (and often do) exist within the same person. I've seen a fair number of these internal wars in my therapy and coaching practices. And when I was an active overspender, I myself used to oscillate between shopping binges and periods of worry when I was scared to spend any money. So, believe me, I know what your client's going through.

If she's willing to accept your guidance in trying to reconcile her divergent desires and behavior, you might begin by suggesting that she learn whom she may be imitating. (For me, it was Dad the worrier and Mom the shopaholic.) Invite her to write dialogues where her "spender" self talks to the "hoarder," and the money avoider talks to the worrier. After she's done these money dialogues several times (it's crucial to complete more than one), these voices will begin to be better integrated inside her and she'll begin to experience some resolution of her inner conflict.

The next step in this exercise is to write down how major financial influences in her life might comment on the dialogues she's just finished. Was her mother, father, a sibling, husband, ex-husband, grandparent, teacher, or friend particularly important in shaping her ideas about money? Ask her to envision just what these people might say—approvingly or critically—about her present attitudes toward money. Finally, invite her to imagine the opinion of God (her higher power or the voice of inner wisdom). This last step is crucial in pointing her in the right direction to reach balance.

If your client does this exercise mindfully, it can be truly transformative in helping her get to a more rational, peaceful state of mind. Coupled with your patient attempts to educate her about her financial priorities, this should eventually lead her to making wiser, more consistent decisions about her money.

AMASSERS AND MONEY MONKS

The 24-Hour Trader

A prospective new client came in recently to ask if I could help her wean her husband away from online trading. He uses his office computer to trade several times a day, then places more trades when he comes home from work. The wife happened to come across a recent brokerage statement and was horrified to see that he paid nearly $1,000 in commissions last month. She'd like me to take over managing their investments. Any thoughts on how we can get the husband to consider giving up his expensive hobby?

The difficulty of this task is expressed in the old joke: "How many therapists does it take to change a light bulb? Only one, but the light bulb really has to want to change."

Addictions in any form are very difficult to overcome, especially when the "addict" is in denial and doesn't see that there's a problem. Nevertheless, I think you can suggest a two-pronged strategy for the wife.

First, at a moment when the husband is more or less accessible, she should tell him (in a non-blaming, vulnerable way) how much she misses spending time with him since he began trading so heavily. She might also mention that she's concerned about what may happen if his employers discover he is distracted by investment concerns when he's at work.

Next, she might say that she thinks it's an excellent idea that he wants to increase their wealth and financial security, and suggest that by working with a professional (you), they might be able to achieve this goal without consuming so much of his scarce and valuable free time. Provide her with your own credentials and references to share with her husband, perhaps including some information about how buy-and-hold stock investors have historically surpassed the returns of frequent traders. She should then invite him to a preliminary visit with you, simply to explore the possibilities.

If and when he comes in, ask him what he likes about online trading. Is it the fast pace, the intensity of being on the edge of risk, the hands-on manipulation of his own portfolio, or the camaraderie of talking to others and sharing tips? Ask him, too, how much he's gained or lost in the last few months, including trading costs.

If you think he's willing to recognize that he may be overdoing it, you might pass along an article or two about the dangers of excessive trading. A scary story about someone who lost a bundle in fast online trading might help wake him up, too. If he won't quit cold turkey, a compromise might be for the couple to set aside a certain sum as his "play money," while you manage the rest of their assets with their longer-term goals in mind.

Remember, though, that unless this man is open to changing his own extreme behavior, you can't "save" him—or his distraught wife. You might be forced to suggest to her that she separate some assets for you to manage, so her husband can't devour everything they own with his addictive trading habits.

Giving Away the Store

A woman almost literally dragged her husband in to see me yesterday, saying she's fed up with his giving away so much of their money to various causes and individuals who hear he's an easy touch. She feels they're affluent enough to replace their shabby furniture, help their married daughter buy a home, and take a nice vacation after many years of skimping. Her husband says they don't really need this money and should continue giving it away to those less fortunate. Is there a happy medium in this situation?

Wealth has negative connotations for many people—particularly for money monks, the personality type this man seems to embody.

When money monks are married to amassers (as is often the case), they create a combination that's hard to help. The monk believes that accumulating money is bad and sinful, while the amasser believes it's powerful, desirable, and fine.

It's important to validate and appreciate his altruistic values and goals, as well as her desire to enjoy some of their money and help out their child. To guide them toward meeting in the middle, you'll need to help them confront their deep, underlying money beliefs and find examples that run counter to their prejudices.

For example, in a recent AARP study, "Money and the American Family," respondents of all ages agreed that wealth makes people feel superior (84%), too greedy (81%), and/or insensitive to others (74%). However, when *Modern Maturity* interviewed several millionaires for its July/August 2000 issue, they turned out to be quite the opposite: very family-oriented, religious or spiritual, frugal, grateful for the independence their wealth offered them, and so on.

Sharing this article with your clients might help change the husband's prejudices about money and wealth. You may also have a few good stories at your fingertips about happy and fulfilled folks who travel, live in a nice home, and help their children financially while making a difference in the world. Perhaps then this couple can begin moving toward a middle ground in their approach to money.

RISK TAKERS AND RISK AVOIDERS

Hooked on High Rolling

My client—a 50ish married executive with three school-age kids—seems to crave speculative "high roller" holdings that most investors in his situation shouldn't touch with a ten-foot pole. Sure, it's exciting when one of these long shots pays off, but why won't he listen when I talk about investments that are more appropriate for his retirement and his family's needs?

Once someone is hooked on risk as deeply as your client seems to be, breaking the addiction can be tough. When you've talked with him patiently about his dreams and concerns for his children, has he been able to acknowledge that these concerns are a higher priority than his own short-term thrill-chasing?

If not, I would advise you to educate him about the appropriateness of high-risk investing at different stages of life. He may have learned this behavior years ago when he didn't have much to lose, but now it makes less and less sense as he contemplates his own future and his desire to provide for his family. To drive this point home, consider exploring with him some past situations where his risk-seeking has backfired with costly repercussions.

When risk-taking patterns are very deeply ingrained, it may take shock treatment to break the trance. Without preaching, you might matter-of-factly caution him (with a true-life anecdote if possible) about the toll a compulsive gambling addiction can take on people's finances, lives, and relationships. If he confides that he'd like to give it up but can't seem to make his intentions stick, nudge him gently toward Gamblers Anonymous, where he can learn how to turn around this compulsive tendency to put his financial and family security at risk.

If you feel comfortable sharing vulnerabilities of your own, you might let him know of a past lack of balance in some area that you yourself have had to struggle with. From your client's perspective, you'll then be in the position of advising him with empathy from your own experience, instead of criticizing him from some superior vantage point.

No matter which approach you take, you may help him get his priorities straight by working on aspects of his dreams and goals where he's connected and rational (for example, maybe he'd love to see his studious daughter go to medical school). Alternatively, see if he has any fears about how his behavior may affect his family (e.g., by prompting his kids to imitate his style and lose their money on risky investments). By playing on a deeply felt longing or fear, you may be able to drive a wedge between him and the addictive "high" of his risk-taker behavior, and prompt him to heed your advice about investing his money more wisely.

Playing Chicken with the IRS

A young man who is an occasional client came in to ask me some tax-related questions. He wants to push the envelope in a few areas, and is seeking permission to do it from me (I'm also a CPA). Some of his proposed tax maneuvers seem merely aggressive, but one or two are decidedly risky. I advised against them, but he shrugged off my opinion. How can I get through to him while also protecting myself?

Begin by acknowledging that in our society, the complexity of our tax code has created many gray areas on which even the tax courts disagree. However, the advice you have given him about his proposed tactics is based on your own familiarity with tax law and recent interpretations of it. Remind him that you have an ethical responsibility to advise him on what he can and cannot legally do.

Scare tactics sometimes work with greedy clients. But even though you may know many examples where the long arm of the law has reached out for wrongdoers, don't allude to them in such a way that he feels you believe he's a crook.

On the other hand, be extremely careful not to give the impression that you are permitting him to cheat in any way. You are not his surrogate parent, even though he evidently wants you to be one. And if the IRS balks at any of his choices, you don't want to be held even partly responsible, by him or anyone else. So be sure to give him your opinion in writing. And keep a copy for your files.

In the final analysis, if he decides to take an action that you feel is illegal, you may have to respectfully part company with him. Let him know that this is a business decision: you would like to help, but you feel it's more important that he find an advisor whose counsel is truly of value to him.

The Rent's at the Race Track

A brother and sister, both in their 30s, have consulted me about working with their father, whose wife (their stepmother) recently left him. They're very concerned about the amount of time and money he spends at the race track. When they broached the subject with him, he accused them of trying to rob him of his sole pleasure in life so they would have more money to inherit. They've asked me if I can get him to stop, but gambling isn't one of my areas of expertise. What can I do to help?

First, you should know that gambling addictions can be highly resistant to change. Gamblers Anonymous, a 12-step program, has chapters all over the country to help chronic gamblers stop this destructive behavior. Unfortunately, these people don't usually seek help until they've created terrible financial havoc in their lives.

Your clients' father obviously is not ready to admit he has a problem, so (assuming you're willing to try) you'll need a less confrontational introduction to him. It sounds to me as though he may be lonely and trying to fill up his empty life with some excitement, to mask the natural feelings of loss and rejection over his wife's leaving him.

You might open a dialogue by sending him an article about what you do. If you have a good file of reference material, I would also send him something that emphasizes the importance of communicating with adult children about money and the future. At the same time, you might suggest that the sister and brother write their father a letter expressing their love and concern, and informing him point-blank that it's concern for his future welfare, not greed, which motivates them.

Again, I would caution that with many gamblers, the only thing that stops the pernicious cycle is "bottoming out"—losing so much money that the reality of their crazy risk-taking at last opens their eyes. There's a slim chance that you might be able to help their father see the light by sending him articles about these kinds of financial tragedies. But he ultimately needs to find healthier ways to "fill himself up"—ways that don't compromise his and his family's financial well-being. A solution might be to encourage him to volunteer at a community center, sign up for a class of some kind, or get involved in other activities where he can make new friends and enrich his life.

The Roots of Risk Anxiety

One of my clients, an entrepreneur in his 30s, insists he can tolerate risk. However, every time the market drops, he panics and I have to talk him out of selling his investments. Recently he told me that his fears stem from a past family crisis involving his father, who was so shattered by the Crash of 1987 that he suffered a nervous breakdown. Is there any way I can help my client get over this still-vivid horror story?

First of all, I'm always skeptical (as you probably are) about accepting a client's declaration of risk tolerance at face value.

Investing is a lot like flying: if we had our druthers, most of us would probably take the train and stay safely on the ground. We "like" to fly because it helps us get somewhere fast, and we believe the chances of an accident are slim (of course, past performance does not guarantee future results). But unless we're coached on what to do when the plane runs into turbulence, our vaunted risk tolerance can easily turn to fear.

Your client's fear is much closer to the surface because his recent family trauma has scarred him deeply. He may need to seek therapy to deal with these wounds, in order to regain his balance and restore his ability to make decisions rationally.

Begin by empathizing with his terror and his loss. You might even share similar stories to let him know you understand what a terrible burden he has been carrying. Once you've validated his fear and pain, you may be able to start vaccinating him against the family virus of stock market doom by educating him with charts and numbers about the market's historical growth over the long term.

I urge you to be patient with your client, and not to push him too hard. The shock waves from financial catastrophe and mental breakdown can be magnified as they pass down through a family, while explanatory details are often forgotten. This makes it hard for younger generations to put the story into perspective. But by persevering with your traumatized client, you should eventually be able to guide him to a more balanced and rational view of the risks of equity investing.

WORRIERS AND AVOIDERS

Take My Money—Please

I've just begun to work with a client who's so anxious about taxes that she overpays enormously every year. In other respects she seems to be very frugal. How can I help her get over this compulsion to give the Treasury an interest-free loan?

I'd begin by taking time to find out why she overpays her taxes. What does she fear that's worse? Did someone she knows have a dreadful experience with the IRS? Does she believe she can't understand the tax rules well enough to be sure of paying just the right amount?

By reviewing her financial goals, you may also glean ideas that help calm her tax-related fears. If you can understand and address what makes her so anxious, without judging her, it may go a long way toward easing her worries and building a bridge toward more rational money behavior.

Remind her of the rules about underpayment penalties, and help her see how she can avoid them more sensibly. For example, she might set up a conservatively invested tax account that will let her keep the interest her money earns, instead of Uncle Sam.

Money Avoiders and Math Anxiety

I don't know if my new client has math anxiety or what, but she has procrastinated for weeks on filling out the financial information forms I've given her. I've considered telling her to bring in all her account statements so I can complete the forms for her, but thought she might be offended by the suggestion that she can't handle very basic financial matters. Should I simply say that I expect her to provide this information, and leave it at that?

If your client does have math anxiety (and the money anxiety that usually accompanies it), neither of these approaches will serve her well. She needs patient, non-judgmental help and support.

I would suggest a third solution: invite her to fill out the forms with your assistance. By allowing her to learn about her financial situation in a safe place, this will be of enormous value to her.

If your client does seem reluctant or anxious about coming to grips with her finances, you may need to calm her down by reminding her that she is not alone. Many people have trouble functioning well in the world of numbers—including filling out forms. Acknowledge the wisdom of her choice to tackle this issue by coming to see you, instead of trying to hide or deny her anxiety.

By meeting this client in the eye of her personal hurricane, you may be able to help her learn about good money management while steering her toward financial well-being. Keep encouraging her to find a way through her emotional turmoil to a calm place where rational learning is possible.

I doubt if your client will feel patronized in this process, unless she senses contempt in your attitude toward her. (If you do feel this way, remind yourself that clients with math anxiety may exceed your abilities in many other areas.) In any event, I believe it's better to run the risk of being perceived as talking down to her than to leave her entangled in her own fears and frustrations.

Should I Abet an Avoider?

A man came in to see me who's made a total mess of his finances. He's what I think you'd call a total "money avoider." He procrastinates about paying bills, filing taxes, investing, saving, and goal-setting. Now that he's come into a small inheritance, he wants me to take it over completely and make all the decisions for him. Is this a good idea for this "out to lunch" guy?

Well, yes and no. Setting up automatic systems such as electronic bill payment and regular transfers to an investment account makes sense for classic money avoiders. But allowing him to totally surrender responsibility would simply encourage him to stay in the role of a helpless child.

So while it's okay to help him clean up his mess, I'd recommend helping him build stronger financial muscles by giving him one financial task he usually avoids, like paying bills. Check in with him regularly to see if he's fulfilling his commitment to do it.

By teaching him to be less of an avoider, you'll foster his self-esteem and self-respect. And helping him grow in ways that go beyond asset management will make you feel good, too.

TAKING ACTION

In general, helping clients with different money styles learn to "do what doesn't come naturally" will be one of the most challenging parts of your job. Although doing it may feel uncomfortable to them at first, it will ultimately give them the potential for more creativity, intimacy, flexibility and choice in their lives. And what could be better than that?

When extreme money personality traits lead to problems, remember that you can help your clients only if they are willing to openly examine their imbalance, fear, compulsion, or addiction. If they refuse to acknowledge and correct the problem, you need to accept that this may be one of the situations where you cannot effect change. Know when to let go, and focus your energies on those clients who will welcome your invaluable help and support in making positive changes in their moneylives.

DEALING WITH DIFFERENCES
Caveat Gender

Over the past several years, the financial services industry has thrown itself wholeheartedly into the task of communicating more effectively to women. Perhaps inevitably, critics have weighed in to admonish that financial advisors should treat women exactly like men—ignoring the fact that there are real differences in perception and priorities between the two genders.

Are you communicating well to both women and men, based on an understanding of where they're coming from and where they are now? As the following examples show, the '60s adage of "different strokes for different folks" truly suits this often-murky area.

Am I a Sexist?

I'm a female advisor who has found I prefer working with male clients. I feel somewhat guilty about this, but it's the truth. Should I make myself seek more clients of my own gender, or just keep doing what I'm doing?

To answer your question, I'd want to know more about why you prefer working with men. For example, are you (like many financial professionals) a left-brain person who feels most comfortable with facts and figures? If so, you may be responding to the more logical and unemotional orientation of many male clients.

Perhaps you feel more validated and respected when a man comes to you for help than when a woman does. That might imply that you value women's opinions less—a bias you might want to work on. Or you may have found that men are more apt to be financially confident clients whose portfolios simply need a little fine-tuning, while women arrive with fears, anxieties, and blind spots that require a lot more empathy and hard work.

In general, if your practice is doing well and you feel good about what you're accomplishing with male clients, there may not be anything broken that you really need to fix.

But if you feel bad about not doing more to help other women, why not experiment? Try taking on one or two female clients, and determine what you like and dislike about working with them. (I would suggest choosing clients with whom you feel a particular affinity, while referring the others to colleagues after the initial consultation.) Don't make this a guilt-trippy "should"—only follow through if you have a real desire to balance your practice in this new and possibly satisfying way.

If you do, you're apt to be pleasantly surprised. Research has shown that women tend to be excellent long-term investors, as well as loyal, consistent, and cooperative clients. They're less easily swayed than many men by tips from friends or get-rich-quick schemes. Also, women tend to be appreciative of the help they get from a good financial advisor, and generous in referring others to you.

Gender Generalizations

I am a woman financial planner who just gave a speech to a group of my colleagues about differences between male and female investors. I made a few light jokes about men's and women's foibles, and was surprised that some of my male listeners took offense at the comments I directed at their gender. Should I avoid humor if I give similar talks in the future?

As a speaker who sometimes addresses this same touchy topic, I try to head off negative reactions by doing two things.

First, I remind my audience upfront that generalizations are false in many cases. In other words, they shouldn't feel that my sweeping statements necessarily apply to them, let alone to "all men" or "all women."

Second, I share vulnerable, personal examples to show that I like and respect men, and think that each sex has a lot to teach the other. In this way, I hope to make it clear for my listeners that I don't intend to put men down or make them feel bad about themselves.

You might try these tactics before making any light-hearted comments in the future. Be aware, too, that many men are brought up to hide their vulnerabilities and hurts, which can lead women into assuming that they're thicker-skinned than they really are. That's a generalization too, of course—but you have no way of knowing the history of the individual men who seemed offended by your remarks.

If you feel you need to repair your rapport with these colleagues, you might try to start a dialogue with each of them. Be willing to apologize for your lack of sensitivity to their feelings. To see if they'll tell you more about why they reacted the way they did, consider sharing with them your own personal journey, if it's not too critical of men in general. (If you do feel angry about men, I'd suggest choosing another topic for your talks. Otherwise, you risk stepping into this minefield again and again.)

Many people need to feel safe before they'll open up to new information. They don't learn when they feel criticized or attacked. So if you hope to enlighten your colleagues, cultivate an attitude of acceptance and compassion—and only then add some appropriate, sensitive lightness or humor.

Playing Dumb?

Although my new client seems to be very knowledgeable about investing, she keeps putting herself down, apologizing for her lack of sophistication, and asking me if she's right whenever she makes a decision. As a male advisor who is almost twice her age, I can't figure out whether she's trying to manipulate me or playing dumb so I'll take care of her. In any case, should I tell her how much this behavior of hers irritates me, or just try to shrug it off?

Unfortunately, there's more to this strange behavior than meets the eye.

In years of doing therapy, I've learned that many American women were raised to believe that they would probably be incompetent with money—but if they were lucky, some guy would take care of it for them. Other women (more than you might imagine) were taught to avoid displaying any financial competence for fear that this "threat" might scare men away or anger them. Some women, in fact, were raised with both messages.

I hope this will help you address your client's annoying behavior with less irritability and more compassion. If so, I would suggest that you tell her something like this: "I find you very knowledgeable and intelligent about investing, and quite sophisticated in your understanding and insight."

Give her a moment to respond, and see if she can graciously accept your sincere compliment. If she shakes her head and demurs, "But I really don't. . .", it's a perfect lead-in to discuss this behavior with her.

You might say, "I've noticed that you tend to apologize for your lack of sophistication, or defer to me in a way that depreciates your own judgment and undermines your power. Can you help me understand what motivates you to respond this way? Were you taught to downplay financial ability when you were younger? Or am I doing something that intimidates you, or makes you reluctant to claim your obvious expertise?"

Once you give her the opportunity to tell you more about what is causing her behavior, you can encourage her further. Tell her you truly enjoy working with competent and savvy investors, and it doesn't threaten you in the least if she's willing to share her valuable ideas with you.

If she can accept all this praise and inspiration without pushing it away, you'll have begun developing a strong relationship with a well-informed client who's easy to work with. Best of all, you'll have helped raise her self-esteem, which is bound to benefit her in other areas of her life.

Stopping to Ask for Directions

Why is it often so hard for men to admit to a lack of financial expertise? When I volunteered to coach a new client who knows very little about investing, he bristled as though I'd insulted him. How can I help him learn what he needs to know without getting his dander up?

When men try to conceal a lack of competence in financial matters (or other important areas), it's usually because they think it means they can't measure up to their peers. That's one of the worst feelings a man can experience, particularly if he thrives on competing and winning.

The best way to approach a client like this is to get in under his radar. Try to teach him what he needs to know without drawing attention to the fact that he doesn't already know it.

For example, you might preface important information with a modest disclaimer: "Some of my clients find it helps them look at things more clearly if we review the basics before getting into a specific recommendation." Or: "If you already know a lot of this, please bear with me. I think we should take it from the top, to be sure we're looking at the same issues together and are agreed on what you want to accomplish." By framing your teaching as an adjunct to what he already knows, you'll soften the agenda and let him know you respect him.

Coping with Provider Stress

During my recent interview with a client couple, I discovered that the husband is very stressed out about feeling that he is the family provider. His fear of having a heart attack and leaving his family in dire financial straits has actually caused him to have panic attacks at work. His wife is totally unsympathetic to this worry of his. In our joint session, she said, "I make more than he does, so why should he feel such a big responsibility?" How can I navigate through these tricky currents?

This situation is an excellent example of the different financial expectations that burden men and women.

While women are often burdened by having to work a "second shift" at home in addition to a full-time job, most men feel burdened by having to be the family's chief provider of stable income. This is usually the case even when a husband makes less than his wife. Why? Because whether or not he's the main economic provider, he doesn't feel free to quit working full-time to do other things: become a house-husband, retire early, pursue a passion, or just work part-time so he can golf or fish more. By contrast, many more wives do feel this freedom.

In my workshops I try to teach women compassion for this burden, which leads so many men to chronic anxiety, depression, and even heart disease. Encourage your female client to empathize with her husband's provider stress (regardless of who actually makes more money), instead of pooh-poohing his feelings.

If you succeed in this emotional bridge-building, you'll lighten his psychic load, making it possible for him to worry less. In fact, it may well come as a big relief to him to acknowledge the reality of her financial success. Once he stops feeling criticized and attacked, and realizes that she is willing and able to partner him in shouldering economic responsibility, I foresee that you'll help create more closeness for this couple.

Am I "Pandering"?

Every year I host an appreciation dinner for my women clients at a nice restaurant. I also take time to send them cards or flowers during the year to acknowledge birthdays and other special occasions. I enjoy doing this, and it comes naturally to me. A woman partner in our practice says I should stop "pandering" to them this way and just do my job as a financial planner. Is she right?

In my experience, most women are what Jung called "feeling types." They tend to care about relationships and about feeling connected to others in all areas of their life. To a greater extent than most men, they're interested in "the harmony of the whole" (a concept developed by Meyers-Briggs adherents, who analyzed personality differences using Jung's types).

To build a relationship of trust with clients like these, you need to make them feel that you're tuned to them as individuals, and that you understand and care about their deeper needs and their lives as a whole. Assuming that you've identified their values, priorities, and dreams, and are helping them make these dreams come true, my advice is to keep trusting your instincts. If your women clients seem to enjoy and appreciate what you've been doing, for heaven's sake don't turn into a cold fish.

In fact, you might persuade your "thinking type" partner to try reaching out to her clients in some way she doesn't find patronizing, and see how they respond to this new behavior. (Many "feeling-type" male clients might appreciate this extra attention, too.) I would caution that any action that feels uncomfortable or out of character may be perceived as phony. But if she can do it in the spirit of meeting clients' need for a more personal touch, it can improve the quality of her client relationships and enhance her practice.

Dealing with Men Who Don't Take Charge

My client, a man in his 30's, is extremely anxious about financial decisions and tries to defer them to me as often as possible. Despite trying to be open-minded, I find this behavior very annoying. Although I'm accustomed to coaching women in similar circumstances, I generally expect male clients to be more independent and willing to take risks. How can I work more effectively with this man?

Financial planners tell me that both men and women often express a desire to have someone else take care of "all this money stuff" for them. Frequently, the client hopes that this person will save them from potential financial disaster, or at least relieve their anxiety and make them feel safe.

First of all, nurture sympathy and patience in yourself by visualizing this young man as someone even younger—an insecure teenager or a child, if you can manage this without feeling condescending or judgmental. Try to find out why he has so little confidence in his own ability to make good financial decisions. For example, was his dad a money manager who constantly put him down? Did his parents disparage his intelligence and life skills?

Once you've gotten him to open up to you about some of the old wounds he carries, it may be easier to encourage him to develop the knowledge, capability, and eventually the confidence to take more of a role in decision-making. In the meantime, by cultivating a sympathetic but not coddling attitude while you work on getting him to let go of his dependency, you'll be temporarily "parenting" him around money till he's ready to become his own parent.

When Rash Choices Lead to Loss

A former client has just returned to me after losing nearly $100,000 on an IPO that a good friend recommended to him. My client's portfolio is in shambles, not to mention his state of mind. I know how to help him recoup his financial equilibrium, but how can I help repair his feelings about friendship and trust?

I often wish I could talk with Carl Jung about men's affinity for acting on hot tips.

In his terminology, men are typically considered to be "thinking" types who make decisions based on linear thinking and logic. But one flaw in Jung's generalization is the tendency for some men to make bad decisions based on tips from friends—which is not rational at all.

In my opinion, this behavior is at least partly motivated by a wish to join a secret society of winners. By belonging to this special clique, the tippee believes he will be able to outperform his colleagues and friends.

Knowing this, you can begin to soothe your client's wounded ego and state of shock. First of all, boost his self-confidence and self-esteem by reminding him of his positive qualities and strengths as an investor (his willingness to explore the unfamiliar, for example).

You might then point out that he is far from alone. Millions of other investors have made the mistake of acting on a tip, often offered in good faith, without making sure of its value. If he did try to check out the IPO before sinking his money into it, he's certainly experienced enough to know that even with all the research in the world, choosing investments is not an exact science. The good news is that despite his bad luck, his fortunes are not irreversibly damaged. Because of his many strengths, you can help him overcome this reverse to get back on track.

Having paved the way with reassurance and sympathy, you may then be able to suggest steps he can take right away to begin turning things around. No doubt you've also thought of ways he can protect himself more effectively in the future—for example, earmarking only a fraction of his portfolio for highly speculative investments.

In general, be aware that behavior you ascribe to "Joe's personality" or "Bob's mindset" may really be an Achilles heel shared by many other men. Whether it's the magical thinking of "This tip will make me rich," excessive risk-taking, over-responsibility, or fear of failure (evidenced in a client's reluctance to acknowledge lack of information or expertise, or to admit and correct mistakes), be sympathetic to their defenses, concerns, and struggles. Pace your teaching interventions and action suggestions so that a client can learn from you without feeling as though you're looking down on him.

As you learn to do this better and better, you'll be in a good position to expand your clientele. The world is full of male investors ready to learn from you and do the right thing, knowing you'll help them overcome their Achilles tendencies without sacrificing their self-confidence.

Do Same-Sex Investment Clubs Make Sense?

A young woman recently consulted me after dropping out of an investment club. (She complained that male club members dominated the discussion and intimidated her out of asking questions.) Though I'm a man myself, I'm strongly in favor of women's financial empowerment. I told her I would be happy to take her on as a client, but suggested that she join a women-only investment club to supplement her work with me and educate herself about investing. What do you think of this recommendation?

Bravo! I applaud you wholeheartedly. First, for being sensitive enough to recommend that your client switch to an all-women club. And second, for encouraging her to keep learning on her own instead of relying on you to make all the decisions.

I've heard other women who have tried mixed investment clubs complain about the way men sometimes monopolize the conversation or talk down to women who are novice investors, making them feel stupid for asking questions. Men's more competitive view of the world can sometimes lead them to claim a louder voice in the group's decision-making. Not all mixed-gender clubs are like this, of course, but a woman who has had this experience would almost certainly feel more comfortable in a women-only group. Most women find learning much easier in a safer, less intimidating place where their questions are encouraged and addressed with respect and understanding.

So I don't see anything sexist in suggesting such a group to your client. And I think it's great that you're encouraging her to continue her own empowerment by learning more about investing. Although she may have considered delegating this responsibility to you as her financial authority figure, she'll feel much more self-confident and appreciative of your recommendations when she has a good understanding of investment principles.

Gender Benders

I thought I was getting better at balancing the left-brain and right-brain sides of this business until meeting a client couple who have thrown me for a loop. The husband is worried about risk and uncertain about what to do with their money, while the wife seems calm, rational, and money-wise. Should I treat them the same? And if so, how?

I think you'll see the best results from treating both clients as individuals with their own fears, concerns, and desires.

In this case, it is the husband who needs sensitive listening, compassion, and a certain amount of hand-holding. If you focus this kind of attention on him and ignore the "rational" wife, it will unbalance the planning process. On the other hand, treating them both this way may make her feel patronized.

I would suggest getting together with each of them separately at first. Frame it as a meeting to acquaint yourself with each client's individual style, needs, and goals, so you can serve them better. This will allow you to walk the husband through his fog to more awareness, without making him feel humiliated in front of his wife. In your meeting with the wife, you can then give her the more sophisticated knowledge and attention she seems to be searching for.

After this brief separation, I would bring them back together when the husband has gotten a little more comfortable with you and with the process. Having identified their objectives and concerns, you'll find both of them more ready to be partners in planning their financial future.

Wives Who "Act Like a Man"

Maybe I'm old-fashioned, but I'm having trouble relating to a new client couple. The wife has a high-paying corporate position, and the husband takes care of their two children while running a part-time consultancy from home. When we discuss financial choices, she acts as if the decisions are primarily hers to make, and he keeps deferring to her. I'm a little uncomfortable with this dynamic. Should I accept her as the alpha decision-maker, or urge the husband to take a more aggressive role?

You're dealing with an atypical couple, if past research about men, women, and power is any guide.

We've learned that when men make more money than women, they generally tend to believe they should have primary authority over how it is spent. This may explain why your male client thinks that his wife has a "right" to this same stance, since she earns more than he does. By contrast, when women outearn men, they usually tend to favor shared, democratic decision-making.

To complicate the picture, American men are trained to be competitive and to view relationships as one-up/one-down, while women are typically raised to be accommodating and cooperative. Thus, most couples conflicts arise when men earn more and insist on having more decision-making power. Obviously, your situation doesn't fit the stereotype.

For the best outcome, I believe you need to help this woman and her husband move toward fully shared power, control, and decision-making—regardless of who earns more money. Advise them that their financial situation might well change at some point in the future. For marital stability, it would be best for both partners (who are both performing vital roles for the family, remember) to have an equal say in what happens to the money.

If they seem unenthusiastic about giving up their accustomed roles, consider suggesting that they switch those roles for a week. The husband should imagine that he is the primary breadwinner, and thus feels entitled to have more say in where the money goes. The wife should imagine that she makes less than he does, and wants to share his decision-making power. If they take on this challenge, she is likely to develop much more empathy for her husband's subordinate position. By the same token, he may become more comfortable with sharing the power and decision-making, regardless of who brings home most of the bacon.

If they refuse to address this issue, hidden resentment can fester. The result will eventually damage their relationship.

In any event, you're right to urge them to take a more balanced approach to decision-making. Persuading couples to share information and power is one of the most important things you can do as an advisor. I wish you luck.

WOMEN'S MONEY MYTHS

I believe many women of all ages still suffer from ingrained beliefs I call "money myths," which keep them paralyzed, anxious, and in the dark about smart financial management. Here are some cases where underlying "myth perceptions" fuel fear, inaction, or other perplexing behavior in female clients, and some suggestions on how you can use your expertise to debunk these disabling beliefs.

"Money Is Too Complicated for Me to Understand"

In my initial consultation with a successful professional in her mid-30s, I was astonished to see her go into what seemed to be a full-fledged anxiety attack when I asked her to summarize her current assets and liabilities and her investment goals. She got very tongue-tied, said she would have to get back to me, and fled. She hasn't returned my calls since. Any idea what's going on here, and whether I can salvage this client?

There's a good chance your erstwhile client is a moneyphobic woman who subscribes to the myth that "Money is too complicated for me to understand."

Although the past few decades have seen some progress in debunking this myth, many women still grew up believing they wouldn't be very good at math or at handling money. As a result, they suffer either from math anxiety, which paralyzes them when they're faced with number problems, or from money anxiety, or both.

My recommendation is to continue trying to reach this blocked woman. Emphasize that you have an idea what she may be grappling with, and that you may be able to help. If there's no way to get this message to her by phone, you might try sending her a letter or e-mail.

Once you've reopened a dialogue, see if you can discover if she does indeed have a full-blown case of math anxiety. If so, you may be able to suggest a remedial math course at a community college or through an adult ed program in your area. She may even be able to find a class offered specifically for the math-anxious, which she'll probably find much less threatening and stressful than the high-school memories that haunt her.

In the meantime, you'll have your work cut out for you. To help her complete the financial profile you need to begin planning, consider breaking the task into smaller chunks, so she'll feel less overwhelmed. You might also offer to let her fill out some or all of the forms in your office, while you're there for moral support. If not, ask if she has a friend or relative who can serve as a "money mentor" to help her complete the information you need.

This overwhelmed client will require gentleness, patience, and warmth from you to begin tackling this paralyzing money myth. Above all, avoid being judgmental or condescending about her fear of not measuring up to the challenge of money management. With your help, she may at last be able to come to grips with this formerly taboo area of her life.

"I Don't Have Enough Money" and "It's Selfish to Put Myself First"

After talking with a new client about long-term care insurance for her mother, I discovered that she hasn't made any financial preparations for her own future. She insists that her main priority is making sure her mother is taken care of, which doesn't leave enough money to invest for her own retirement. Obviously I don't want to tell her to neglect her parent, but how can I help this woman see the need to plan for herself?

There's a good chance this client is being affected by two different money myths. First, like many women, she was probably brought up to believe that good daughters, sisters, wives, and mothers take care of others first and themselves last. This myth might be expressed as: "It's selfish to put myself first. I'm supposed to take care of everyone else."

Many women also subscribe to the myth that "I don't have enough money to do anything with." That's often a very valid concern, considering that the average woman earns only 76 cents for a job that pays a man $1—assuming, of course, that she hasn't given up her paycheck entirely in order to raise children.

One effective way of helping your client overcome the "selfishness" myth is to point out that if she doesn't take care of herself now by safeguarding her financial security, she may be sacrificing the future choices of others in her family—most likely her children. Financially insecure and dependent, she may force them to care for her in a way that could deplete both their resources and their energy. As giving and unselfish as your client wants to be, I'm sure she will not want to live out this scenario.

To find money she can begin putting aside, help her look at where she spends her money now. Again, I recommend encouraging her with inspirational stories of other women (ideally, other clients) who have taken charge of their own future and are now reaping the benefits of financial security. If a splash of cold water is called for, remind her that half of all women over 65 are widowed or divorced, so it's crucial for her to build her savings now.

"If I Take Risks with My Money, I'll Lose Everything"

Although my new client is well off, she's extremely nervous about taking any chances with her money. I've tried to educate her about the tremendous potential of starting to invest in equities at her age (late 20s), but she says she's just not ready to move out of CDs and money market funds. It drives me crazy to see her waste an opportunity she'll later regret. What else can I do?

Women are much more likely than men to believe the myth that "If I take risks with my money, I'll lose everything." The fear of ending up as a penniless bag lady lurks behind every potential reverse, no matter how affluent a woman is. A few years ago, even Katie Couric admitted to me that she had bag lady fears. If your client is an heiress who didn't have to do anything to make her wealth appear, it may seem all the more likely to her that it could vanish again just as suddenly and inexplicably.

In guiding her toward a more balanced view of investing, you need to help her understand that risk is not the same as loss. You might steer her toward *Money Shy to Money Sure: A Woman's Road Map to Financial Well-Being*, my recent book co-written with Sherry Christie, to help her overcome her preconditioning against risk.

While encouraging her to become more knowledgeable about investing, you also need to persuade her to trust your judgment. Reassure her that you don't believe in taking extreme risks. Tell her success stories of other women clients who have increased their wealth and financial security with sensible, long-term investing strategies you've recommended for them.

The bottom line, of course, is that your client is right to worry about the really big risk—that her money won't be there when she needs it later on. However, it's more likely to be inflation, not the stock market, that takes it away from her. I know you must have lots of charts, graphs, and tables to illustrate this.

Remember, though, that she's not interested in abstractions; her fear is very personal and immediate. So if you use examples, couch them in personal terms ("I know you're concerned that you could lose money by getting into the stock market at the wrong time. Let's suppose that every year for the past twenty-five years, you were unlucky enough to choose the very worst day to invest. . . .")

Once your client understands that total risk avoidance is really quite risky, she'll have taken the first step toward smart investing—and because of your patient coaching, she may well become one of your most grateful clients.

"I Don't Have Enough Time to Manage My Money"

As a woman planner, I believe strongly that women should know what they want their investments to do, even if they leave the heavy lifting to professionals like me. So I'm a little perturbed by the attitude of a young executive who recently instructed me to invest her inheritance from an aunt in "something safe," after telling me she's far too busy to discuss such details as goals, risk tolerance, and an investment strategy. This feels like an accident waiting to happen. Without preaching, how can I get her to make time to be more involved with her money?

The belief of busy women that "I don't have enough time to manage my money" is one of the hardest myths of all to debunk, perhaps because it's so often rooted in reality.

Though many women do suffer from second-shift fatigue after working for an employer all day and for the family every night and weekend, I believe your instincts are absolutely correct.

To begin getting this woman to take ownership of her financial plan, consider insisting that she take a short course on Investing 101 from you (many planners I know make this basic education mandatory for new clients). Or you might be able to refer her to a course elsewhere, and provide carefully chosen financial articles and investment reports to keep her learning. Meanwhile, do your best to help her identify small chunks of time—at the breakfast table? before meetings start? while "holding" on the phone?—when she can glance through this reading material and in small but significant ways stay connected to her money and what's happening with it.

The harder you work at this, the more likely it is that this client will ultimately come to appreciate your respect for her, your insistence that she should not neglect an area which is so crucial to her life, and your willingness to become her money mentor. In fact, if you continue being committed to your role as a financial educator, I predict that your women clients will reward you with appreciation, loyalty, and copious referrals. Once women cross over from the shadowlands of money myths to greater knowledge and financial power, they're likely to become some of the best clients any advisor could ask for.

"If I Take Charge of My Money, I'll Antagonize Others"

When I first realized that one of my clients was an overspender who enjoys taking extreme financial risks, I expected his wife to help me get him going in the right direction, since her approach to money seems much more sensible and balanced. In my conferences with the couple, however, I haven't been able to get her to speak up with her opinions and ideas. How can I encourage her to be more of a participant in this process?

Many women believe (not without good reason) that "If I take charge of my money, I'll antagonize others and might end up alone."

It's true that husbands who are accustomed to controlling major financial decisions will at first see their wife's encroachment on their power as a threat. This will disrupt the normal communication patterns between husband and wife, and may lead to fights, withdrawal, sulking, and the like. But I firmly believe that if the marriage is fundamentally solid, a woman's strengthening voice in this area will ultimately lead her mate to a sense of relief at being able to share the financial responsibility with her.

One woman who wrote to me while I was researching my recent book on women and money put it this way: "At first, after I attended these marvelous women's empowerment workshops and got into the pleasure of tracking my finances on the computer, I had to manage my money AND my husband, too! But now he seems quite pleased at my newfound expertise, as if a burden had been lifted from his shoulders."

If you know any anecdotes about client couples who made progress in sharing financial power, tell these success stories to your reticent woman client, perhaps in a separate consultation with her alone. Tell her how much value she can bring to the planning process with her sensible input, and encourage her to take the risk of sharing her thoughts and opinions as sensitively as she can with her husband. You may want to consider advising her of the downside: that many women who kept quiet about money decisions to avoid rocking the boat have ended up financially devastated by their husband's poor judgment, death, or divorce. Although I prefer to teach through inspiration rather than fear, be guided by what your expertise and sensitivity tell you will motivate your client to change.

"Someone Else Should Be Taking Care of All This for Me"

My new client, whose husband recently died of a heart attack at age 48, seems confused and uncertain about where their money is and what to do with it. I get the idea that she hopes I can take the whole thing off her shoulders, allowing her to stay clueless while feeling cared for. Is it fair of me to try to push her into getting more involved?

Even in the most feminist of families, girls are often raised to believe in the subtly pervasive myth that "Someone else should be taking care of all this for me." Many of my female clients tell me they consciously or unconsciously absorbed this message, which ran counter to all the other empowering pep talks they were given about careers and competence. As a matter of fact, it's just what my own parents unwittingly imparted to me.

I suspect your new client is laboring under the weight of this myth, and is probably hoping you'll be the next knight to ride in on a white horse and save her from having to make decisions about money. However, I think you're correct not to push her too hard right now. The grieving phase may last as long as a year, which means she'll probably be in shock about her husband's death for a while—not a great state in which to begin learning about money management.

Take it slow and gentle as you work with your client, but resist the urge to do everything for her. Encourage her to read articles about personal finance, attend a seminar for new investors, or at least discuss financial matters with friends she considers knowledgeable about money. (A friend may be less amenable than a relative to stepping in and taking over where her husband left off.) Stress to her that the more knowledgeable she becomes about her finances, the better you'll be able to work together to determine the best course of action for her.

Once she starts flexing her financial muscles, I believe she'll experience such a jolt of self-confidence and satisfaction that you may well have a very good client for life. Just remember to resist the temptation to be her savior, since enabling her dependency will undoubtedly backfire in the long run.

Taking Action

If our Darwinian destiny is for men and women alike to evolve into a better balance of thinking and feeling, one day we may all want exactly the same blend of sensitive, emotionally tuned communication and solid factual information. Until then, it will be up to you to find out what each client needs in order to make well-informed and well-integrated financial decisions.

If he or she is anxious and underconfident, then compassionate listening may be just what is needed. By contrast, a straightforward informational approach may be more appropriate with a client who is knowledgeable and confident.

You can reduce the risk of condescending to anyone by cultivating patience and sensitivity to their individual needs and quirks, and by making them feel respected and understood. Ultimately, this will allow you to become a fuller partner in helping these clients make sound decisions about their money.

DEALING WITH DIFFERENCES

Coming from Different Places

It's a small world—but there are still big differences within it. At a recent conference, I was warned that my talk was being translated into Cantonese, Thai, and Spanish, which meant that some of my comments—particularly the humorous ones—might not be clear to these other cultures. Knowing this, I made a special effort to be sure that the multinational group of participants could appreciate what I had to say.

This experience reopened my eyes to the importance of understanding the ethnic orientation and cultural norms of clients. The more you know about the values that underlie their attitudes, the more successful you may be in building relationships—as these examples suggest.

Emigrés from Shaky Economies

My new client is a software engineer who recently emigrated from Russia. Because he lost all his earlier savings due to the economic turmoil in his country, the only investment he trusts are U.S. Treasury bonds. Is there some way I can help him get past this limitation?

It's often hard for Americans, with our faith in our essentially self-righting economic system, to appreciate the emotional scarring of clients who have survived the panic and frustration of explosive inflation, stagflation, depression, or other kinds of severe economic malfunctioning.

Proceed cautiously with this client, taking plenty of time to help him air his fears and feelings about his experience in his homeland. Along the way, you can educate him about other investment options, and about the differences between the Russian economy and our own.

In working with clients who carry this kind of emotional baggage, it's vital to take their anxieties into account in pacing your educational efforts. If you push this economically insecure Russian into the market before he's ready, he may well bolt. The result: you could lose a client who might have come around, had you taken the time to deal more sensitively with his financial trauma.

Parental Expectations

A young entrepreneur of Pakistani heritage has asked if I can help him. The only son of immigrants who run a small restaurant, he is having a hard time dealing with his parents' expectation that he will take care of them in their old age. He thinks they ought to be setting aside funds to protect their own financial security, but feels unable to discuss this with them. How should I handle this?

Unfortunately, there is no easy solution to this problem. In certain cultures, children have been conditioned for centuries to accept the responsibility of caring for elderly parents. If your client acts on his Americanized belief that his parents should try not to be a burden on him, he may be haunted for the rest of his life with feelings of being a selfish, "bad" son, at least in their eyes.

Dialogue and compromise may be possible, but you need to begin by empathizing with the vast gulf between the viewpoints of both sides. I would suggest interviewing your client to find out more about his parents' values and the extent of their openness to our own cultural beliefs. This will tell you whether meeting with them is likely to be productive.

In exploring this possibility, be sure to tread slowly and carefully. In the meantime, you might encourage your client to buy long-term care insurance for his parents, so that a health crisis in their later years won't cost him his own financial security.

Even folks whose great-greats came over on the Mayflower often struggle with this issue, and solutions are almost never neat and easy. But if you help this young man air his fears about losing his independence, and see what financial plans you can devise to address his anxiety, you will contribute significantly to his peace of mind.

Veiled Tale

I was recently consulted by a husband and wife from a Middle Eastern country. He didn't seem to have any difficulty in dealing with a female planner, but I was taken aback by his blueprint for his children's future. He intends for his two sons to attend an Ivy League college, while settling large sums on his two daughters when they marry. He has discouraged the girls from thinking about college, and won't pay the cost if they want to go. His wife said virtually nothing during the entire interview. I found myself biting my tongue to keep from protesting his sexist assumptions. If I work with him, can I possibly make a difference?

Whoa! First, back up a few steps. Do you honestly feel able to set aside your own beliefs in order to work compassionately with this couple?

If your client's lack of interest in educating his daughters makes you want to clobber him every time you get together, I'd back away even farther. Refer him to someone who is less emotionally involved, or at least capable of more patience and tolerance in trying to change the father's attitude. Perhaps a planner from a similar cultural background would find it easier to understand and accept the conditioning that informs your client's point of view.

If you do feel able to continue, you might ask the wife how she feels about educating her daughters. Her passivity during the initial interview suggests that she may be unforthcoming, unwilling to disagree with her husband's position, or even in total agreement with him. But in the event that she does voice a wish for the girls to have an opportunity to attend college, you may be able to gently nudge this couple toward a more egalitarian view.

The deck will be stacked against you, though, if your client thinks you are trying to force him to change his views. People are more likely to change when they feel totally accepted for who they are—not when they feel judged or condemned.

East vs. West: Family Values

My client, a teacher whose modest inheritance I manage, has asked me to help resolve a conflict with the Vietnamese immigrant she recently married. A moderately successful seafood wholesaler, he regularly sends $1,500 a month to relatives in his homeland. This upsets his wife, since it leaves them unable to build up any savings of their own. Is there any way I can do some good for this couple?

This type of situation calls for a great deal of diplomacy. If you are willing to step into the breach and help build a bridge between these two partners, I would first invite them to discuss the cultural beliefs and values influencing this conflict. Then, try to summarize their differences in a way that clarifies the issues and opens the door to negotiation.

For example, you might say something like this: "In Vietnam, you [the husband] grew up believing in the duty of a successful family member to support his relatives. But to you [the wife], brought up in America where personal responsibility is more prized, it seems a higher priority to protect your own financial welfare and that of your children. Is there a compromise that would help you both achieve the sense of well-being you seek?"

Eventually, the husband may feel less obligated to send away so much of his wealth, and be more willing to meet some of his wife's needs and concerns. But unless and until he is willing to compromise on this point, it would not be wise for you to push him too quickly to deviate from his own cultural norms.

Color Blind

I think I've just blown it with a prospective client—a sales professional referred to me by his manager. First of all, he was reluctant to open up to me about his money (maybe because I'm white and he was African-American). When I asked if he had established a college fund for his two children, he told me in no uncertain terms that they would have to pay their own way—that it was not his job to support them once they turned 18. I then asked about his level of experience with stocks, bonds, and mutual funds, and he said that real estate was the only investment he wanted in his portfolio. I ended up feeling I'd put my foot in my mouth big-time. What could I have done better?

You are probably being too hard on yourself. But it could be helpful to reflect on the experiences that lead many African-Americans to distrust the market system, and to prefer tangible investments to those that are more abstract.

With any strongly biased client, the best approach is to respect his investment preference, discuss the pros and cons with him, and present the options at his disposal. Make time to let these clients ask you questions, voice their concerns and fears, and see for themselves that you are working to meet their needs while respecting their values.

In a case like yours, the course of action I would suggest is to answer the client's questions honestly. Be patient with his skepticism until you have earned his trust. If his attitude stymies you to such an extent that you can't empathize with him, you may want to ask if he would be more comfortable working with an African-American planner. However, don't rush to suggest this unless you are sure you can't work it out. Otherwise, it may appear that you're rejecting him as a client, which could well increase his sense of distrust toward you and other non-African Americans.

Cultural Obligations

A middle-aged couple recently asked to meet with me after we got acquainted at their oldest son's bar mitzvah. They're committed to sending their three children to college and graduate school, but when I looked at their portfolio, I had to tell them that this goal might be out of reach. When I started talking about student loan programs, the parents said emphatically that they won't consider letting their kids start out in the world under a financial burden. What now?

First, you need to understand that many (if not most) Jewish families consider it of prime importance to provide for their children's education. Failing to do this makes them feel they have failed as parents. So before you start trying to change this couple's minds about what they can achieve within their financial limitations, you need to honor the depth and power of this cultural belief.

Let them know that you understand and respect the position they're starting from. Then, ask if you may help them explore ways to achieve their goal despite their limited resources—for example, with PLUS loans or home equity loans that they (not their children) would repay.

Over time, you may be able to help this couple accept that they can be very good parents without having to pay 100% of the cost of their kids' education. By telling success stories about other families' experiences, you may even be able to help them see that it could be beneficial for their children to share this financial responsibility. But take it slowly before presenting this alternative to them.

One Man's Joke Is Another Man's Slur

I recently started working with an estate attorney who has been an excellent referral source. Since he's of Italian descent, I thought he'd enjoy a joke about Italians that my wife (also an Italian-American) recently told me. Instead, he seemed to *freeze up* and quickly changed the subject. The more I think about this, the more I wonder if I should apologize to him. Ironically, having been married to an Italian for so many years, I feel like a member of the clan.

Many of us have made this common faux pas, causing a fair amount of hurt feelings all around. Though it may be hard for you to accept, being married to an Italian is not the same as being one (at least not in the eyes of some other Italians).

I would feel the same way if someone who wasn't Jewish made Jewish-slur jokes with me—no matter how long he or she had been married to someone Jewish. In fact, I might even feel upset, stung, or offended if it was another Jew making really slamming remarks about our common culture.

So, all in all, it's safer to avoid this area of humor altogether. In the meantime, I think your instinct is right. The next time you see this attorney, apologize for your inadvertent rudeness. Tell him that although you feel as though you're almost an Italian yourself because you're married to one, you can understand why he took offense. If you assure him of your future sensitivity, I think the rift will heal. This is a no-man's-land that you can surely avoid stepping into in the future.

TAKING ACTION

When working with clients like these from diverse ethnic backgrounds, try to understand the weight of the traditions and values that they bring to your office. Remember that each culture has different norms when it comes to matters of wealth, children, the elderly, spouses, education, and so on, and accept these differences with respect. This is slow and painstaking work—especially when attitudes are the result of centuries or even millennia of conditioning.

None of this will be possible, of course, if you are convinced that your views are right and theirs are wrong. If you do find yourself in that place, be flexible enough to refer your clients to an advisor who is more sympathetic to their background. But if you are honest with yourself and work toward cultivating cultural sensitivity, you will know when to try to expand your clients' horizons, and when to simply help them find financial options within their own framework of beliefs.

Family Matters

When you deal with family issues, a certain amount of intensity comes with the territory. Families are supposed to be nurturing places to come home to; but sad to say, many of them are places to run away from, or at best perilous terrain strewn with emotional landmines.

This section of the book will help you create some order amid unexploded bombshells of love, money, death and dying, control, fear of change, old resentments, dependencies, and intergenerational power struggles. These strong, primitive passions will sometimes be intense enough to make you feel like throwing up your hands and running out of your office screaming. Rest assured, this feeling is perfectly normal.

Given the complexity of most families' dynamics, sorting out feelings from facts can be tricky. In most cases, the more you know about family history, traditions, and legacies (both financial and non-financial), the better equipped you will be to help your clients make grounded decisions.

Marital tensions are a source of many family-related issues. Even though you aren't a therapist, conflict-ridden couples will often seek you out to provide an even-handed viewpoint. You'll need to put on a "therapeutic mediator" hat to urge choices based on fairness and justice, not rage or spite.

When dealing with the effects of divorce and blended families, still more challenges crop up. Divorcing or newly divorced couples often want to act out their desire for revenge, or get "war reparations" for past suffering. In this bitter game, children are sometimes used as unwitting pawns. New marriages may be sabotaged from the outset by damage inflicted in earlier, unsuccessful unions. In these situations, the support of a good marital counselor can siphon off some of the most intense feelings, allowing you to help clients gradually return to a more rational state of mind. Divorce therapists or mediators may help, too.

Speaking of children, you've probably noticed that even highly rational people are sometimes a little unbalanced where their kids are concerned. At times of great stress, parents may ask you to help them resolve issues they can't handle themselves. (As the mother of a son who's now in college, I've had to learn over the years how to set limits, say no, and back off to let him struggle through problems on his own—all very painful lessons for me, if not for him.)

Many other clients in the prime of life belong to a "sandwich generation," grappling with issues that involve their children while trying to deal with the emotional insecurity of having increasingly frail parents. Meanwhile, the older generation may face dilemmas of their own in inheritance planning.

Then there are family businesses, where struggles for dominance often play out on subtle and not-so-subtle levels, along with attempts to be recognized, loved, and validated. In many closely held businesses, open and respectful emotional communication is not the norm. Daughters are treated differently from sons. Younger generations may carry around emotional baggage from childhood hurts or injustices. To put it bluntly, you have your work cut out for you.

Remember that in troubled family relationships like these, money is never just money. It represents love, power, security, and a host of other emotions. If you can help clients learn to view money simply as a tool to accomplish certain goals, and not as the key to emotional fulfillment, your work will be infinitely easier.

Finally, if dealing with family matters exhausts or overwhelms you, get help. Convene supportive colleagues to brainstorm client solutions. When necessary, refer problematic clients to therapists or counselors. And be generous in forgiving yourself if you have to send individuals or couples to other planners who are less vulnerable to emotional conflicts that resurrect traumas of your own, or make you feel too judgmental, angry, or anxious to do your best work.

I would go even farther and recommend developing a resource network for all sorts of peripheral problems that may come to you. For example, your network could include people or organizations that focus on working with acting-out adolescent children, places that provide good child care so parents can hold jobs with less guilt and anxiety, and so on. Consider spending some time and energy to expand this area of expertise. I think it will not only give your business a competitive edge, but also fill a large gap in your clients' lives.

When you do succeed in resolving painful matters, you may be instrumental in making a family more functional, and its members more respectful and loving with one another. Congratulate yourself, for that result is priceless—and an achievement that may well stand for generations to come.

FAMILY MATTERS

Couples Conflict

Conflict between intimate partners often leads to irrational thinking and unproductive behavior. Sometimes one appears to be the instigator, while in other cases they both seem entrenched in their power struggle. You may not know if they both want your help, especially if only one of them asks you for it. Should you try to restore fairness in situations like these?

Maybe, after weighing professional detachment against personal ethics, you decide you can't ignore a client in distress. If so, is there a way to intervene sensitively? And at what point does intervention risk overstepping its bounds into therapy?

Difficult questions, every one of them. Perhaps seeing how they're answered in a variety of circumstances will help you handle spousal tension among your own clients.

Why Do We Need an Advisor, Honey?

Recently, the wife in a client couple visited me by herself to discuss a ticklish issue. She would like me to review their total financial picture, but her husband, an economist, feels he can handle most of their life planning himself. Although she believes he has made some bad financial decisions, she doesn't feel knowledgeable enough to confront him. Should I agree to revisit these areas with the two of them, as she wishes?

If you're willing to tackle this, I think there are a couple of important steps to take before you see the couple together. First, consider meeting with the husband separately to spell out just what aspects of your expertise he is interested in. Then get together with the wife to clarify her views. At that point, you will be in a position to bring both partners together in your office and lay out the differences in their wants and needs. Take care to understand and validate where each is coming from; nobody is "right" or "wrong."

See if you can devise a plan that meets both partners' needs, addressing some of the life planning issues that concern the wife while allowing the husband to retain enough decision-making control to preserve his self-esteem. Praise him for what he did right, but gently suggest that new developments make it nearly impossible for anyone who isn't a full-time planner to stay on top of everything.

He may be more willing to move toward his wife's life planning approach if you proceed slowly, after building rapport with both of them. If he's still resistant, consider serving as a life planning coach for the wife, teaching her what she needs to know to participate with him in planning their future. This is riskier for the marriage, though—the husband may perceive that you're challenging his expertise and authority, instead of understanding that you're trying to educate and empower his wife.

War Reparations

A client of mine has just discovered that her husband of 22 years is having an affair. She intends to file for divorce and "take him for all he's worth." She is a small business owner with a higher income than his, and a substantial investment portfolio. I sympathize with her need to provide for their two children, but am uncomfortable with the vindictiveness of her plan. Should I try to talk her out of it?

First, this couple should consult a marital therapist to see if their marriage can be healed, in spite of the infidelity. Even if they still choose to divorce, therapy may help cool the heated emotions surrounding their breakup and allow them to give their long relationship a more respectful funeral.

Meanwhile, be assured that your client is more typical than you may think. Although many women in this situation would say, "I don't care about the money; just get me out of this painful and humiliating mess," many others will try to salve their hurt and anger by using money as war reparations.

Divorce therapy can help couples like this devise solutions based on fairness and justice. I recommend it highly to my own clients, particularly when there are children involved. Vicious, vengeful negotiations can damage youngsters permanently, in addition to making it hard for either spouse to trust anyone else from then on. If your client is truly ready to divorce, you can help her by suggesting a fair financial arrangement that she'll be able to live with when her rage and pain subside. This will be a far better solution for the children, as well as for the parents themselves.

Joining Financial Forces

I'm facing an awkward "his and hers" money situation. The husband and wife, who are both in the military, each have young children from previous marriages. So far each parent has been supporting his/her own kids. Now the wife, who is higher in rank, wants to merge their money to emphasize the blending of the two families. The husband prefers to continue with separate finances. What should I advise?

This is an unusual reversal of roles. More typically, women in relationships want money of their own—often so they don't have to account to their partner for every purchase. Another reason is to ensure their own autonomy in the midst of intimacy. In addition, today's high divorce rate makes many people skittish about overmerging, and women are notoriously apt to end up poorer after a divorce.

I would explore this couple's reasons for wanting either merged or separate money. Is the husband uncomfortable with experiencing more closeness in their relationship—the usual motivation for other men who are okay with merging money? Is the wife concerned about the children's vulnerability if anything should happen to either parent?

Once you understand each position more fully, you might recommend an experiment in partial merging for agreed-upon joint expenses and savings. I would not recommend total merging. Women need to have money in their own names, and many men prefer some financial autonomy, too—especially when they've been married before, as in the case of this blended family.

Caught in the Middle

After working with a client couple for several years, I got an almost hysterical call from the wife yesterday. Her husband just told her he's filing for divorce in order to marry a woman he's secretly been having an affair with. He said he wants a fair and amicable parting of the ways, but she doesn't know whether to trust him after learning that he has cheated and lied to her. She asked me whether she could rely on me to keep looking out for her financial interests, or whether my loyalty is now to her husband, an executive who has generated all their wealth. I stammered something reassuring and said I'd get back to her. What's the best way to proceed?

This is a very tricky situation, because of the primitive feelings involved in dissolving a long-term relationship.

For you, the important thing is to assess your own comfort level in dealing with an intense emotional situation, the good will (or lack of it) of your clients toward each other, and your personal preferences in terms of client rapport. When you weigh and analyze all these factors, you can decide how best to proceed.

In this case, there are no universal answers. Financial planners are not like attorneys, who can only represent one of the two clients. You have the option of working with both members of the couple through this painful transition, if they're willing and you truly desire to continue with them (perhaps with the aid of a good divorce therapist—a growing specialty of couples therapists, sad to say).

So the first step is to ask yourself whether you would be comfortable continuing to deal with them as a couple, with the goal of achieving a win-win financial settlement for both. This will depend on the intensity of anger and hurt of the wife, as well as the husband's emotions about the split. Perhaps a joint meeting with them, or a phone call to each of them, will clarify the issue.

If their feelings about each other are so bitter, explosive, and antagonistic that you can't ethically work with both clients, you have two options. One choice is to continue with just the husband or the wife, while referring the other client to a good planner who can protect his or her best interests. (Caution: Although business priorities might lead you to choose the high-earning husband as the "keeper," he may be the likelier of the two to want a change—leaving you with no clients once the wife, feeling you too have abandoned her, moves to the advisor you've suggested. Consider, too, whether the moral satisfaction of helping the wife manage her divorce settlement wisely might outweigh any lesser financial reward.) Alternatively, you could step out of the fray completely by referring each of them to a new advisor.

Whichever path you choose, I wish you luck. Remember that when a marriage breaks up, something alive is being ripped apart. Whether or not they're conscious of the emotional cost right now, both spouses will eventually feel the pain.

Credit Tightening at the Bank of Mom and Dad

My client couple are fighting about whether or not to pay their daughter's student loans after she graduates. They funded the first two years of college, and she borrowed to pay for the last two. The mother has told her daughter that they will repay these loans. Knowing her husband is against this, she didn't consult him before making this promise. Now he insists that their daughter is responsible for paying back these debts. Neither parent will give way. Help!

What is fueling the disagreement between the mother and father? Is it a difference of philosophy about parents' role in educating their children, perhaps based on different cultural backgrounds or upbringing? Or is it strictly a financial issue, with the dad realizing that they just can't afford to pay any more without sacrificing their own security?

Once you have encouraged them to get to the root of their feelings and examine their financial situation, you may be able to help them find some common ground. The mother probably needs to acknowledge the unfairness of promising payment without first getting the father's agreement. If they don't have the resources to make good on her promise, the daughter may need to step up to the plate and pay off part or all of her loans. A financial and emotional compromise that might work for all parties would be for the couple to pay half or a third of the loan amount, while the daughter pays the rest.

It would be a good idea to suggest that these clients try harder to work out their differences in the future, with the help of a money therapist or couples counselor if need be, to avoid dragging their child into the midst of their own unresolved conflicts.

Tax Attacks

Over the past six months, I've made a lot of headway in helping a young married couple to settle on mutual financial goals. But as soon as I asked them to start getting their tax documents ready, it turned into a scene from "The War of the Roses." She attacked him for spending too much on his sports-fan hobbies, and he blamed her for buying extravagant clothes and home furnishings. There's nothing in J.K. Lasser about this. How can I de-escalate their hostilities?

Tax time is one of those stressful yearly occasions that make many of us regress to our oldest and most dysfunctional survival modes of behavior. Since couples often polarize around different priorities when it comes to spending money, it's not unusual for them to use this club against each other when dealing with Uncle Sam forces them to confront their financial flaws.

Often, real fears lurk beneath the fights. She may fear they'll end up on the street with nothing. He may fear they'll be audited and their life will become a living hell. Perhaps they're both imagining the modern equivalent of debtor's prison.

The first step is to calm your clients down. Find a time to talk when neither is tired or feeling otherwise pressured (outside the normal pressures of tax time, that is). Urge them to think separately about their own stress reactions and consider how to minimize this dangerous behavior. Do they need to divide the tax-preparation tasks? In the future, how far in advance should they begin getting organized in order to avoid these blowups?

I would also explain to them that it's normal for couples to have different priorities about where the money is spent. With patience and compromise, they will probably be able to work out a way to have what they both truly need to be happy. If they are willing to look at their spending habits and consider modifying them somewhat, you might suggest that they each keep a spending diary for a month or two. Writing down everything they spend and how they feel about it may help show them where they could tweak their choices a bit.

But as far as your own peace of mind is concerned, don't take these polarizing struggles at tax time too seriously—they're just an inefficient way for your clients to let off steam about a process they hate having to focus on.

Sell Low, Sell High

My clients' behavior has me baffled. He's a physician, she's a corporate lawyer, and they both have strong opinions about their shared portfolio. The moment a stock loses ground, he's ready to sell it. By contrast, she's eager to sell whenever a stock racks up significant gains. What gives here?

It sounds as though your male client is suffering from loss aversion. In other words, he feels so bad at losing money that he's willing to give up the opportunity to make money. You need to help him see that a downturn is a risky time to sell, and that panicking at this point will probably cost him a great deal.

What about his partner, who is anxious to sell winners? If she doesn't need the cash and isn't eager to give the IRS a windfall, perhaps she's just uncomfortable with success. It's another version of the "devil you know" syndrome—but in this case, she may fear that if the stock continues to outperform, she'll be swept away to a place she's never been before. Many people have upper limits of wealth and abundance above which they are ill at ease.

In discussing these possible explanations with your clients, you need to be a model of calm, patient therapeutic education. Remember that choices which may seem to you to be self-sabotaging merely feel safe to a scared client's psyche. The more you can teach them about patterns which do not serve them well, the better equipped they'll be to choose a new path.

Prenuptial Jitters

A new client asked to consult me privately before bringing his fiancee in with him. It seems that in his recent divorce, his ex-wife ended up with half of the assets he was hoping to leave to his children. He'd like me to tell his fiancee that he insists on having a prenuptial agreement to protect his children's inheritance if the new marriage breaks up. I understand his motives, but I'm cringing at the thought of trying to handle this hot potato. Any suggestions?

Your client's no fool. He knows very well that whoever says the words "prenuptial agreement" will be branded as a cold-hearted brute who's thinking about divorce and death instead of romance, eternal love, and the bliss of marriage.

So if you're willing to help him look less like a bad guy with his betrothed, go ahead and meet with both of them. To begin this educational financial planning session, you might share the old adage that the only people who have a chance of being pleasantly surprised by life are those who have already prepared for the worst.

You just might get through to them if you can empathize with them both—with her need to look ahead with romantic anticipation, and his need to take care of his children. For example, I would ask him (in front of her) how the divorce affected his kids, emotionally and financially. When he explains that the inheritance he had meant to leave them was cut in half after all his years of hard work, you could observe that if he and his fiancee can agree to an arrangement now that helps the kids feel more secure, it will pave the way for their accepting her more openheartedly (something she would certainly want). Also, ask her what she would want and need in order to feel taken care of, and listen with compassion to what she says.

Finally, in your role as a therapeutic financial advisor, you may want to point out to the couple (largely for the fiancee's benefit) that a second wife often has the difficult task of accepting her husband's prior loyalty to his children—a much longer-standing relationship than this new love. She needs to realize, however, that he cherishes her in a different way than he loves them. You might also comment that in your experience, it's very common for someone who has been financially burned by divorce to want to protect himself or herself in the future. When your client's fiancee sees that his insistence on a prenuptial agreement is not a personal affront to her, she may be able to go through the painful (to her) process without feeling unloved or fleeing.

I have worked with similar polarizations in remarrying couples, and have been able to help them eventually find a true win-win solution. Once this couple begin consulting attorneys to draft the agreement, the most difficult part of your job with them will be done—and you'll be entitled to heave a huge sigh of relief.

Danger: Exploding Temper

The couple who have just been to see me are definitely from different planets—and unfortunately, I don't feel I belong on either one! The wife is timid and meek, a real nervous Nellie. The husband is a tyrant who rages at her, the government, and the world in general. I'm concerned that he may be a time bomb waiting to explode. Should I suggest that he get therapy, or maybe that they see a therapist together? If so, how can I bring this up?

The best way to handle this exceedingly tricky situation is to meet with each person separately. (You might explain to the control-freak husband that this is simply part of your work method.)

When you get together with him, see how much of his past and present motivation he's willing to talk to you about. Try to educate him about the need to share decision-making more fully with his wife.

You may also be able to ask him tactfully about his anger. If you yourself have ever struggled with your temper, you could suggest ways you've learned to contain it, channel it, or medicate it. Consider suggesting therapy at this point, if he seems open to the idea.

When you work with the wife, ask her how she feels about asserting her own opinions and desires more strongly, about money as well as other issues. After finding out more about her, you may be able to encourage her to be somewhat more assertive around her husband. However, I would advise against making comments about him that she could use as ammunition in future fights (if she ever feels strong enough to fight with this bully).

Whether or not you've proposed therapeutic help to him, you may want to consider recommending couples therapy to her. In my experience, women are generally more open to getting this kind of assistance. If she says, "He'll never agree!", suggest asking him to do it as a favor to her, not because he has a problem that needs to be fixed. Sometimes husbands will consent to therapy for their wife's sake—which opens the door to help for both.

Fault Lines

A gay couple has asked me for help in resolving a difficult situation. The more financially experienced of the two began trading online (with her rather skeptical partner's consent) and lost cnearly half of their savings. Her partner of 15 years is furious that they now can't afford to adopt a child from an orphange in the developing world, as they had planned. Thought somewhat sheepish, the trader asserts that she has learned from her mistakes and can trade more productively next time. What's the best way to handle this?

One tends to think that men are more prone to such compulsions as frequent trading, but clearly some women also fall prey to fantasies of windfall profits, getting something for nothing, and the trance-like thrill of the ride.

Your trader client sounds like a typical addict in quasi-denial. She needs to understand that taking on more risk than her partner can tolerate simply will not fly.

I would encourage her to acknowledge her penchant for excessive risk-taking, and seek help in dealing with it. Consider steering her toward a good therapist and Gamblers Anonymous group. Since these clients are polarized around different priorities as well as risk tolerances, I'd also suggest finding a couples or marriage therapist they can consult together. When two intimate partners are very far apart, they need to learn how to meet in the middle so each can realize at least part of their cherished dreams.

Your clients need to rebuild trust and openness, and initiate shared decision-making about their finances. With professional help, they may be able to work through the wounded partner's feelings of insecurity and betrayal.

This can be a slow, slow process—but so, alas, could be the task of getting their savings back on track. I encourage you to pursue both avenues, in hopes of helping them restore their mutual trust as well as their financial security.

Leaky Assets

I only see my client's wife when she needs to sign documents concerning her family inheritance. Both spouses are quite well off, but I've noticed a steady trickle of assets making its way from her accounts to his. She shrugs off my attempts to explain what she's signing, and glances at her husband constantly as if she's afraid of saying or doing something he might not like. How should I deal with this?

Since you handle both spouses' financial affairs, suggest that they get together with you to revisit their goals and their respective (or joint) plans. At this meeting, ask innocent questions such as, "Mr. X, help me understand your objective in transferring your wife's funds into your accounts, so I can advise you more knowledgeably."

The husband may try to browbeat you into silence, but continue your patient questioning until you're sure the wife gets the message. If she keeps checking to make sure he's okay with what she says, don't comment on it. Just keep encouraging her to voice her own opinions and needs.

In this discussion, your ultimate goal should be to open the door for the wife to talk to you whenever she's ready. You might even say that since it can be easier to explain complex financial matters in a one-on-one consultation, you'd be glad to see her separately.

Personally, I think it's vital to educate a passive wife so she can carry the financial ball if something happens to her spouse. By assisting this woman, you'll help breathe healthy air into a stagnant situation. And instead of risking a backlash by directly confronting or attacking the husband, your tactful intervention may prompt him to deescalate his domination.

Golden Handcuffs

My client just told me that she miscarried last year when her husband pushed her down a flight of stairs. No one believed her when she tried to report it, since he's generally viewed as a pillar of the community. She wants to leave him, but is afraid she can't make it on her own. How can I assist her?

The most important thing you can do is help your client develop a plan to secure her future, so she can freely choose whether to leave her marriage. Besides investment strategies, this plan might include seeking work in a well-paid field, earning a degree if she lacks qualifications, and/or moving in with a friend or relative until her situation stabilizes.

At the same time, I'd refer her to a women's center. This can be a good source of the strength, sustenance, and practical guidance she will need to move on with her life.

Along with financial expertise, you can provide some emotional support as your client makes this transition. But beware of allowing her to depend too much on you as her knight in shining armor. Sure, it feels good to rescue damsels in distress—but you're an agent of empowerment, not Sir Galahad. If your client needs more emotional assistance than you can realistically provide, refer her to a good therapist or counselor who can help her heal while she creates a better life for herself.

Deadlier Than the Male

One of my clients just called to let me know that he's been laid off. When he told his wife, whose substantial paycheck will now be more important than ever, she hit the ceiling. It turns out that she's been very abusive lately—screaming at him, humiliating him in public, and even throwing a glass paperweight at him. I know I've only heard his side of the story, but I'm inclined to believe him. He wants me to enlist her emotional and financial support in his job search. Should I agree?

The idea of spousal abuse makes most people think of the husband as the bad guy. But in *The Myth of Male Power*, Warren Farrell offers many cases of wives who are the abusers: punitive, psychologically unstable, accusatory, dishonest, even physically violent.

If your client's wife is willing to come to his aid once she calms down, invite them to review their financial plans with you in light of his job crisis. See if you can gently arouse some compassion in her for her husband's inevitably shaky feelings of self-worth.

On the other hand, if she continues to react to his joblessness with anger and contempt, consider suggesting marital counseling for both of them. Consult your own referral sources and colleagues (if needed) to offer them a choice of two or three good marriage therapists.

If either spouse refuses counseling, you may want to advise the husband privately to consult a lawyer who can protect his interests. The risk is that if the wife hears about this suggestion, you will have compromised any possibility of a future professional relationship with her.

A cautionary note here: since temporary marital discontent can often seem quite intense to an outsider, it's best to proceed carefully. Don't suggest specific actions until a distressed spouse is ready to make a move. Ideally, your experience with these clients will tell you when to keep quiet and listen, and when to come forward with concrete suggestions.

Abuse and Consent?

I'd always thought my clients (I'll call them Dick and Jane) were an ordinary suburban couple. But when Jane came by last week to pick up some papers Dick had requested, she was wearing sunglasses and a long-sleeved dress on a gloomy, sultry day. She evaded my question about how she was doing, never took off the sunglasses, and winced when I shook her hand. Could this have been spousal abuse? Was I right to say nothing? I didn't want to look like a fool.

The problem isn't really looking foolish. It's the danger of using loaded terms like "spousal abuse" without knowing the full story—especially if the putative victim hasn't even admitted that anything is wrong. By assuming a therapist's role without suitable training, you might unwittingly offend a client who's not in distress, or touch off an already incendiary situation.

So you were right not to jump the gun. In your place, I would have asked Jane, "Are you okay?" in a gentle tone that encouraged her to share more. I might have taken extra time to inform her about the papers she was picking up and what consequences they might entail, to remind her that I cared about her well-being.

When a woman is in denial about an abusive relationship, or protects it for fear of greater violence or of being left destitute, it's essential to proceed with great caution and patience. Follow her cues. If she drops hints about abuse but thinks she has no recourse, you might share a story about a client in similar circumstances who has reshaped her life in a healthier, more satisfying way.

Most important, don't be a know-it-all. It would be truly foolish to assume that you have all the answers, or even that you fully understand how ready she is to leave a troubled relationship. By being too hasty, you might cause her to panic and act too precipitously about her marriage.

A House Divided

My client says his wife has left him and taken the children, and he wants to move his assets where she can't reach them. However, I know from a reliable friend that she and the kids are actually under medical care in a shelter for battered women. What should I do?

If the couple together are your clients, I would refuse the request. Since you represent them both, it would be neither fair nor equitable to align with one of them against the other. If your relationship is with the husband alone, there's no conflict of interest—but think hard about whether you really want to assist him in cutting off funds to his family.

Even if both spouses are your clients, don't grab the phone to notify the wife of her husband's plan. Your sympathies may be with her, but you could actually intensify the conflict by barging into it. If she contacts you, however, be forthright in letting her know what's going on. You might also recommend marital counseling to her—or divorce counseling, if that's the way the couple is headed.

In the event of divorce, you'll have to decide whether to continue working with either of them. In the meantime, try to be even-handed (at least when disseminating information), while remaining sensitive to the wife's plight. You've obviously entered a war zone, and would prefer not to end up as cannon fodder! So keep your boundaries clear, and don't rush too impetuously into this emotionally intense and painfully polarized situation.

Counseling for a Shaky Marriage

I'm getting nowhere in trying to develop a financial strategy for a couple who are so divided about how to handle their assets and their estate planning that I suspect they'll end up in divorce court. It may be none of my business, but I think they might really benefit from seeing a marriage counselor. If I suggest this (a big "if"!), I'd like to be prepared with specific recommendations. But how do I find good people to refer them to? And how many choices should I suggest?

The dilemma about how to address personal issues that are harming a client's financial well-being isn't as rare as it may seem. A simple way to do it that isn't too heavy-handed would be to tell these clients about another couple (perhaps composite or fictional) who sought counseling and improved their relationship as a result.

Before you take this step, ask people you trust to refer you to good couples therapists in your area. Interview these professionals (at least on the phone) to find out their experience with issues of money and inheritance, and to ascertain how comfortable you would be in referring your clients to them. (If you don't know where to start getting names, check the Bibliography for professional referral organizations.)

But personal recommendations from people you trust are always more useful than mere lists of names that meet abstract criteria. By interviewing these therapists yourself, you'll feel more at ease suggesting them to your clients.

If you're undecided about how many to recommend, three is a good number. This helps give clients a real choice, allowing them to select the individual they feel the best rapport with.

The best therapist, in my view, is someone who can both support and confront a client. Some people need (and learn more from) being challenged, while others need more support and safety. Although the precise mix of these two elements varies from individual to individual, you may be able to steer your clients to the "right" therapist if you know them well and have good instincts.

If you do, you'll be giving them a priceless gift. Even if a couple is irrevocably headed for a split, therapeutic help can allow them to give the relationship a respectful burial and minimize emotional damage to their children. This last reason alone, I believe, is justification enough for making it your business to encourage these clients to seek counseling.

Getting help is still somewhat stigmatized in our culture, especially when it comes to that scary word "therapy." I personally feel that maturity comes from realizing how healthily interdependent we all are, and recognizing that any of us may need help to cope with the challenges in our life. Knowing when to seek help is a sign of that maturity. And when your caring and knowledgeable support leads clients to the assistance they need, I believe you'll see the benefits in your practice—and in yourself, through the satisfaction and inner peace that comes from doing right by the clients who trust you.

TAKING ACTION

You can be enormously helpful in encouraging clients like these to meet their demons head on, before proposing any action or behavioral change. But with the scariest and most explosive couples, be sure to use caution before barging in where angels fear to tread. You need to balance your desire to help (even if only with well-meaning suggestions) against the risk of getting in over your head. Learn when to refer out, when to make therapeutically helpful suggestions, and when to listen to the fear, anger, and pain in the couples who visit you. In this way, you'll help your clients—men as well as women—develop a more balanced approach to sharing money and power.

FAMILY MATTERS

Children of All Ages

As a financial advisor, you can be especially valuable to your clients if you come to understand the often irrational and passionate financial decisions that parents make regarding their children. For example, it's hard for many parents to say no—especially those of us who can't stand seeing our loved ones deprived, frustrated, or in pain.

As children grow up, parents often struggle to find a balance between keeping them too close and pushing them too forcefully out of the nest. Attitudes about nurturing independence are often laden with deeply held beliefs and family traditions about how to express love and support. In situations like these, your clients' attitudes and behavior may complicate the planning process in some emotionally ticklish ways.

You can help most by building bridges between the generations, while making sure your clients' giving to their children does not come at the cost of their own future security. If you do this well, your clients will view you as a "life coach" worthy of their respect. And they'll thank you for helping to make parenting a little easier for them and the children they love.

College Mom vs. Credit Cards

My client, a divorcée, is worried about letting her only son go off to college several hundred miles away. He has not been good at managing money, and she fears he may get in over his head with credit-card debt. How can I help her?

There are no quick answers to this serious problem. Many college students with little or no money experience are bombarded with credit-card offers. Some do end up deep in debt, and may even be forced to quit school to pay off their bills—a tragedy that could be avoided with better financial education up front.

Encourage your client to share her fears and concerns with her son at an unstressful time and in a non-confrontational way. For example, she might say something like, "Honey, I've heard so many horror stories about college kids piling up hundreds and thousands of dollars in credit-card debt. Let's talk about how I can help you avoid this situation." If she herself has not been the best role model for financial prudence, she should be open about it.

The main thing is to help the son learn to set limits on his spending without making him feel like what therapists call "the identified patient." Suggest that they discuss what's important to him, and how his spending choices may affect whether he meets these goals or not. (If you're willing, you might volunteer to meet with him by himself to talk about this.) Your client may also want to take him to a local meeting of Debtors Anonymous, so he can hear for himself how overspending and debt can wreck otherwise functional lives.

From a practical standpoint, the two of them have several choices. For instance, they can head off the whole issue of indebtedness if he uses a card that is pre-loaded with cash, such as Visa Buxx or MasterCard's i-Gen. Or he might start out with a debit card and graduate to a credit card after showing that he can spend responsibly. I would suggest that the statements be mailed to his mother, and that he send her a check to pay them off. That way, she can monitor the balance and see if he's getting into trouble.

Consider doing everything you can to support your client before her son goes to college and gets overwhelmed with debt. Together, the two of you may be able to avert a financial train wreck.

"But Everybody Else Has One"

My client recently moved his family to a wealthy neighborhood with an excellent school system. His problem is that his two sons, aged 11 and 13, are now besieging him for the same expensive clothes and electronic gadgets that their schoolmates have. My client has asked me how to help his kids learn the value of money. Any ideas?

The best thing he can do is also the simplest: to talk with them about the perils of trying to keep up with the Joneses.

Sitting down with them individually or together (whichever feels more comfortable), he should tell them that he understands and sympathizes with their desire to fit into their new surroundings.

He can emphasize that he wants to help them. But instead of handing out the funds they want for gizmos or trendy clothes, he should challenge them to think up ways they could earn at least half the money themselves.

I'm generally a fan of recounting personal experiences or anecdotes that support a point of view. That might work here—although many tweens and young teens find that their parents, formerly the fount of wisdom, now seem absolutely clueless. (Mark Twain once noted that when he reached his 20s, he was amazed by how much smarter his father suddenly became.)

In any event, encourage your client to set firm limits by asking his sons to help pay for the costly peer-prized items they covet. He'll be helping them learn to work hard and delay gratification to reach a goal—important lessons in our "gotta have it now" society.

Making Allowances

After opening a $1.5 million account for a new client who recently sold his business, I was startled when he asked me if allowances would help teach his children (aged 4 and 5) financial responsibility. If so, when should he start paying them? How much? Should the money be tied to specific chores? Should they have rules about how to spend it? As a single guy, I'm in the dark about this. Help!

My opinion is that kids should be given allowances as early as they can count money and understand how to use it. I'm all for giving children experience in spending, saving, and contributing to charity, with the space to make their own decisions. Allowances facilitate these lessons.

A wonderful idea I heard about from another financial planner was to give each child three containers, perhaps painted different colors. One is for money to be saved, the second for money to be shared or given to a church or charity, and the third for money to be spent.

I don't have any problem with parents saying something like this to a child of 4 or 5: "Here's $3.50 for your weekly allowance. A dollar fifty should go into the savings jar. When you have $25 saved up, we'll take it to the bank together. Fifty cents should go into the sharing jar. Once you have $10, you can decide where to give away the money. The remaining $1.50 should go in the spending jar, to be used for whatever you want."

Children need the freedom to learn from mistakes they make with their own money. So you might counsel your client not to rescue his children regularly if and when they spend all their allowance and ask for more.

As far as tying this money to chores is concerned, I believe that kids should be given an allowance for being members of the family—not for work done. Parents can help children learn how to work for pay by compensating them separately for tasks above and beyond what's expected of every family member. As for the amount, that's an individual decision based on the going rate in the area, as well as your client's own values and financial situation.

There's one other recommendation I would suggest you pass along: not withholding a child's allowance as punishment, except in unusual circumstances. Reflexively shutting off the financial faucet sends the message that money is a form of love and approval which will be withheld if the child is "bad." This makes money more emotionally charged than it needs to be, and can create problems later in life.

Guilt Trip

I never really knew what an "embarrassment of riches" was until I talked to a 40s-ish couple who are in a dither about $500,000 they recently inherited. They want to use some of it right away to bankroll two of their dreams: a Mercedes convertible and a five-star cruise. But they're concerned that these purchases will make them poor role models for their three children, whom they've tried to bring up to be sensible with money. They're not sure how *to defend their behavior if the kids start pressing for goodies of their own. How can I help them deal with their conflicting feelings?*

The children need to know what went into their parents' decision to give themselves these long-desired rewards. Your clients should explain that these expenditures are not impulsive; they've wanted to take this cruise and own this wonderful car for years, but couldn't afford either one until now.

To help alleviate their concern about being poor role models, they might slow down the spending process a bit by deferring one of these purchases. Even if they're not willing to do this, they can still communicate to their kids that they intend to invest most of the inheritance for retirement, college tuition, etc.

The parents might also consider giving each child a lump sum to use as desired to celebrate the windfall. Again, they should be sure to emphasize that the bulk of the money will be earmarked for future needs.

A thoughtful discussion with the kids can go a long way toward allaying your clients' fears. But I would advise them to keep an eye on how their children deal with money, since overspending and money avoidance habits usually begin at a young age. By helping each child learn to save, spend, and share money with others in a balanced way, they'll be more likely to nurture sound financial values in the next generation.

Merging Family Values

A couple I've just begun working with each have a child from a former marriage. The wife, who is somewhat wealthier, has a 15-year-old daughter to whom she denies nothing. The more frugal husband has a 14-year-old son who has been earning extra money for years by mowing lawns and shoveling snow. The father is concerned that his son's values will be influenced by the extravagant spending habits of his stepsister and stepmother, while the mother acknowledges that she has not been the best of role models for her daughter. How can I help them?

I would begin by recognizing their wisdom in being concerned about this issue, and in bringing it proactively to you. Then I'd advise the mother to tell her daughter that her own lavish spending may have set a dangerous example of instant access to wealth without limits.

She should explain that, after deep reflection, she has decided that things will change in their new family. From now on, the daughter will receive a regular allowance (slightly bigger than her stepbrother's, I imagine, since she is older). Impulsive spending will be discouraged. In other words, the girl will no longer be able to run to her mother for money and be granted it without a second thought.

Her mother may want to point out that blended families can be quite complicated. She could say something like, "I know this change will be a real challenge to you at first, but I do believe that a consistent family philosophy will benefit us all in the long run."

At the same time, the father should communicate a similar message to his son about the planned allowance and family expectations. This discussion shouldn't be as difficult, since the son is already following his thrifty dad's example.

Finally, both parents should decide in advance what to say at a family meeting that includes both children. They should respond lovingly to the kids' questions and protests, while holding firmly to the decisions they've agreed upon. The process should prevent inequalities and resentments, helping to launch this blended family with consistent and harmonious values.

The ABCs of Inheriting Assets

An older couple I work with are finally getting their estate in order. They want to leave a substantial sum to their grandson, now 15, who seems to have no ambitions beyond hot music and cool clothes. They worry that it's too late to begin educating him about the responsibilities of wealth. How should I advise them?

It's never too late to start this learning process. If you feel comfortable serving as a mentor for their grandson, you might volunteer to teach him about investing, borrowing, and so on. Or you may be able to recommend a good personal finance book or video to begin educating him about ways to grow money and put it to work.

In any event, I'd suggest that the grandparents discuss their plans and their philosophy with the young man. They could also talk to him about his goals and potential uses for his inheritance. This may be a meeting you'd like to be involved in, if everyone else is willing.

A toe-in-the-water tactic would be for them to give him an advance on his inheritance, and have him work with you to choose stocks or funds in categories he's interested in. This advance might be held in a custodial or 529 college savings plan account, if the grandparents want to retain control. Once he begins tracking these investments, he'll be on the road to understanding what money can do for him, other than simply satisfying his immediate needs and appetites. The grandparents could also get his input on earmarking some of his money for a charity of his choice.

I must say, your clients are truly enlightened. By devoting time and effort to educating the next generation, wealthy families are much likelier to raise young people who use money wisely to benefit themselves and the community.

Overspending for the Kids

Although I've dealt with spending problems before, I'm getting nowhere with a new client who insists she's only doing what's in her children's best interest. The pricey house in an exclusive suburb was chosen so the kids could make the "right" friends; the private schooling is an investment in their future; the big car is for their safety; the $50 birthday gifts for their little friends are to help them fit in. I know children are important, but this *lady's spending leaves no financial slack for her and her husband's future security, or her kids' college education. How can I convince her to be more sensible about her priorities?*

First of all, figure out whether she's an overspender in all areas, or just when it comes to the children. If it's the latter, try to discover why she has such a strong need to give so much to her kids. If she was deprived as a child, she may have vowed to herself that her own children would never have to go through what she did—wearing hand-me-downs, suffering social rejection, and generally feeling ashamed and inferior. Or was she a spoiled child who now overspends on her kids in emulation of her parents? There's also the possibility that she's simply driven by a competitive desire to keep up with the Joneses at all costs.

If a candid conversation with the mother reveals that childhood traumas are fueling her need to overgive to the kids, it's entirely appropriate to empathize with her painful past experience. I would advise you to gently counsel her (perhaps with anecdotes from your own experience) about kids who got everything and turned out poorly, partly because they never learned to set limits themselves or deal with the everyday deprivations that are part of growing up in the real world.

Then try to get this couple to start setting goals for themselves, not just for the kids. Do they want to retire early and travel? Do they have elderly parents they may have to support? Do they want to pay for their kids' college education in full themselves? How about graduate school?

This discussion can help the mother see that unless she moderates her spending so they can take care of these long-term needs, the kids will be poorly prepared to look after themselves once they're on their own. What's more, by failing to assure their own financial security, the parents run the risk of having to ask the kids to support them in retirement—an outcome your clients would surely go to great lengths to avoid.

Equality in Education Spending

A recent marriage was the second one for both of my clients, each of whom has a child in college. Her son is going to a state university, while his daughter is enrolled in an expensive private college. The difference in the cost of education is causing some friction between the spouses, even though they entered the marriage with fairly similar net worths. How can I help them deal with this?

Blending families is never easy—and couples polarization patterns are challenging, whether it's a first marriage or the fifth. The important thing is to help this couple hash out their priorities and communicate openly with the children about their differences as well as their shared goals.

I would begin by finding out whether you are dealing with two different money personalities. Is the father a spender who tends to buy what he wants, whether he has the money or not? By contrast, the mother may be a hoarder, frugal and self-denying even if she has enough money to spend on the important things.

Encourage both spouses to think about and write down their goals as individuals and as a couple. By sharing their separate lists and trying to integrate them, they can see where the areas of alignment or disagreement lie.

Then I think they need to sit down with their kids, either together or one on one, to discuss the choices that have been made in colleges and college costs. Encourage the children to talk openly with their parents about their feelings, and explore whether their treatment needs to be equalized in any way. For example, if the state-school son resents the disparity in funding, would he be satisfied with a more generous spending allowance, or is he longing to transfer to a private school with better courses in his major? If so, is the mother willing to increase her spending to make this happen? Would her husband be willing to contribute, in order to level the playing field?

By helping this couple take the time to listen to each other's needs and search for creative compromises, you could play a vital role in improving their marital and financial harmony.

Big Heart, Small Budget

A retired widow has asked my advice about her learning-disabled son's request for help in buying a house. He's 26, and up to now she has readily provided the money he's asked for to buy a car, pay for school, and otherwise supplement his low income. However, the death of the boy's father left her in modest circumstances, and giving her son the $50,000 he's requesting will seriously compromise her finances. How can I help her see the risk in being so generous?

It doesn't get much tougher for a parent than this: trying to take care of a child in need without sacrificing one's own financial security.

I think it's probable that your client has been overgiving to her son out of guilt—guilt about his learning disabilities, and possibly even guilt associated with the father's death. She needs to recognize this tendency in herself, and this time tell him openly that she can't give him the money to buy a house without putting her own financial security at risk.

But there are still ways she can help him. She might provide a certain amount every month to help him afford a good rental. Or if you think it's feasible, she could agree to a "matching grant" to supplement his own saving for a down payment. You might also suggest that she help him brainstorm ideas for bringing in more income so that he can buy a house on his own.

Your client needs to work out her guilt in a way that doesn't compromise her own well-being, while still emotionally supporting her special-needs son. His interests, and hers, will be best served by helping him to become more independent. I think the old adage applies here: "Give a man a fish, and he eats for a day. Teach a man to fish, and he eats for a lifetime."

"Wastrel" on Welfare

My client, a now-wealthy entrepreneur I've worked with for many years, is growing exasperated with his "wastrel" son. Now 25, the young man has drifted from job to job since college. Without being asked, the father provided his son large amounts of cash on two occasions when it was advantageous from a tax standpoint (once as an investment in a business startup which failed). My client has asked me for my advice. What would you suggest?

It's good that you have a strong relationship with this client, for I think you need to help him see that his generosity may be making the situation worse. Throwing big chunks of money unexpectedly at his son keeps the son dependent and off-balance, never knowing when large windfalls will come his way or when they will dry up. My advice would be to encourage the father to sit down with his son (perhaps with you as a mediator, or with a therapist if the relationship is emotionally charged), and express his fears and concerns about his son's lack of direction.

If the father truly thinks it's best to help his son get on his feet financially, I would suggest that his support take the form of a regular, predictable allowance that the son can count on consistently. On the other hand, the father may decide that these handouts are preventing his son from developing his own financial muscles. In this case, encourage your client to offer love and support in ways that are not tied to money, instead of trying to bail out his child or push him to mimic his own entrepreneurial success.

The Good, the Bad, and the UGMA

My clients' son will soon be 18, giving him legal ownership of the UGMA custodial account they funded for his college education. He wants to withdraw the assets so his struggling ska band can buy new sound equipment, hire a manager, and embark on a national tour.. His parents are appalled. They want me to help them say no to him, but what can I realistically do?

A separate meeting with the son may yield more honest feedback from him about going to college versus his music. Once you know this, you'll be in a better position to help the parents recover from their "freak-out" and suggest a compromise plan that all three can live with. For example, maybe he would agree to his parents underwriting a loan for the new equipment and six months of the manager's salary, on the condition that he leaves the custodial assets untouched for now.

As much as your clients may want their son to have a college education for broader choices in life, they need to remember that he soon will have free rein with this money. If they come down too hard on him about the impracticality of spending it on the band, or their anger and hurt that he wants to defy their wishes, he may retaliate with an adamant refusal to attend college. Worse yet, they may provoke a rebellion that will drive him away from them. Use your understanding of the son's personality to figure out how you can help build a bridge between him and his parents.

Ready for Responsibility

The 23-year-old daughter of a client couple recently consulted me about a trust set up for her by her grandparents. She'd like me to persuade her parents (the trustees) to let her have the assets outright so she can learn to manage them. I'm somewhat sympathetic, since I know a recent divorce has left her quite short of money. But I'm reluctant to get in the middle of a wrangle between her and her parents, who think she's financially irresponsible. Should I step in? And if so, what's the best way to handle the situation?

If you're comfortable mediating this dilemma, ask the daughter what she can do to show her parents she's prepared to make responsible decisions about her money. You might lead up to this by empathizing with the breakup of her marriage, her difficult financial situation, and the awkwardness of her parents' controlling her trust fund. Ask her to think about how she would handle the assets if they distribute them to her. Does she have any fears that she may spend everything on purchases or activities that she'll regret later?

Ask her, too, about her money management habits during the stress of divorce. During particularly difficult life events, people tend to be less rational with their money and revert to old, dysfunctional behavior—their primitive survival mode. If she has been defaulting on bills, overdrawing her checking account, or otherwise behaving irrationally, her parents may be justified in keeping a tight rein on the money, at least for now.

If her responses convince you that she's ready to take on the responsibility of controlling the money her grandparents left her, you could suggest a compromise solution that allows her to receive an appropriate chunk of the trust assets. Set up a future meeting with her and her parents to see how this distribution has worked out.

It's important to remember that your primary clients are the parents. If you swing too far toward the daughter's view, you could not only lose her father and mother as clients but contribute to widening the family rift. So proceed carefully, mindful of their desire to take care of her by keeping some control over her money, and of her need for more independence, trust, and income.

If you're tuned to everyone's objectives, you may be able to narrow the gulf between them in this way. It can be a touchy process, however, and you may not be completely comfortable with the counseling and mediation required. In this case, consider asking the parties involved whether you may invite a therapist to conduct the meeting with you. Or you might suggest that they consult a family therapist first, and come back to you to work out the financial details when matters are less emotionally charged.

College Finals

A stressed-out couple just left my office arguing fiercely about their son, a junior in college. His grades have been slipping badly, and the parents aren't sure why. His father wants to cut off the boy's educational funding and make him get a job, but the mother is willing to give him another chance. How can I resolve this?

Take some time with the parents to determine what approach might be most successful with this young man. When he has disappointed them in the past, what (if anything) has worked best in getting him back on board: limit-setting with strict consequences, second chances to mend his ways, or perhaps a middle course that defines the steps he must take to restore the parents' trust?

Consider meeting with the son to explore his feelings. How does he account for his falling grades? Young people in their late teens and early 20s sometimes aren't really ready for the college experience. I've known quite a few who have taken time off, then gone back to finish college with greater maturity and a much better attitude about learning.

Ask your clients' son if he can help his parents by suggesting a workable plan. If he is toying with dropping out, for instance, he might propose taking a leave of absence for a semester or two, and then coming back when he's ready to work harder for his education. Or if all three of them are agreed that he should stay in college, you might explore a multi-tiered incentive plan. For example, the parents might commit to funding the next semester, but will cut their support for the following semester in half unless he brings his grades up by x number of points. Ask the young man what consequences of academic negligence would feel appropriate to him.

In general, I find that a several-step approach works better than either extreme of unilaterally lowering the boom, or offering another chance with no consequences for failing to take advantage of it. Good luck in helping all three navigate this difficult situation without sinking into angry recriminations.

Ready to Fly

My clients' son, 22, has had some initial success with an Internet-based freelance business. He's looking for financial backing to start his own company, but his parents are worried that this is a risky move. They're trying to persuade him to go to graduate school instead, and have offered to pay for his MBA and provide seed money for a business later. After meeting with the young man at their request and reviewing his business plan and ideas, I think he has a good chance of making a go of it right now. He has no interest at all in being diverted to grad school. What's the best way to present a conclusion that's not what my clients hope to hear?

To soften the blow of your unwelcome news, you might remind the parents of some of the successes achieved by other contemporary entrepreneurs who are MBA-less. And though they may hope that grad school will help make their son's risk-taking less risky, it's an unfortunate fact that even MBAs aren't immune to making mistakes.

You might also point out that if they bribe him to go back to school when his heart isn't in it, flunking out could damage his self-esteem far more than a business failure might. It's important not to squash his passion and work energy at this point in this life.

Ask the son if he's willing to limit how much personal financial risk he'll take in his new venture. If he agrees, you can feel more confident in recommending to the parents that they let him give it a shot. They should feel even more reassured if you're satisfied that he plans to raise enough start-up capital, especially if he promises to shelve his plans in the event that this level of financing doesn't materialize.

In any case, the parents should listen to you without being alienated if you have a strong relationship with them. However, it sounds as though you're concerned that your relationship will be destroyed if you tell them what you honestly think. If you're really attached to holding onto clients who are somewhat rigid in this way, you could take a safer route and stay out of this family debate altogether. Just tell them this isn't your area of expertise, and wish them well in sorting it out with their son. But if you are at all therapeutically oriented in your style, I'd invite you to take on this challenge.

Move Over, Mom and Dad

I've been helping an elderly couple with their retirement planning and estate planning. Lately, their two adult children have asked to be included in the meetings. The parents and I are open to this, but the kids are beginning to call me directly with questions about their parents' portfolio. What's the best way to deal with these calls?

You need to inform the children in a nice way (if you haven't already) that they're not your clients; their parents are.

You can encourage intergenerational communication when you meet alone with the parents, and in your family-wide meetings as well. But as you're already aware, it's important to understand and respect the parents' reluctance to tell all, and to know when and how they intend to share their plans with their children. If you push them too hard to divulge everything, or allow the kids to pry information out of you, you risk losing their trust in you.

Though I personally feel that older children should know the realities of their parents' moneylife, this issue is highly sensitive and emotional. If their parents aren't open with them, grown-up children often fall prey to old feelings of resentment, deprivation, or being cheated or lied to. Similarly, old hurts and resentments may revive in parents who feel pressured to give up their financial privacy. It's not uncommon for elderly clients to fear that knowledge of an impending inheritance may affect the judgment of a child—someone they may have to depend on later to make financial or health-care decisions on their behalf.

Whether or not your clients are distressed by this particular fear, take care to preserve their sense of safety and security in dealing with you. If you proceed slowly and cautiously in helping everyone express their needs, fears, and wants, you may end up with a family whose money communications you've helped to improve—or even to heal.

"Equitable" Isn't Always Equal

I've begun doing estate planning with a couple who have both been married before. Each has a child from the previous marriage—but while one of these youngsters is on her college dean's list, the other is mentally and physically handicapped. I know that the mother of the child with special needs feels that much more money should be left to him than to her husband's able child. However, she hasn't said this out loud, and I know she wants me to bring it up at our next meeting. How can I tactfully approach this?

I would take on this touchy subject by first ascertaining whether both parents feel the same way about providing for their children. Do they have similar or different philosophies about how much money to leave to children in general? Does each have a good-enough relationship with the other's child, and do they have a good-enough relationship with each other?

Once you've gleaned some of this information from being with them and asking subtle questions, you can proceed to talk about the serious complicating factor of the handicapped child's life situation. By positioning your suggestions carefully ("As many couples in similar circumstances have done"), you may find the stepparent receptive to providing more generously for this disabled child, perhaps through a trust overseen by a reliable family member or friend. If he seems to feel that his able child is being overlooked, be sure to take the time to address his needs, concerns, and wishes for her.

Eventually, it may be a good idea to meet with the parents and the able child to see how she feels about the fact that her handicapped stepbrother is being left more money to be sure his needs are cared for. Ideally, she will understand and accept this differential treatment. In partial compensation, perhaps other more sentimental gifts could be left to her.

At any rate, it's important to help both parents see that "equitable" is not always the same as "equal"—certainly not in a situation like this. A lot will depend on how long this second marriage been going on, how well the two families have blended, and what scars have carried over from the first marriages. But the determining factor in the success of these negotiations, I suspect, will be the degree of commitment, involvement, and love of the husband for his wife's disabled child.

In general, there are a few rules of thumb that can help you in broaching touchy subjects like these. First, get as much background information as possible so you can put these issues in the right context. Use anecdotes, articles, and other tools to make a thorny topic seem more general and less personal. And remem-

When One Kid is More Responsible than the Other

I'm trying to head off a future blowup in a family I've been advising for years. The father is determined to leave money outright to the younger of their two children, a levelheaded young man who just graduated from law school, while setting up a trust for the older child, a daughter. While the young woman does seem immature (she's a college dropout who has held only menial jobs and has repeatedly defaulted on her debts), the mother worries that her daughter will be upset and furious to learn after her father's death that she doesn't have free access to her inheritance as her brother does. The father says he's too angry with her to care. What do you advise?

As painful and difficult as this situation is, I think the mother has the right instincts. My advice would be to open up a dialogue by getting the parents together with their daughter (and with the son in a separate session), and telling each of them what the father is thinking of doing and why. Even if the daughter is initially outraged by the apparent unfairness of the way the money will be distributed to her, there's at least the possibility of further discussion and progress while her father is still alive.

But before this meeting, I'd explore with the father whether he would be willing to change his mind about leaving his daughter's money in trust if circumstances showed that she had become more responsible. If he agrees to this, he would then be able to tell her, "I know this arrangement must seem unfair to you, but I'm afraid that if I give you the money outright, it will be gone so quickly that you won't have it when you might need it later on. Is there anything you can say or do to reassure me that I don't need to put it in trust to protect you from yourself?"

I can predict that at first, she will probably be too hurt, angry, and defensive to say anything her father can rely on. But if he pursues the dialogue (perhaps in several stages), she may be able to come up with a solution that would reassure him and allow her to feel less like an untrustworthy child.

In your estate planning, you've probably found it ironic that "trusts" are so often based on distrust. When this is the case, they're capable of causing deep, permanent wounds, like other emotionally loaded ways parents choose to dispose of their assets. The best solution is always to air these decisions while both parties are still around to discuss them. I hope you can help this father find the courage to take on his daughter directly in trying to come up with a solution they both can live with.

Generation-Skipping Distrust

I'm doing estate planning for a strong-willed elderly man whose family I've known for years. He has a difficult relationship with his only daughter, and doesn't want her to inherit any of his assets. Instead, he's decided to leave quite a bit of money in trust for her son (his grandson). He's hoping his daughter won't find out about this plan until after he's gone. I know the daughter well, and am convinced that his course of action will compound her already strong feelings of rejection and hurt. How can I urge him to reconsider?

Though this man wants to take the easy way out, he is essentially cursing his daughter. After rejecting her anew, he will force her to deal with this pain after his death, with no possibility of reconciliation or healing. What a cruel legacy!

Though you're not a therapist, you can take on the role of a therapeutic educator with this client. Share anecdotes with him that illustrate the healing power of openness, compromise, and forgiveness. Even if you're unable to change his mind about the way he chooses to dispose of his assets, try to open his angry mind and closed heart to the possibility of beginning a dialogue with his daughter (probably with a therapist's help), so that they may improve their relationship before he dies.

If she doesn't find out until after his death that he has ignored her and left his money to his grandson, she may view it as such a slap in the face that she will do something irrational to sabotage this "gift" from the father who rejected her. She may even feel rage and resentment toward her son, who got the goodies that were denied her. That's why I feel it's vital for your client to discuss his plans with her now, in the spirit of fairness and perhaps eventual reconciliation.

Great Expectations

A brother and sister in their 20s recently came to me to complain about their widowed father. They had been counting on financial support from him (and a substantial inheritance afterwards), but it seems he has just remarried and acquired two young stepchildren. My clients are upset that their father's financial focus seems to have shifted away from them and toward his new family. They want me to speak to him about their expectations. How would you suggest I handle this?

I think they're the ones who should approach their father, not you. They need to talk to him about their sadness, hurt, and fear that he seems to have deserted them to bond with his new family. In fact, I would recommend that they address only this emotional aspect of their relationship with him, not the money—at least not right away.

Second (or better yet, simultaneously), you should encourage these siblings to let go of their dependence on their father's money. They need to realize that it's his money after all, not theirs. And for their own good, they ought to be planning how to take care of themselves if their worst fears come true and their dad does abandon them financially for his new family. If it came down to a choice between supporting two youngsters or two able-bodied adults, in all likelihood he would expect his older children to be able to make their own way.

Facing up to this challenge may be a positive, maturing experience for them. In a similar situation I've encountered, a wife was counseled by her husband to stop waiting for her parents' money. Though following this "tough love" suggestion was hard at first, she subsequently took it to heart and strengthened her sense of financial competence and autonomy, while building a stronger and closer relationship with her mother and father.

So even if your clients have a hard time accepting that their father's money is his own and not theirs, I believe you'll strike the right balance if you nudge them in this direction, while encouraging them to let him know that they need to stay connected to him. This two-pronged approach will hopefully move them past their desperation and panic, and toward more creative action.

Heir Conditioning

One of my clients, the CEO of a very successful Internet company, would like to endow a family foundation. However, he and his wife have always tried to hide their wealth from their 16-year-old daughter. They're concerned that if the girl learns the size of the foundation's endowment, it may discourage her from trying to earn her own way in the world. How should they proceed?

Though each family has different temperaments, money personalities, and dynamics, I believe that open communication is almost always better than secrecy. Your clients should stop pussyfooting around the subject of their net worth, and explain to their daughter about the creativity, hard work, and sacrifice that engendered it.

Presented in this light, the revelation of their wealth (which probably won't be as much of a surprise as they think) may not do much damage to her work ethic. A further option might be to involve her in managing the foundation, where she would have an opportunity to develop valuable expertise in allocating resources to deserving recipients.

This could do wonders for her financial confidence and competence. I'm reminded of a young woman I met some time ago who had been involved in her family's foundation since her mid-teens. Though only in her early 20s, she was very skillful and balanced in her understanding and use of money—a true example of what I call "money harmony." Grateful for what she'd been given, she was eager to put this legacy to good use as a true steward of wealth. In my opinion, a good deal of the credit for her wisdom was due to her parents' willingness to involve her in this endeavor at an early age.

It isn't easy to raise children with sensible values, long-term goals, and a balanced view of money when we live in a society of instant gratification, overspending, and feel-good-now messages. The best tool that parents have is a willingness to share their own struggles and vulnerability, model balanced money attitudes and behavior when they can, and set loving limits for their children.

As a financial advisor, you can be instrumental in encouraging the development of intrinsic values in your clients' children. Nothing could be more important in ensuring the financial well-being of generations to come.

Taking Action

When parents are at a loss about how to handle money matters with their children, often the money is a stand-in for love and approval—love lost, withheld, yearned for, denied, or even overgiven in a way that may disempower the kids. As an objective financial professional, you can help your clients find the right balance in encouraging their children to stand on their own feet, and learning to let go without relinquishing their love and support.

FAMILY MATTERS

Issues of Aging

In your practice, you're apt to deal with adult children who fear inheriting their parents' illnesses and weaknesses and resist facing their own mortality. Older clients may deny their own aging, making rational decision-making next to impossible. Mix in unresolved issues between generations, and you have the potential for a maelstrom of guilt, fear, anger, denial, and even outright panic.

If age-old problems like these are troubling your clients, consider how you might handle some typical situations.

The Age of Reason

My client's 87-year old father is slowly failing. Although he can't remember to pay bills or deposit checks, he refuses to give her a power of attorney so she can take care of his financial affairs. My client, who has always considered herself close to her dad, feels hurt and bewildered by his apparent lack of trust. How can I help her deal with this?

From personal experience, I can tell you that this father's behavior probably has nothing at all to do with your client.

In all likelihood, his refusal to give up his financial independence stems from denial of his own growing lack of competence and a need to retain his dignity at all costs. If he has always been very capable, as my own father was, surrendering control will feel like a humiliating defeat to him. In addition, he may not want to burden his daughter with having to take care of him.

So, as frustrating as this situation is, encourage your client to take her dad's attitude less personally. Over time, she may be able to find a way to reach him and soften his inflexibility. To make him more comfortable with her offer, she might try telling him how relinquishing money management to an adult child has helped other super-competent parents feel relieved and able to enjoy life more. I think she should also remind her father how much she loves him and respects his competence in other areas.

If he still won't budge after she's given it her best shot, she has a choice between letting go and loving her dad as best she can, or taking control more forcibly at the risk of damaging a long and loving relationship. Only she can decide which option is preferable.

Policy Exclusions

My client was named sole beneficiary of her mother's life insurance policy, with the understanding that the proceeds would be used as a college fund for my client's and her brother's children. However, her brother is so furious about being excluded as a beneficiary that he has vowed to take the money earmarked for his children's education and spend it on himself. My client was ready to set up college accounts for each of the grandchildren, but now she isn't sure what to do. Any advice?

Before your client does anything with the money, I would recommend that she urge her brother to join her in consulting a counselor or family therapist. He needs to work out his feelings of hurt and humiliation at having been excluded from his mother's legacy.

I strongly believe that the mom should have talked to each of her children about her plan. If she was unsure whether the son was mature enough to co-manage the insurance proceeds, she should have explained her feelings. As painful as that discussion would have been, it might have led to greater trust over time. At the very least, your client's brother would not have experienced the shock of this apparent rejection after his mother's death, with no way to salve the wound except to pour out his hurt on his sister.

That said, your client should try to heal this painful rift for the sake of present and future family relationships. If she feels bad that her brother was denied a role in administering the insurance benefit, she may need to explore ways to correct the imbalance with him. She definitely owes him a heartfelt apology if she knew about the plan but kept it a secret from him.

If the brother refuses to let go of his anger, your client's only recourse is to carry out their mother's wishes, perhaps by opening 529 plan accounts for the grandchildren that would keep the money out of his reach. To make the best of a bad situation, she might meet with the brother's children, explain what she has done and why, and say that she would like to make amends with their father if he ever feels open to it.

Sadly, even if the two siblings become reconciled, the son's legacy from his mother will always include residual feelings of anger, hurt, and betrayal.

Fear of Aging

I've been urging a client couple to buy long-term care insurance, but the husband has balked. I thought the issue was the expense, but the wife recently confided that his father has an advanced case of Alzheimer's. She believes her husband is in denial about the possibility of ever needing long-term care himself. Under these circumstances, I feel this coverage is more important than ever. Without using scare tactics, is there a way to encourage him to consider it?

Watching parents forget who you are as their personality slips away is nightmare enough for any child. Worse yet is fearing that you might eventually suffer the same fate yourself. It's perfectly natural to flee in panic and horror from having to deal with such a dreadful situation.

You'll need to be exceedingly gentle and sympathetic to help the husband face his fears about his own future. I would start by asking him to discuss (in his wife's presence, if possible) his feelings about what is happening to his father. If his mother is alive, how is she coping? How is his dad's situation affecting them financially? How well off will his mother be after his father's illness has run its course?

Finally, when you have fully heard his concerns, you can slowly broach the subject of long-term care insurance, why you think it's the right action for your clients to take, and why now is the right time. Consider positioning it as financial protection for each other, so that neither will have to bear the full burden of tending to the other, and the cost of one partner's prolonged care will not impoverish the survivor. If any of your friends or other clients have benefited significantly from long-term care insurance, share these stories with this couple.

Don't urge your clients to act until you've given them enough time and space to air their feelings. In particular, you may need to meet with the husband alone if he won't open up about his fears in front of his wife. Encourage him by offering an optimistic overview of Alzheimer's research, with its hope of mitigating or even preventing this terrible illness. It may be worthwhile to meet individually with the wife as well, to see whether anxieties of her own are contributing to inaction.

However you decide to address the situation, be prepared to provide patience, support, and a sympathetic ear. It may take a while for the husband—indeed, for both of them—to stop reeling in shock and begin thinking in a more balanced way about their own future.

Taking Risks to Increase an Inheritance

A man of 79 and his daughter are both clients of mine. He is a very conservative investor, with enough money in annuities alone to live well for the rest of his life. His daughter would like him to convert some of his Treasury bonds into stocks to provide a more substantial inheritance for his children and grandchildren. However, he's too worried about the possibility of needing the money himself to agree. Any ideas?

For people who were scarred by the Depression, it's often difficult to appreciate the reality of having enough income to last the rest of one's life. If your older client can't quite believe it, take time to draw him out and empathize with his past trauma. Have you shown him charts, facts, figures, and analogies to drive home the unlikelihood of his ever running out of money? Generate numbers for the worst-case scenario so he can see that even in the direst situation, his future will be secure.

You might then ask whether he would like to pass on greater financial security to his family. By investing a small portion of his assets more aggressively (tell him what a small percentage you're talking about), he may be able to leave them much more than he otherwise would.

If he doesn't respond positively to this suggestion, so be it. After all, it's his money. You'll just have to tell the daughter that you've tried your best to help him open up to her reasonable agenda, and if she still wants him to change his mind, the ball is in her court.

Making Amends for Neglect

My client has been trying to encourage his 82-year-old mother, whose health is fragile, to move to an assisted living facility near him. However, she doesn't want to move hundreds of miles away from her small town, friends, and extended family, particularly since he has been too busy to visit or call her often. He says he would stay in closer touch if she lived nearby, but I have my doubts since I know what a workaholic he is. How can I talk to him about this?

One of the hardest things for grown children to do is to let their parents deal with issues of aging and dying in their own way, even if the children are convinced that they could do it better themselves.

I would address this gently with your client in an unstressful setting, perhaps over coffee or lunch. Begin by sympathizing with his predicament—how busy he is, and how he'd like to do more for his mother than he has so far. Empathize with his sadness at living so far away from her, and not being able to remedy the situation in a simple way that works for both of them.

I would then ask him about the support system she has in her small town. Is it a strong one? If she needed help locally, could she obtain it? Assuming he agrees that she would be well cared for, you might observe that his mother seems to know what is best for her. Instead of uprooting herself to a place where a hardworking and very busy son might be her sole source of support, she feels it's better to stay close to her comforting friends and familiar surroundings.

Perhaps there are other ways he can express his concern for her (or work out his guilt). For example, you might suggest that he schedule regular phone calls or more visits, pay for some of the cost in an assisted-living facility in her area, and/or devise a mutually agreed-upon plan to take effect if she needs hospitalization. If you have any personal experience with these issues (direct or indirect), share it with him.

When children with busy lives of their own live far away from a parent in declining health, there's no perfect solution. Allowing one's mother or father to grow old in familiar surroundings, with friends, cousins, churches or temples they know, can often be a greater gift than insisting they relocate in order to meet a son's or daughter's need for peace of mind.

Sacrificing for a Parent's Security

A new client in his 50s has come to see me at the insistence of his wife. I can see why: virtually all his resources are going toward caring for his ailing father, who lives with them. My client and his wife have no retirement savings, and only a negligible amount put aside for their two sons' college education. When I suggested a more balanced way of allocating his income, he shrugged off my concern by saying, "One of the kids will take care of us later, if it comes to that." How can I get through to him?

It can be very difficult to challenge and change a family tradition of caring for an aging parent in one's own home, no matter what the emotional and financial costs are to the spouse and children involved.

Don't try to talk this client out of taking care of his father. You'll get nowhere, and he'll think you are heartless. All you can do is slowly, gently, patiently nudge him to widen his horizons by considering his other responsibilities to his wife, his kids, and ultimately himself. You may be able to convince him that his all-encompassing devotion to his father doesn't necessarily mean his own sons will take care of him when he's old and infirm. On the contrary, his present neglect and indifference to their needs may drive them away, filled with feelings of resentment and deprivation that they may pass on to their own families when and if they marry and have kids.

You may know some case histories to tell him, either about clients who found the right balance in taking care of a parent, a partner, children, and themselves; or about others who martyred themselves in servitude to family traditions, dramatically compromising or endangering their health and well-being along with the other important relationships in their lives. Sometimes parables work better than straight talk—but whatever you do, I urge you not to stop talking to this fellow. He needs your help, and so does his family.

Giving More Than You Can Afford

What should I advise a client whose adult son has welshed on a debt? A widow in her 60s, she was left with barely enough money for her needs, which forces her to live very frugally. Five years ago, she lent $20,000 to her son, who promised orally to repay her. Although he's now financially well off, he's never repaid a penny. His mother doesn't want to "nag" him about the money for fear he'll be annoyed and prevent her from seeing her grandchildren, but I can see her resentment is building about this.

I feel for your client—but it's tragic to see how many widows and widowers overgive to their children, or bail them out in a way that compromises their own financial security and well-being.

My advice for this woman would be to find an unstressful time to talk to her son, and broach the delicate subject in language like this: "There's something I need to talk to you about that's bothering me. If you can, I need your reassurance that you'll hang in there with me until we resolve this subject, and that we won't let it come between us, or between me and your kids, whom I adore. Can you try to promise me that?"

Ideally, the son will be moved enough by his mother's concern and her love of him and the kids to respond in a way that makes her feel safer in sharing her feelings. I would then urge her to emphasize her need for the money to be repaid now. If he doesn't make a believable commitment to pay her back, she should share her hurt and disappointment at his failure to live up to his promise, to describe the price she has paid in terms of comforts forgone and sacrifices made, and to ask her son how he feels about this loan. Does he think it should have been a gift?

In general, lending money to children is a big risk. Many experts advise avoiding it at all costs, or at best considering the cash a gift for which you don't expect repayment. Of course, there are many cases where kids have borrowed money and paid it back promptly with (or without) interest. But all too often, the child thinks instead, "Considering all the ways you were an imperfect (or worse, lousy) parent, the least you can do is give me this money and expect nothing in return." In other words, the "loan" becomes belated compensation for the unconditional love we wish our parents had given us while we were growing up.

In a perfect world, parents would always teach their children to support themselves well, and help them develop into responsible adults who wouldn't repeatedly rush home to be bailed out or compensated for the pain of childhood wounds. But because most of us are far from perfect, I believe it's smart to keep money transactions between parents and children as clear and direct as possible.

Bailing Out Grandpa

One of my clients, a man in his 30's with a young family, has asked my advice in resolving a difficult dilemma. His father came to him recently (not for the first time) asking to borrow $10,000 to pay off creditors, and hinting that if refused he would cut off the relationship with my client's two children. After many years of bailing out this alcohol-abusing parent from financial and social scrapes, my client is in torment about this decision. How can I help him?

In this situation, I would recommend to your client that he gather family and friends for an "intervention" with his father. By giving his dad vital feedback on how his drinking is affecting all those around him while expressing their real concern for his welfare, this intervention may succeed in pushing him into an alcohol-treatment program. (It's a good idea not to undertake this without the support of a professional trained to facilitate interventions. See the Additional Resources section for suggestions.)

Of course, interventions don't always work. If this one doesn't, in your place I would do everything possible to help your client learn to let go of his father and disconnect from any expectations that he will be a safe and loving grandparent.

Sometimes a temporary disconnection can create the space family members need to look at themselves and their lives, and realize how important good, solid, loving connections really are. I would hope this might be the case with your client's father. But there are some families where the dysfunction is so deep, and the repeated wounding is so emotionally and spiritually destructive, that its members need to turn away and look for loving and nurturing connections in other places—with close friends, with mentors at work, in spiritual or religious communities, in places they volunteer, or in activities that nurture the spirit, such as meditation or walking in places of beauty and meaning. In this case, your client's children may eventually be able to find grandfather-like substitutes who will be more consistently reliable.

In any event, caution him about bailing out his father at his own expense and that of his family. Past experience has shown him that this rescuing hasn't worked. If he can find ways to support his father emotionally (such as through a group intervention), he will at least know he tried his best to help his father get the real support he needs.

Confronting Fears of Frailty

An older couple recently visited me for advice on planning their estate. They've done well with their investments, but the glaring omission in their preparations is a lack of long-term care insurance. I'm a little gun-shy about this, since discussing the same thing recently with my own parents brought up painful questions of who would care for whom, home care versus a nursing home, and other emotionally touchy issues. How can I handle this to avoid upsetting my clients unduly?

Getting these terribly painful and scary issues on the table is never easy. To expect your clients to think and talk about these topics in front of you may be unrealistic—and perhaps more than any of you could handle.

A gentle way to initiate thoughtful conversation about this topic would be to send them home with an article on the subject, along with a list of questions for them to think about separately and discuss before they see you next. These questions might include their preferences about home care vs. nursing homes under various scenarios (e.g., what if home care is not possible?), as well as issues that might be handled with living wills or powers of attorney.

After you've given them this homework, you can schedule an appointment to discuss the financial planning aspects of their choices. However, talking about the death or frailty of loved ones, our own dying, and who takes care of whom can make the most self-possessed of us regress into primitive, childlike states of need, fear and deprivation—so be prepared for emotional eruptions and undercurrents to permeate the discussion.

Like most of us, your clients may find it hard to wend their way back to an adult level on these topics. If so, it may be helpful and soothing to recount any experiences you've had with other clients who have worked out these decisions and gone on to reap the fruits of their wise choices.

Incidentally, if the intense emotions generated stir you up a lot too, you may want to talk to colleagues for support before or after you see these clients.

Stubborn Parents, Stymied Children

I'm stumped on a life planning issue that involves a longtime client. His 84-year-old mother is ailing, and he has asked me to help research assisted living plans and home health care. However, she's dead set against these options, and keeps insisting she's just fine living on her own and driving wherever she wants. My client is afraid she may be endangering herself. Is there any way I can improve his peace of mind about this?

Droves of baby boomers are beginning to experience this difficult situation with their aging parents. Unfortunately, I don't know of any magic answer. Why not invite some planner colleagues to a roundtable discussion on helping adult children who are in conflict with their parents' needs?

Sympathize with the worry your client must feel while his mother remains unwilling to give up her freedom. You may be able to lessen his anxiety by educating him on long-term care alternatives. Reassure him that if her life situation worsens, he will at least be armed with practical information and potential plans to help her.

Be careful not to overstep your limits by advising your client to take charge of his mother's affairs, unless he is ready to make this aggressive and adversarial move. Otherwise, if he tries to seize the reins of control and it backfires in any way, he could well blame you for pushing him in this direction and ruining his relationship with his mother.

Help!

My partners and I are feeling overwhelmed as we try to work with baby boomer clients who are struggling with the dilemma of caring for failing parents. They need help choosing nursing homes, Alzheimer facilities, and hospices, but we're inadequately prepared to advise them. Is there a source we can turn to?

The downside of advances in health care is that more and more people are facing agonizing decisions about how to care for elderly parents with a debilitating or terminal illness.

I believe that the most creative way for you to deal with this is to expand your knowledge of referral sources for a host of related problems—not just good nursing-home facilities and hospices, but firms who can provide live-in help, and even support groups for adults caring for failing parents. (Many of your grown-up clients are likely to feel helpless frustration and grief at having to parent their parents, which may leave them feeling like the children they once were.) Consider sponsoring a fact-finding workshop with your colleagues to brainstorm and share ideas on eldercare resources in your area. The more knowledgeable you become, the more your clients will appreciate being able to consult you as part of a support team helping them get through this difficult transition.

TAKING ACTION

Helping older parents or adult children is an enormous challenge that will tax your clients' ability to think calmly and clearly. Emotionally close relationships raise issues of love, support, and care, while more troublesome feelings surface when the relationship is strained, distant, or hostile. When you deal directly with older clients, you may be swayed by reminders of your relationship with your own parents.

To help these clients, take steps to resolve your own personal issues about aging and mortality. From this relatively calm place, you can take time to hear your clients fully. Then gently help them consider creative ways to make the best of a situation that's inherently fraught with difficulties, but is as old as mankind.

FAMILY MATTERS
Family Business

Blood is thicker than water, they say—and few situations prove the point more effectively than trying to work with family members who are in business together.

The working relationships of unrelated people can be complicated enough. When you mix in emotionally charged family dynamics, the result may be a tangle of love, fear, envy, distrust, and betrayal worthy of the Corleones (who started out with a family olive-oil business, if you recall).

If you encounter situations like these, here are some ways to help your clients sort out the business issues while preventing blood relationships from becoming too bloody.

A Clinging Mother

My client is supposed to be taking over the family business from her mother, a successful entrepreneur now in her sixties. The problem, according my client, is that her mother won't (or can't) let go. The daughter has asked for my advice on how to maximize her future financial interest in the business, assuming she can encourage her mother to pass the reins of leadership to her. What's the best way to approach this?

Entrepreneurs often have a hard time giving up control because their self-worth is tied so closely to the success of their brainchild. When they're also parents with real children, even thornier complications come into play.

As a therapist, my first suggestion is to remind your client to be sensitive to her mother's feelings about aging, loss, and letting go in general. These are all terribly difficult things for people to face as they get older.

If your client is asking you to get personally involved, you'll need to gauge your own comfort level with serving as a therapeutic bridge between the parties. Are you okay with helping the mother discuss her feelings about letting go and passing the torch, and helping the daughter open up about wanting to take on her mother's legacy and prove herself worthy of trust?

Your client may feel that her mother's reluctance to let her take over is due to a lack of confidence in her. Actually, it may have absolutely nothing to do with the daughter's competence, and everything to do with the mother's fear of feeling empty and worthless once she gives up control. By helping to allay this fear (perhaps by suggesting other challenges she could take on after retiring), you might pave the way for better discussions about the needs of both women, and of the business as well.

Although your client has also asked you to help her plan her future once she has taken over the company, I believe she must first explore her hurt feelings about her mother's perceived lack of trust in her business acumen. Only after this component has been "lifted off the top" will she be able to think calmly and rationally about what she wants to accomplish with the business. Individual counseling for her and her mother, or a family session, may be just what the doctor ordered to separate personal feelings from professional considerations.

An Unsuitable Job for a Woman

I've always been impressed by the independence and common sense that characterize one of my clients, a mid-level executive in her 30s. She recently learned that her father, who lives in another state, plans to retire and pass on his manufacturing business to her younger brother in the next five years. My client, who has an MBA, is much more interested in running the company than her brother is. However, her father won't take her interest seriously, insisting it's "no job for a woman." She is frustrated and upset, and has asked if I can think of a way to get him to reverse his impending decision. Any ideas?

Unfortunately, this painful family situation is not uncommon. Outdated sexual stereotypes and traditions about the line of succession in a family business can create emotional havoc (and bad financial outcomes) for generations.

To begin with, I would urge you to help your client assess her financial and managerial strengths, so she feels in a solid position to press her case. Then encourage her to talk to her brother, assuming they have a good enough relationship to communicate honestly and openly. She needs to ask him how he feels about her managing the business and leaving him free to pursue whatever he'd rather do. If he's willing to support her, they can approach their father together. I would recommend an initial approach in writing, followed up by a face-to-face meeting a little later. This gives the siblings an opportunity to present their argument clearly and free of emotion, while allowing their father time to absorb the message without feeling ambushed or railroaded.

Their obvious caring about what's best for the business may eventually win their father over, prompting him to change his preconceived notions and open up to the real strengths and divergent interests of his two children. If he does, he'll not only advance the cause of family harmony, but also take an important step to help the business flourish in the future.

Patching Up a Sibling Rivalry

My client inherited the family business when his widowed father died recently. He tells me that his sister is so outraged about being excluded from this inheritance that she won't speak to him. Though he believes his experience and abilities make him a better choice to run the company, he feels somewhat guilty about his father's decision. How should I advise him to proceed?

In families where the father or mother gives preferential treatment to one sibling and ignores the others, there are bound to be feelings of hurt and betrayal that go deep. Reestablishing the connection between the hurt one (or ones) and the favored one is very important family healing work.

In this case, I think you can serve as a "connection coach" for your client, helping him to re-establish a loving connection with his sister. I would begin by suggesting that he think about whether he could offer her some financial compensation, or even a role in the company, to make up for his father's one-sided inheritance. (Caution: the father may have purposely excluded one sibling from the firm because the two can't work together. If so, offering her an active role in the business may not be the way to go.)

In any case, encourage him to reach out to his sister in phone calls, letters, and in person to communicate his understanding of her resentment and injured feelings. Did he persuade their father to leave the business solely to him? If so, why? By explaining his motives to her, he may help her see the situation more clearly (even though it may not improve their relationship, at least initially). She also needs to know right away if he was totally uninvolved in the decision.

Your client may need to give his sister time and space to process her sense of hurt and betrayal. (These feelings should really be directed at their parents, who unfortunately are no longer around to help work things out.) But by communicating his own feelings of guilt, sadness, or embarrassment about the decision—ideally in writing, so she can read it over and over—he can help her see that this "gift" had a high price tag attached to it for him too.

Assuming that your client can get through to his sister, and offer her either profit-sharing participation or a place in the business that they both feel good about, you can help cement their reconnection by meeting with both of them in your office. But even if they can't find an immediately satisfactory solution, encourage them to keep talking about what bothers them (provided this painful topic doesn't take over their entire communication). If the sister still has unresolved anger, it's better for it to be directed at their deceased father, who concealed his decision so she had no leverage to change his perspective.

Eventually, she may be able to find peace despite this imperfect state of affairs. In the meantime, as long as she and her brother stay in touch, you'll have helped strengthen the loving family connection between them.

Stagnant Heir

My client dropped out of college to work for his uncle, who inherited 100% of a family business that had been owned by my client's father. His cousin (the uncle's son) also joined the business at about the same time. The problem: the cousin has received several promotions and pay increases and is clearly heir apparent, while my client complains of being over-

worked, underpaid, and unappreciated. I learned all this as we were discussing how to improve his investment return, but it seems to me that a change of scenery would help him a lot more than a different asset allocation. How should I proceed?

This messy situation is fraught with emotional pitfalls, and probably with deep festering hurts and resentments as well. One old wound I imagine might be there is that the uncle, once in his brother's shadow, may now be getting even by slighting his brother's son.

There's not much point in appealing to the uncle to give his nephew preference over his own son—that's been tried unsuccessfully since at least the days of the Caesars. And to be fair, the owner's son could have some stellar qualities your client lacks, perhaps including a better education or a more enterprising personality.

All in all, the nephew would be better off positioning himself to be of value to a company with less emotional freight for him. To start with, he'll need that college diploma. If he can get the family business to support him in obtaining it, why not, considering the time he's already put in?

So my first suggestion would be for your client to write a list of his current job responsibilities and personal strengths, discuss it with his uncle, and ask if the company will pay for him to finish college. Perhaps the uncle can see that this investment will be good for the company. If not, and if your client realizes that the job is compromising his sense of self-worth, it may be worthwhile to find another way to pay for completing his education. Going back to school will expose him to other work options, perhaps encouraging him to pursue another avenue after graduation.

If your client resists quitting the firm his father founded, remind him that most people experience several changes of career in a lifetime. Tell him about similar situations you're familiar with, to reassure him that he is not alone. Even if he still opts to stay put, you may have planted a seed that will eventually prompt him to free himself from an environment where he feels unappreciated and put down. The sooner he recognizes the need to move on, the more opportunity he will have to shape a life to please himself—not his uncle.

A Dilemma Fit for a King

Several years ago, I helped a client set up a family limited partnership as part of his estate planning. However, his son and daughter now tell him they want more say in how the business is run, as well as a greater share of the income. My client has no intention of giving up control of the business at this point, and doesn't want to provide them more money. The catch is that he wants me to explain this to his children! Any ideas?

Since your client wants to pass the buck to you, it sounds as if he's hoping you'll find a way to communicate with his children that won't hurt his personal relationship with them.

Instead of serving as his proxy (a role you're understandably not comfortable with), I would suggest that you coach him to take the lead in this tricky task. In a one-on-one meeting, discuss what he wants to achieve with his money and in his relationship with his daughter and son. See if there's any negotiating room between his desire to maintain total control of the business and his children's wish to share more of its financial resources.

Encourage him to think about all of this long and hard. Then, he should write them a thoughtful, loving letter outlining his goals, desires, and plans (emotional as well as financial). This would permit him to assure them that his primary motive in setting up the FLP is to save on taxes—a move intended to benefit them later on.

Last, if you are comfortable playing a mediating role in this conflict, you could sit down with the three of them and try to help them reach agreement. But watch out. It's very likely that all three are carrying around the emotional baggage of unmet needs and hurt feelings from the past. The children may be seeking payback for their wounds by making demands on the father, and he may be warding them off because of old hurts, angers, and disappointments of his own. If their discussions get too intense, you need to be ready to recommend good family therapists who can help them sort out their differences.

Also, be clear about your own allegiance before you take on this challenge. If the father's position as your client makes you feel you must support his views, be sure to spell this out for his offspring. Even so, you can still help him communicate better with his children about love, money, and the family business.

Nepotism Lives!

The owner of our financial planning firm has just told us he intends to bring in his relatively inexperienced daughter as vice president of client services. Many of us feel sandbagged by this news. After working here for years, we expected to be rewarded for our loyalty and effort by being able to move up in the company. Now we feel merit no longer matters, since a successor has obviously been anointed. Is the only solution to leave this business where we've invested so much of ourselves?

If you and your colleagues are agreed on this issue, perhaps a sensitively worded letter to the boss from all of you is the way to address this explosive issue. Bear in mind that you won't have much bargaining power unless he knows you're willing to leave the firm if his daughter comes in.

Still, it's worth a try. The key is not to be confrontational, but to emphasize positive aspects he'll want to agree with, such as the enjoyment and satisfaction you all get out of your work and the respect you have for him. You might add that you understand his pride in what the business has achieved and his desire to involve his children in its continuing success. (I wouldn't harp on his daughter's inexperience or other inadequacies—after all, love is blind.)

You could delicately remind him that although he started the company, you feel that you're stakeholders too, by virtue of the time, energy, and ability you've invested in it over the years. Explain that you'd all greatly prefer to continue working for a firm that demands and rewards merit and hard work, no matter whose it is. Your boss should get the message that he risks losing his entire staff (or at least your enthusiasm, dedication, and loyalty) unless he reconsiders his decision to bring his daughter on board.

When family loyalties cloud their professional judgment, people like your boss often have no idea of the havoc their ill-founded plans can generate. So try to approach him patiently and considerately, but with firm resolve to have your needs heard. The reason I would suggest having other job options in your pocket is to eliminate any trace of desperation from this negotiation. If you have other choices, you can devote all your energy toward getting the outcome you want, without being tempted to compromise too much just to keep your job.

Taking Action

When business and family mix, remember that old grudges, hurts, and feelings of deprivation or low self-esteem are often intensified. More and more family firms these days are seeking outside help—"business therapy," I call it—to sort out what's best for both the business and the family. Regular meetings or staff retreats with these business therapists are an excellent way to breathe fresh air into a dysfunctional family system and open it up to healthier possibilities.

I encourage you to help your clients lighten the load of their disabling baggage, by yourself and/or with guidance from a psychological expert. This tremendous service will improve the chances of their business growing across generations, and of their personal relationships continuing to flourish as well.

Stress and Trauma

Stress comes in many forms. Remember the "stress scale" that made news years ago? Even good events, such as a move to a bigger house, a marriage, or an unexpected windfall, can cause tremendous stress to the point of impairing health. Sudden radical changes in financial worth—not only losses, but inheritances and other windfalls—can make people feel detached from reality. Personal loss, such as a loved one's medical crisis or death, reduces many normally rational individuals to a barely functioning mode. And the type of stress we've all experienced since September 11 has filled many of us with a sense of free-floating anxiety and vulnerability.

For advisors, a key question is how to help clients deal with stress and trauma when you yourself may be under considerable strain. I think it's vital to practice self-care and self-nurturing so you can project balance and healing to your more stressed-out clients. Identify the places, practices, or devices that help you regain a sense of serenity, and make time to benefit from them. If you're overly anxious, upset, or even just irritable from sleep deprivation, it will be hard for you to find the patience to listen carefully to your clients' fear and pain.

And listening is crucial. Before you can lead them back to more rational decision-making, you need to provide a safe space for them to vent their problems and anxieties. If they are dealing with personal loss, give them time to grieve before nudging them to move forward with their financial plans. People who are profoundly affected by stress tend to retreat into a primitive survival mode, which is always somewhat dysfunctional. In extreme cases, some clients may even suffer from post-traumatic stress disorder, where they keep re-experiencing past trauma as if it is happening in the present.

But even if your clients act oddly or unpredictably, never label or treat them as "crazy" or "sick." In cases of extreme trauma or stress, it may well be appropriate to refer them for supportive counseling or therapy to help them cope.

In any event, empathizing with their feelings of being overwhelmed or out of control is an essential first step in building a bridge to better decision-making. If you are managing to survive similar stresses and traumas, sharing some of your own small successes can inspire your clients. But be careful to focus on connecting with them first, then guiding and helping. Even if you feel you have mastered their dilemmas, avoid the temptation to get impatient and push them forward too quickly. A tone and attitude of compassion and respect will make you much more effective in leading them back toward balanced thinking.

All this takes time and patience. Learning how to connect well, when to listen, when to empathize, when to suggest therapeutic help and support, and when to gently move clients toward action is part of the advisor's art that this section of the book will help you cultivate. Indeed, I'm convinced that as more and more clients come to advisors burdened by stress and trauma, the skill to help them cope with these pressures will fast become a necessity.

STRESS AND TRAUMA
September 11, 2001

We Americans like to feel we're a "can-do" nation, strong and adaptable. With jaw-gritting determination, we began after September 11 to adjust our horizons to a new world of vulnerability, risk, and loss. But despite this resolve, all it took to send us back to Ground Zero in our hearts was a plane crashing in nearby Queens.

The stresses on your clients may accumulate on many levels: the possible (or actual) loss of friends, colleagues, or even family members; the lost sense of security in everyday life; and the backdrop of economic and market loss that may have drastically affected their plans for the future. Here are some ways to help them deal with these stresses.

The Loneliness of the Long-Distance Runner

After losing a couple of close business colleagues in the World Trade Center, I find I don't want to get close to other people I have to contact every day. Yesterday a bond trader I've known for a long time asked me if I had something on my mind, because I wasn't really listening when he told me about his kid in Little League. I don't like being this way, but what can I do about it?

Considering the trauma of your recent losses, it's no wonder you are pushing away former friends and trying to hold them at arm's length. All intimacy, closeness, or connection carries within it the possibility of hurt and loss—it's a sad but universal part of life.

Though the distance you have created is perfectly normal and understandable, the fact that it's beginning to bother you is a good sign. You may be ready now to share your feelings with a counselor, a spouse, or someone else who can help you mourn your losses and let go of some of the pain you are undoubtedly carrying. It would be a courageous act to tell your bond trader colleague what you've been going through, and express your regrets that you've been pushing him away to avoid the possibility of more pain in the future.

In the meantime, be gentle with yourself. Do what you need to do to heal and soothe your soul. When you are ready, encourage yourself to risk opening your heart to friends and colleagues so that even more healing can occur.

And if you're feeling bad about yourself for cutting off your connections to others, try to practice compassionate listening to your own inner thoughts and feelings. Remember that humans are somewhat fragile creatures who tend to pull into their shells when hurt or endangered. (What's a turtle's shell for, after all?) We need time to feel safe enough to emerge into the light again. If you take it slow and steady, and share when you can with those you trust, I believe you'll eventually come out of your shell.

Fear and Anxiety in Children

At a portfolio review session, a client who is a divorced mother of two asked me for advice about her young children. Even though her family knew no one who died on September 11, the kids are having temper tantrums when she leaves for work, and refuse to sleep alone. She's concerned about whether this reaction is normal, and if not, what she should do. Obviously, this is beyond my area of expertise. Help!

Whether or not the children knew any of the victims personally, it is very normal for them to experience these symptoms of high anxiety. Many kids are hypersensitive to what goes on around them, and they've probably tuned into the underlying vibe of apprehension that has swept over many adults in waves since 9/11.

While reassuring your client that this reaction is natural, consider suggesting some resources that might help. Has she talked to anyone at the children's school? If not, she might start by discussing her concerns with their teachers and guidance counselors.

Also, encourage her to keep talking to her kids about their fears. It's not a good idea to paint an unrealistic picture ("Nothing like this will ever happen again"), which may fly in the face of alarming announcements they will hear about or see on TV. Instead, she should try to reassure them with truths suited to their ages and worries ("Sweetheart, brave soldiers from many nations are helping us find these bad men so we can stop them" or "Honey, haven't I always come home from work?").

If the kids won't open up about their specific anxieties, she might try telling them a story (or acting it out with stuffed animals or dolls) about "other kids" with similar symptoms, asking her children to suggest why the imaginary kids are upset. For more in-depth therapeutic support, consider assembling a list of good psychological resources for children and adults. This mom may need a little counseling herself right now.

Eventually, you may be able to shift your client's focus to her financial situation. But unless you first address her worries about her children, she probably won't be ready to hear a word you say about her portfolio.

Emotions Out of Whack

At the start of a year-end review of their investments and insurance, clients of mine erupted in a terrible fight. The husband complained that his wife is making his life crazy by overreacting to the threat of terrorism. She is extremely wary of crowds and unexpected mail, won't travel, and insists on having a survival and evacuation plan. She accuses him of being in total denial about the danger. I felt as if my office had become a war zone. How should I deal with these folks?

Remember that in times of high anxiety, people tend to revert to their oldest, primitive survival mode. This couple is doing it in spades.

To address their divergence of reactions, you need to seat yourself emotionally smack in the middle between them. Assure them that even though the ways they are handling this stressful situation look extreme to each other, both responses are normal. Some people are comforted by taking action against the danger they fear, while others find it more calming to return as quickly as possible the routines of everyday life. Both approaches can be healing.

If you're willing to serve these clients as a therapeutic educator, ask if they can possible move toward a middle ground. You may want to mention my comment about people's tendency to retreat under stress to survival mode—which, although totally normal, is rarely the most rational or functional way to act. If you can help the husband agree to take some steps that will reassure his wife, and encourage her to pull back a bit from her hypervigilance, they may be able to move on to a discussion of their real financial needs.

Who Would Your Clients Turn To?

As a sole practitioner for 15 years, I was taken aback when a client recently told me she'd be totally lost if anything happened to me. She's also concerned that if my records are destroyed through some calamity, her finances could be ruined. Her worry struck me as a natural reaction to the turmoil we've all been experiencing. I think I reassured her, but how can I head off this concern with my other clients?

This vital question is one you need to address in detail. If anything did happen to you, whom would you want your clients to turn to?

Do you have an associate who is ready to be trained for more responsibility? If not, should you think of hiring someone to back you up? Or you might prefer to make an arrangement with other sole practitioners to take each other's clients in case of necessity. Whatever the solution, let your clients know you have put in place a succession plan to ensure continuity in their moneylives. It's important for them to know that you've thought about this long and hard, and paved the road to a smooth transition.

On the matter of financial records, make sure you have backup systems in place so clients' account information will be safe even if your office disappears. By addressing these two concerns promptly and firmly, you can assure your clients that they are well protected against the risk of disconnection and loss.

Providing a "Holding Space"

A longtime client was badly shaken by the death of old friends on one of the hijacked planes. She has asked me about selling her mutual funds and buying annuities, so her grandchildren will be guaranteed a death benefit no matter what happens to her or the market. And even though she is well provided with life insurance, she plans to quadruple her coverage instead of buying the vacation home she's wanted for a long time. When I ask her to consider whether she's overreacting to recent events, she doesn't seem to focus on what I say. What should I do to help her?

This client needs to be able to air her fear and sadness about what has happened before she can think rationally about what makes good financial planning sense. If you can provide a safe "holding space" for her to talk and be listened to with compassion, she may be ready sooner to make truly appropriate new decisions about her loved ones' needs and her own.

You'll probably want to schedule several visits with her about this, if you can. In between, she may be willing to read literature you provide about her choices. But be prepared to find that at a deep level, she's still in shock and may need extra patience and guidance to make good decisions.

Underneath all the angers and fears triggered by the cataclysmic events that have unfolded, many of us feel a profound sense of sadness that life will never again feel as safe as it once did. Even if that safety was an illusion, our perception of it was tremendously comforting. Without it, we need to connect more deeply with one another, and with our own personal sources of healing and nourishment, to rediscover our strengths and our serenity.

Portfolio for Peace

A client of mine is so upset about our country's military response to terrorism that he wants to move all his assets into a few stocks focusing on peaceful values. I have no problem with his willingness to stand behind his beliefs, but abandoning his well-diversified portfolio could prove disastrous in the long run. How should I handle this?

It's perfectly natural for this tense world situation to inspire a reevaluation of our life course, including the causes we support financially. But action should come after careful thought, not on impulse—especially not if it's prompted by a feeling of desperation about the future.

I would address this client's request by empathizing with his desire to make a difference in the world. Ask him to share his values and ideals with you in more detail. Once you have respectfully explored these avenues, you may be able to suggest more balanced ways to achieve his goals. For example, giving directly to causes he believes in, or volunteering his own time and abilities, could be personally fulfilling as well as effective.

If he remains firm in wanting to invest in these chosen stocks, be sure he's clear on the risks they present. Investors with survivor guilt, or guilt at our society's affluence, may even choose certain stocks purposely to lose money. If you suspect that this may be the case, you'll need to address the issue with great sensitivity so he doesn't feel judged or attacked.

After some discussion, he may be willing to keep at least some of his portfolio in more broadly diversified investments. This would assist you in protecting his longer-term financial security, while helping him feel that he is expressing his values in a forceful way.

Now Is the Time for Client Guidance

All my clients seem to be struggling emotionally these days. Many appear dazed and distracted, others so needy and anxious that I hardly know how to respond. How can I help them return to normalcy?

A forward-looking financial planner I know wrote a thoughtful letter to all her clients about the events of September 11. She began by empathizing with what many of them must feel, validating their feelings of vulnerability in a scary new world.

Her letter continued by calmly suggesting ways for these clients to cultivate a long-term perspective. She discussed her view of the financial marketplace in the near term and in the long run. By the closing paragraph, she had built a bridge from emotion to rationality, making it possible for her clients to communicate with her in a more centered fashion devoid of panic.

Your own clients may be waiting for you to take the lead in discussing the future. This could be a good time to organize a client appreciation event or a "What Now?" financial seminar. By meeting in a group, they can share their anxieties and ideas while being coached on ways to get through these difficult days.

These are stressful times, indeed—so we all need to be much more aware of the messages we're sending and how we're delivering them. In fact, I'm with those who feel our government needs more psychologists on board to advise on how best to communicate with an anxious public; warnings about vague and unspecified imminent danger do nothing but fan the flames of panic. Our goal should be to support true preparedness and assuage people's intense anxiety.

Helping Panicky Clients to Focus

After the terrifying attacks, a panicky client asked me for an appointment to discuss his financial plan. He's insistent on doing the right thing for his children, but when I asked him to sit down with me and revisit his goals, he just couldn't seem to think straight. In view of his anxiety, how can I help him see if his plan is still appropriate?

Like most of us, your client will need time to heal. In the wake of a cataclysm like the one we have experienced, this is a process of moving past the primitive survival mode to rediscover one's rational, thriving self.

To make this easier for him, listen patiently to his feelings and fears. Help him explore what he needs to do to reestablish balance in his own life. This might entail spending more time with his family and friends, volunteering to assist the relief effort, or simply doing whatever calms and relaxes him.

In the meantime, if you allow him to hang in there with you, your patience will be rewarded. As he finds more inner peace, he will slowly be able to turn his mind toward his financial goals. Eventually he will feel rational enough to review his needs, and explore with you whether his money is in the right vehicles to meet them.

When Grieving Clients "Need" to Act

My clients lost their only son in the World Trade Center. They know they need to change their estate plan, but whenever we try to talk about it, the father chokes up and the mother begins weeping. I know they need time to come to grips with this tragedy, but since they're already in questionable health, I hate to delay too long. How can I help them make these important decisions without losing more time?

You can't, so don't even try. Now is not the time for decisions. It's time for them to mourn their horrific loss, as they begin moving through their grief and anger toward healing.

The best way you can help them now is to listen compassionately. Allow the mother to cry to her heart's content, and the father to grieve in his own way. As you sympathetically witness this wrenching process, you can ever so slowly begin discussing their choices with them. You might also consider sending them articles that suggest options, such as leaving a gift to a meaningful charity or starting a foundation in their son's memory.

Despite their shaky health, I can't emphasize enough the importance of giving them time to make the right decisions clear-headedly. If you push them to take action before they're emotionally ready, they may make decisions they'll later regret, or flee your insistent urging and never return. The better you can connect with their sorrow and pain, the sooner they'll be receptive to your suggestions.

Space for Sorrow

I lost a brother-in-law at the Pentagon on September 11—he was about my age, and we'd been close for years. I thought it would be best to get back to my job as quickly as possible, but I find myself unable to concentrate, doing poor work, and being easily upset by clients and colleagues. My sister and her family are leaning on me for emotional support that I feel less and less able to give. What should I do?

It would be wonderful to keep letting your sister's family lean on you, but if your own emotional engine is running on empty, you can't be much help to them or yourself. Your first priority should be your own need to mourn your brother-in-law, and to heal the raw wound of his loss.

Make time to take stock of your own thoughts and feelings. Writing them down may help you deal with them. You might even write a letter to your late brother-in-law, along with an imagined response from him, to promote your own emotional release and healing. Or stop multi-tasking for a while and listen quietly to great music that opens your heart. Consider a visit to your own source of comfort—a church, synagogue, or community organization—and participate in a way that helps you feel more connected to life and more hopeful about the future.

If you don't feel up to taking on this effort by yourself, or it doesn't seem to be helping you, consider seeing a grief counselor or therapist who can lend a hand. By caring for yourself in this way, you will not only restore your own emotional well-being, but be of greater service to your family, your colleagues, and your clients.

Claiming Respite for Yourself

Since September 11, my clients have inundated me with phone calls—sometimes about their portfolio, but often about other aspects of their lives. I'm exhausted by this outpouring of their needs and emotions. How can I handle it without getting swallowed up?

Consider writing your clients personal letters or emails sharing your compassionate understanding of what they're going through.

You might mention that even though you want to be fully accessible to them, you have sometimes felt overwhelmed. To help yourself stay balanced and able to help them, tell them you are setting aside a certain time each day for their calls—perhaps an hour in the morning, or half an hour at each end of the day. Let them know that you intend to be fully present for them during these times.

This letter or note would also give you an opportunity to suggest other healing resources your clients may want to consult, such as charitable or community organizations, religious groups, and therapists or grief counselors. Include phone numbers and Web addresses if you can.

You want to do this in a sensitive way that makes clients feel cared for, not rejected or abandoned. By suggesting these alternatives, and limiting the impact of their emotions on your own schedule, I think you'll feel more whole-heartedly available to them when you are willing to be consulted.

In the meantime, don't feel the slightest bit guilty about being unable to cope with their intense neediness. Your reaction is perfectly natural. In fact, the very reason why psychotherapists like me so often burn out is because we forget to practice healthy life balance and self-care. So I understand completely what you must be going through, and hope you can be a model to your clients in restoring your balance.

Getting Away from It All

My client's fiancé has been so unnerved by the terrorist attacks and the prospect of war that he's asked her to liquidate her investments so they can buy land in Canada, build a cabin, and live self-sufficiently. She's deeply in love with him and feels she should go along with this. I think it could be a huge financial mistake. How far should I go in making my opinion felt?

Don't be surprised if your client doesn't seem like her usually sensible self. Being in love is an altered state like a trance, in which one's own personality and values may be subsumed for the sake of the love relationship. Recent events like 9/11 only intensify this temporary lack of groundedness.

I think your approach should be to honor her commitment to this relationship, while encouraging her to step back and assess her goals. Point out the importance of basing a marriage on mutual respect, with enough space for both individuals to live out their desire for a meaningful life. Is she really sure this kind of lifestyle is right for her, or is she surrendering her own needs to her fiancé's fears?

If you are willing and she agrees, you might ask him to join the two of you to discuss the action he is contemplating. See if you can empathize with his fears and stresses, while reminding him that many other people feel equally worried and even panicky. Don't reject outright his idea of moving to a cabin in the woods (this crisis, after all, may be a long-awaited opportunity to make a major change in his life), but do counsel him to consider all the options calmly and rationally. See if you can lead him into a less drastic long-term strategy for himself and his fiancée.

If he's still determined to head for the hills, get together with your client by herself and help her understand the risks of losing her nest egg. What if she and her husband find that this lifestyle isn't quite what they expected? Or what if something happens to him, leaving her alone? You might suggest that she set aside her portfolio (perhaps in a revocable trust) while she tries on this new life to see if it works for her. By making it possible for her to return to a more traditional lifestyle if she wishes, you could be giving her a gift of incalculable value.

Turning a Loss into a Legacy

A new client came to me after inheriting close to $200,000 from his father, who was killed aboard one of the hijacked airliners. When I asked the young man what his goals are for this money, he said vaguely, "I just need to take care of it." Some of it is in fairly risky and illiquid investments, but when I suggested trying to unwind these positions, he said, "My dad was smart; he knew what he was doing." I'm not really sure why he came to see me in the first place. What should I do?

Your client's behavior is a very common response to grief and loss. Trauma to the heart and soul takes as much time to heal, if not more, than injury to the body. So allow him a period of recuperation before you suggest any changes to the portfolio.

If he's willing, you might encourage him to talk about his father. What means most to him about the kind of person his dad was, and how he lived his life? By helping your client honor his memories of his father more fully, you may eventually be able to open the door to a discussion of the specific financial legacy he has received.

When he is certain that you've come to respect his dad's gifts, he may be willing to listen to your recommendation that he move the money into more suitable investments. It may be possible to frame this as a fulfillment of the father's deep desire to help his son feel true financial security and serenity in his own unique way.

In all these cases, the essential first step is making time for clients to get over their shock and move through the natural stages of mourning and healing. If you rush these stages or are not adequately attuned to them, you risk leaving your clients feeling upset and slighted. By slowing down and empathizing with their shock, grief, or fear, you will be able to lead them toward sensible financial decisions when they are willing and able to move forward.

Taking Action

Amid the reality of terrorism, the threat of biological warfare, and other horrific possibilities, it's often difficult to help people slow down enough to reintegrate their thinking and their feeling functions. Remind your clients (and yourself) that learning to cope with constant stress is a long-term process, requiring creativity and as much supportive human contact as possible. The more you can encourage clients to reflect on their long-term values and goals, the more rational their decision-making will be.

Be sure to give yourself the same space. Replenishing your mental and emotional coffers will allow you to provide wiser and more balanced counsel, making you a better advisor for having "walked your talk." Proactive steps like volunteering to help a charitable or community group can make it easier to return to some semblance of normalcy. Even though what's normal now will probably never be the same as what was normal before September 11, the main positive outcome may be more interpersonal contact and deeper connections.

STRESS AND TRAUMA
Sudden Wealth

Is there any of us who hasn't thought at some point, "If only I had a lot more money, my life would be fantastic"?

Unfortunately, sudden wealth doesn't automatically lead to happiness and fulfillment. On the contrary, it can raise completely new problems and dilemmas.

In the situations below, I've looked at some of the difficulties unexpected prosperity can create, and suggested ways to cope with an embarrassment of riches.

The Overnight Millionaire

It shouldn't be a problem to have a client who just made $6 million on an IPO, but he and his wife seem completely overwhelmed by this vast increase in their net worth. While working on a financial plan for them, I feel I also need to help them make the emotional transition from being moderately well-off to becoming truly wealthy. Any ideas?

Instant wealth can often be more of a curse than a blessing—initially, at least. Why? Because it threatens to sweep the beneficiary off into a fantasy in which it is virtually impossible to make calm, rational decisions.

You can expect all of your clients' financial fantasies to surface—those dreams we all have about "If I had enough money, I'd. . . ." That's fine in itself, but rushing to act out these fantasies is dangerous. It's important to take time to calm and center oneself enough for wise decision-making.

While celebrating your clients' good fortune, I would caution them about others in similar situations who spent their windfall money without thinking, and regretted it later. To slow down the action process, encourage them to rethink their goals and dreams in light of this amazing new situation. I advise my own clients to write down their short-, medium-, and long-term goals at least three times over the course of a month. This gives them some time and space to before making impulsive purchases that they may regret later on. (Also, newly wealthy people are sometimes unconsciously tempted to sabotage their windfall by getting rid of the money as fast as they can, so they return to more familiar circumstances.)

You might also refer them to resources that will help them think productively about their new situation. (See the Additional Resources section for some suggestions.)

In any event, you'll be providing a priceless service if you can help your clients relax and think about how much of the money they want to invest or use to benefit others, instead of getting carried away with the euphoria of wanting to spend it all right now.

No Sympathy for the Suddenly Rich

All of a sudden, I have several clients who are "victims" (don't laugh) of instant wealth. Some have inherited large sums sooner than expected, while others have sold their businesses or done well in the stock market. I find myself increasingly unsympathetic with these clients' lamentations about "problems" that result from swimming in money. A big part of my resentment, I'm sure, is that I've suffered recent financial setbacks due to a divorce and family illness. I sense that I'm endangering some good client relationships—but how can I change my feelings?

You can't. Feelings are feelings, and they tend to have a life of their own. But you can begin to ease the pressure of these strong emotions and improve your attitude toward these wealthy clients.

I would not hesitate to suggest that you talk about what you're experiencing with a therapist or counselor. At the very least, take some time to write down your feelings—your resentment, disappointment, pain and fear. If possible, share this with trusted friends or colleagues.

Try also to think about very wealthy people who have been miserable and unhappy. As those perceptive philosophers Lennon and McCartney noted, "Money can't buy me love." Remember that instant wealth is certainly not an unmitigated blessing—though of course it can lead to more choices and more freedom, which are certainly good things if handled well.

In the meantime, it's important to keep nourishing yourself emotionally, so you won't feel so deprived in the presence of these newly wealthy clients. Don't condemn yourself for your negative feelings. Though they're natural in your situation, you want to gently steer yourself through and past them to some more loving, accepting place for yourself and your clients.

By being aware of your own feelings about wealth and privilege, you can slowly become less negative and judgmental in dealing with clients like these, and more able to serve their needs. Remember that becoming instantly wealthy is like being shot through with too much energy. It lifts the recipients way off the ground, and makes them temporarily "crazy," or at least overwhelmed and overstimulated in a way that clouds their rational thinking and such normal considerations as goals and values. You can help your clients slow down to address their real goals, needs, wants, and even their fears and their guilt. Then they'll have the time and tools to clarify these important factors before making any decisions about their newfound wealth.

Rich Dad, Poor Dad

My client had no idea that when her father died, he would leave nearly a million dollars to her, his only surviving child. She can't seem to get over her anger at him for not talk-

ing to her about this beforehand. I think, too, she feels some remorse for her behavior toward him before his death. In any event, she's now very reluctant to move her inheritance from the antiquated investments he put it in, and shies away from spending it in ways "Dad wouldn't have liked." How can I help her get past these feelings?

Before trying to move her forward, take time to hear your client's maelstrom of feelings and conflicts on the subject. Reassure her that you won't push her to take action before she's ready.

While advising her to proceed carefully and wisely, I would also suggest that she consider seeking out a trustworthy friend who really understands her feelings and who is willing to talk things out with her. If she's not afraid to bring the issue out in the open like this, it may help her become more comfortable with her inheritance. On the other hand, she may worry that telling certain people about her woes will make them treat her differently or begin acting weird with her. After all, most of us have as many emotionally charged feelings about wealth and inheritance as your client does (or perhaps more). For this reason, she does need to choose her confidant carefully.

If she can't think of anyone she'd feel comfortable talking with, you might suggest consulting a therapist who is comfortable with wealth issues. Your client may be more open to this approach, since these conversations will be completely confidential. You might also recommend that she consult some of the resources in the Bibliography for valuable insights from others who struggled with similar dilemmas.

A self-awareness exercise I mentioned previously might help here. Suggest that she share her feelings with her dad, either by having a "discussion" with him or writing him a letter. Ask her to imagine or write an ideal loving response from him. This can help her resolve unspoken feelings and unsettled issues.

Once she has calmed down, you can talk to her about preserving her father's legacy without being wedded to the form that his investments now take. At this point, you may find her more willing to use her new wealth for her deepest fulfillment, pleasure, and financial security.

Who Says the Rich Are Just Like You and Me?

For the past 10 years, I've dealt mainly with middle-class clients. Now, having inherited the practice of a late colleague, I'm suddenly working with extremely wealthy people—and find I'm not very comfortable doing it. How can I get over whatever's bothering me, to serve these clients as I should?

First, you need to step back and determine why you're so uncomfortable. Do you worry that people who have more money will be more difficult clients, or will look down on you for being less wealthy? Or are you concerned that you don't know enough about financial and estate planning strategies for the very wealthy? Whatever your fears are, taking time to sort them out will help reduce your anxiety and discomfort.

If the problem seems to be a lack of practical experience or education, reach out to a fellow advisor who does have that experience and is willing to coach you, or at least steer you toward sources of information. If your concerns appear grounded in your emotional outlook, another colleague who works with very wealthy clients may be willing to discuss how he or she deals with any personal feelings of envy, insecurity, or inadequacy.

Remind yourself of other instances when you helped a client or clients who had much more wealth than you did. Make sure you acknowledge and appreciate your past competence, and imagine it expanding to include, one by one, the new clients you've taken on.

Finally, if you decide to continue working with these very affluent clients instead of referring them to a competent colleague, be sure to take good care of yourself during this transition. Do whatever makes you feel more connected to your own positive nature, so you can keep reminding yourself of who you were before this influx of people, money, and energy entered your life.

The Winning Ticket

I never thought I'd see the day, but a man just entered my office in a daze, having—yes, really!—won the lottery. He's being bombarded by relatives, friends, and strangers hinting that he should give them some of his windfall, and has even had a few bizarre marriage proposals. Fortunately, he knows that without a solid financial plan, the money may run right through his fingers. I can assist with the planning, but how can I help prepare him to handle the other issues connected with his new wealth?

As you probably know, winning the lottery really can destroy people's lives. Many winners consume their windfall in a few years and end up back where they started—except for the newly added burden of screwed-up personal relationships with friends and family who coveted the money.

No matter how eager your client is to share his good fortune (or to assuage his guilt at having been undeservedly singled out for such bounty), make sure that he slows down the decision-making process. He should review all his goals, needs, desires, and options, and carefully consider (with your assistance) whether he wants to help out family members or friends with loans or gifts.

Giving or lending to intimates is tricky. It almost always makes personal communications more awkward, and can lead to feelings of obligation, resentment, unjustified entitlement, betrayal, and/or estrangement. If you and your client agree that it makes sense for him to share some of the money with needy loved ones, help him explore ways to translate his generosity into a clearly-spelled-out contract, so that their current closeness and harmony won't be jeopardized if anything goes wrong.

Ask him whether he has expectations about what they'll do with the money. Is he comfortable offering it a gift, or would he prefer to make it a loan? If it's a loan, what would he do if it isn't paid back promptly (or at all)? Once he sorts out all these issues, and balances the choices with his own desires and needs, he may feel better prepared to handle his newly-won wealth. Just remind him to take it real slow, and commit only to action he truly feels comfortable with.

The Princess Bride

A new client with $1.4 million in inherited wealth tells me she doesn't plan to share any of it with her fiancé after they're married. He is very hurt by her stance. I know pressure from her parents is involved, but this doesn't seem a promising start to a marriage. What advice should I give her?

Though it's more usual to see women who are predisposed to "give away the store" for love, your client is obviously concerned that if her marriage doesn't work out, she might lose her financial security.

My suggestion would be to set up a plan which protects her financially, yet also allows her to share more of her wealth over time as trust builds in the marriage. Without some arrangement like this, her fiancé may understandably feel that she is withholding her trust on the eve of a commitment that's intended to be permanent.

You need to talk with her about this—perhaps alone at first, and then together with her fiancé. Try to ascertain whether her hesitation to share her wealth is a result of her own feelings or her family's influence.

If the family is responsible, talking about this can help the two of them reduce the polarization of their positions, and perhaps help them find a mutually acceptable way to share some of her assets. Ask your client how she would feel if the situation were reversed and he were unwilling to share any of his wealth with her. If she can empathize with him, she may be willing to moderate her stance and begin including him in the benefits of her affluence.

I do caution couples against plunging into marriage with the idea that they'll merge all their money in the name of true love and lifelong commitment. Since most people have money secrets, money personality quirks, and/or intimacy fears, you often don't really know whom you've married until you've been down the road a bit with him or her.

Merging money gradually over time is a much sounder strategy. But when the assets are unevenly weighted, the wealthier partner's refusal to share the riches can lead to bitter acrimony. Again, patience is necessary, with a more balanced relationship as the goal.

From Blue Jeans to Pinstripes?

My client, a millionaire entrepreneur in his mid-20's, feels that his workaholic lifestyle has cost him friendships, love relationships, family ties, and even his health. He's asked me if it would be a good idea for him to sell his business and perhaps return to an Old Economy corporate environment, where he can mentor others, be mentored himself, and balance his work and personal life more effectively. Obviously, he needs more than just financial advice. Help!

Disenchanted with a life that revolves around work and money, many young people like your client are beginning to choose a more balanced and personally rewarding lifestyle. I personally applaud this choice as a sign of maturity, but it needs to be made with calm deliberation, not in a state of panicked burnout.

Assuming you accept this task, resist the impulse to nudge your client in one direction or the other. Instead, help him carefully assess the costs and benefits of his various options. If he needs your permission to scale back his workaholic behavior, gently point out that the permission must come from inside himself, not from you. You're there simply to help him air his concerns till he can come up with a solution that feels really right to him.

In the process, consider encouraging this young man to make time for whatever restores life balance to his psyche: exercise, rest, writing down his thoughts and feelings, or some creative hobby. This will put him in a better state to think this dilemma through and take action when he feels the time is right.

A Teen with Net Worth

While still in high school, the teenage daughter of one of my clients started a Web-based business which is now very successful. Her mother has asked me to help educate this young woman about business finance. But as soon as we begin talking about money matters, the daughter becomes short-tempered and defensive. How can I overcome this?

Let this young woman herself guide your approach and your subject matter. I'd begin by asking her how she feels about being in your office. Does she have any questions she would like to ask you? What goals would she like you to help her accomplish?

If you initially saw both the mother and the daughter, schedule the next consultation with the daughter alone to see how the interaction changes sans mom. Even if they have a wonderful relationship, her mother's presence could be complicating her ability to learn from you—or to learn at all.

If she's willing to try, begin giving her small amounts of "homework"—articles to read or action steps to take with her new wealth. Encourage her to identify what she wants to achieve in the near term and in the years to come. She should write down her dreams and desires at least two or three times, to see which ones surface again and again. Ask her to discuss this list with you.

Early in this relationship, be sure to make space for her to air her feelings of anxiety or helplessness about the new responsibility (and burden) that wealth has brought into her life. Let her know that these emotions are natural. And reassure her that the more she learns about managing her money, the less overwhelmed she will feel. If you're patient, I think her defensiveness will abate and she'll become not just a willing student but a good client.

Overcome by Options

My new client, a 24-year-old woman, unexpectedly inherited $300,000 a few months ago. Now she's trying to choose what to do with it: quit her job, buy a house, send her nephews to college, take a trip around the world, give it all to charity, etc.—or just sock it all away and pretend that her life is still the same. The possibilities have completely overwhelmed her. How can I help her sort out her priorities?

Big windfalls often hit people like a bolt of lightning. The recipients may feel as if they're floating off the ground, somewhere up in the ozone.

So the first thing I'd do is reassure this client that her feelings of being overwhelmed are totally normal. Encourage her not to rush her decision—the money won't evaporate while she thinks about what to do with it.

Suggest that she write down her thoughts and emotions about this windfall. If she is being wracked by feelings of guilt, unworthiness, superiority, shame, or anxiety about making a mistake, getting them out in the open can lessen their intensity.

I'd then urge her to let herself fantasize about all the things she would like to do with this inheritance. The desires that come up time after time are the ones she can trust and act on. Explore these dreams and goals with her, and brainstorm ways she can begin to achieve some of them. This process will help her panic subside, and allow her to start enjoying her newfound wealth.

Breeding Suspicion

A client whose $2 million inheritance I manage has fallen in love with a young fellow she met at a party. He wants her to provide capital for a new venture that has something to do with cloning racehorses. This lady has been looking for Mr. Right for a long time, and she's thinking seriously of funding his idea. Needless to say, I fear he's a con artist. I've explained the importance of doing due diligence before risking money in any business venture, but she doesn't seem to hear me. How can I get her to see reality before she loses her fortune?

Many heirs and heiresses have conscious or unconscious guilt about wealth they haven't worked for. In various ways, they may try to sabotage their own best financial interests.

Combined with the fact that love is blind (particularly in the honeymoon stage), it's likely that your client won't respond well to rational arguments against this investment—at least not initially. She certainly doesn't want to hear that you fear her boyfriend is dishonest and plans to use her. If you take this approach, she'll only push you and your advice away, to her own detriment.

Instead, encourage her to help you figure how much money she may need for her future financial security. Then you can estimate how much will be left for her to share with loved ones and charities, invest in high-risk opportunities, and otherwise play around with.

If she is willing to discuss this cloning scheme with you, ask her to consider whether it will help her reach her long-term goals. Remind her that before recommending an investment, you always try to estimate the downside risk as well as the upside potential. What does she think the worst-case scenario might be if she invests in this deal? If her answer echoes your own fears, you might try to help her see the risk more clearly by telling her about someone else's emotionally motivated investment that had disastrous results.

If your client is willing to lose the money despite all these cautions, you need to let go. Just be there to catch her if and when she falls, without saying smugly, "I told you so."

Taking Action

The more sudden the wealth, the more ungrounded your newly wealthy clients will feel and act. By slowing down the decision-making process to determine their abiding goals and values, and encouraging them to think and act deliberately with these goals in mind, you can help them get what they truly need and want.

STRESS AND TRAUMA

Financial Loss

Staying cool in the midst of a severe financial reverse isn't easy. Whether it's an investment loss, a corporate downsizing, or a business failure, it may drastically affect people's lives. A major drop in portfolio value can devastate an older client who's ready to retire. And try to explain the value of "corporate belt-tightening" to a father of three who's been cut back to part-time, or a working woman who's been laid off for the first time in her life. All their best-laid plans now look pretty shaky. And even though they've been told there's "nothing personal" about it, feelings of anxiety and failure may still haunt them.

If your clients go into throes of shock, anger, or panic following a job loss or market meltdown, it may take focused TLC to restore them to order and sanity. Here's how cooler heads might prevail in these difficult situations.

Back in the Job Market

With his portfolio decimated by the market slump, a distraught client has begun to realize that he may have to abandon his long-awaited early retirement and go back to work. I can't see any other good alternative, but is there anything I can say to cushion the loss of his dreams?

You can definitely sympathize with his profound sense of disappointment, without encouraging him to wallow in it. Though it may mean a major shift in his life plan, he is far from alone in having been set back by the market. Once he knows you understand his frustration, see if you can help him brainstorm ways to make a return to work more exciting and satisfying—perhaps even rejuvenating.

What did he really enjoy about what he used to do? Is there a type of job that will let him do more of it? Or has he always wanted to try another productive line of work? Now might be a good time to experiment.

In addition, you may be able to help him reduce the drain on his assets by downsizing his lifestyle. Many people who have chosen this route have ended up feeling happier and more peaceful as a result. A reduction in living expenses could also make the difference between having to work full-time versus just a few hours a week.

This exploration will put you somewhat in the position of a career coach. If you're not comfortable with this role, suggest that your client consult a career professional for help in positioning himself for a fulfilling return to work.

Loss of Faith

I'm deluged with calls from clients wanting to dump all their stocks and move into gold or real estate. I've encouraged them to keep the faith, but it gets harder and harder as the market keeps falling. I feel like King Canute trying to sweep back the tide with a broom. What more can I do?

My first suggestion would be to define for yourself exactly what your philosophy and outlook are. What do you believe is the wisest action to take in the midst of this maelstrom? If you have general guidelines to share with all of your clients, state your perspective in an email or letter to them.

Begin by letting them know that you understand why they feel so shaken, mistrustful, and uncertain about how to proceed. Try to reassure them about the future without being unrealistic. For example, you might suggest broader diversification, noting that the great majority of companies play by the rules. If you have taken steps with your own portfolio, you might share your course of action as a way to reinforce openness and trust. You could also point out positive signs of change, such as many companies' decision to clean up their earnings statements by treating stock options as a compensation expense.

Financial advisor Dick Vodra, author of the superbly commonsense guide *Enough Money* (see Additional Resources), recently wrote an excellent letter of this type. A suggestion of his that I particularly like was for clients to use some of their assets to build up their "career development fund." This fund can be used for workshops, continuing education, improving skill sets in their existing line of work, or exploring a new field—anything that broadens their employability in this rapidly changing world.

Once you have written your clients about where you stand and how you think they should proceed, follow up with individual conferences to revisit their goals and needs. Whether these meetings are face-to-face or over the phone, don't try to rush clients into action without hearing and addressing their feelings of fear and disillusionment. If you give them time to share their concerns, you'll help calm them and reassure them of your dependability at a moment when everything else seems to be changing around them.

The Blame Game

When my client wanted to sell his telecom stocks last year, I recommended that he hold onto them. Since then, he's lost a bundle. He says that after this experience, he finds it hard to trust my judgment. Should I address this with him, or just let it blow over?

I feel for you—he's certainly put you in a tough position. I think it would be a fine idea to conciliate him, perhaps by inviting him to lunch at a good restaurant to acknowledge that you truly regret his losses. (If you lost money too, let him know he wasn't alone.)

But don't grovel unduly. Even the smartest analysts in the business were misled about the strength of these companies' earnings. To make sure he doesn't heap all the blame on your shoulders, you may also need to remind him that while your recommendations are based on your best professional judgment, the ultimate decisions are always up to him.

Finally, remind him of the contributions you have made in the past toward his financial security and peace of mind. Ask what it will take to restore his trust in your advice, which for the most part has served him well so far.

By encouraging him to remember the advantages of working with you, you may be able to bring him back to a more balanced perspective in assessing your relationship. If you give him an opportunity to fully express his sense of loss and disappointment, he may be able to move past these feelings to continue honoring your expertise in the future.

Faith Healing

I thought I was prepared for market volatility, but the simultaneous plunge of the Nasdaq, the Dow, and the S&P 500 really shook me. If I can't take this in stride, how can I expect my clients to cope with it? And if they can't have confidence in me, what value do I have to offer them over the long haul?

When investors collectively lose more than $4 trillion in portfolio value in a single year, crises of confidence can affect even the most seasoned pro. To regain your sense of balance, share your fears and doubts with colleagues who can help you put this loss into a more positive context.

I would also suggest using this setback as an opportunity to reassess your professional strengths and talents. If you've built your appeal to clients around being a stock-market fortuneteller, you may need to reorient your practice to take advantage of more relationship-focused skills.

Evaluate what you like best about your job. Revisit past successes with clients, and consider how you might replicate these highlights in the future. How about exploring a professional niche that has always fascinated you, such as eldercare, educating young people about money, or coaching neophyte investors?

Even if you don't make any changes in your business model, this exercise may help you calm down and recommit yourself to your career. I would also advise you to seek out ways to nourish your spirit and restore your self-confidence. Take time for whatever replenishes you—exercise, writing, golf, music, spending time with family and friends—to get away from your constant awareness of market gyrations.

In general, market downturns needn't leave you at a loss. It's a tremendous help to have educated your clients beforehand about the likelihood of economic turbulence. But in any case, listen empathetically to their feelings before revisiting their financial strategy in light of this unpleasant development. If necessary, make time to reassess your own professional commitment. By caring, coaching, and listening during a period of financial loss, you may end up with a net gain in renewed energy and client satisfaction.

Clinging to Ivy League Hopes

A client who works for an energy trading company has just been cut back to part-time at a lower salary. To make matters worse, his investment in company stock is down to a fraction of its earlier value. He still hopes to send his son to an Ivy League college, while paying private-school tuition for his young daughter. When I explained to him that this meant a choice between going deeply in debt or raiding his retirement savings, he looked devastated. I think I could have handled this better, but what should I do now?

For a client like this, nothing is more destabilizing than to have his worklife and financial life crumble unexpectedly and simultaneously.

It's important to make sure he knows he has your full support. Focus on building up his self-esteem by reminding him of his talents and strengths, and assure him that you understand and empathize with what he is going through. You might tell him about other people who are even worse off, so he can feel he's not alone and still has things to be grateful for.

Once he feels that you have heard his anguish, help him explore more financial choices. What if he steers his son toward a state university? How about the possibility of grants, student loans, and other financial aid? Because of the change in his situation, his daughter might be eligible for a scholarship at her school, too. What lifestyle changes could he and his family make to free up more money for the children's education?

You may also want to inspire your client to keep looking for full-time work. The possibility of having a larger income than his new downsized salary will make him feel less trapped and desperate.

If it still seems necessary to tap his retirement savings, help him develop a plan to restore the funds when his situation improves. Encourage him to focus on the light at the end of the tunnel. With luck and effort, these dark days will eventually be behind him.

A Matter of Trust

What can I say to a client who appears to have lost confidence in me? He says that after buying wholeheartedly into my view of stocks as the engine of investment success, he feels "betrayed" that I am now advocating bonds. Incidentally, his portfolio is down about 20% since the stock market's height. How can I regain his trust?

The difficulty of explaining a more conservative viewpoint has become a concern for many planners, and no doubt for more than a few of their clients. So before focusing on this particular individual, I would take some time to consider just how many of your clients understand why you have changed your tack lately.

Have you written or called them to discuss the changing economic outlook and how you recommend coping with it? Some planners have invited their clients to group events or one-on-one get-togethers to thank them, calm their fears and soothe their losses, and communicate how to handle the changes life may have in store. Consider your own personal strengths in deciding which approach would best strengthen client relationships.

In any case, this message is probably just what your "betrayed" client needs to hear. Empathize with his disappointment and frustration, while reassuring him that your goal is to help him protect his portfolio against future losses. Make sure he understands that you have not changed your long-term fundamental views, but merely advocate a tactical shift to reduce volatility and adapt to current market conditions.

Panic over a Pension Change

A single woman in her early 50s just came to see me in a panic. She had counted on her company pension allowing her to retire early and live out her dream of teaching in Africa. However, her employer's recent switch to a cash balance plan means her pension probably won't increase enough to fund this goal. She was practically in tears as she told me that all her hopes and plans have been dashed by this development. How can I help her?

The recent hullabaloo about cash balance plans may have made your client's employer more sensitive about shortchanging older workers. Her first step (if she hasn't already been this route) might be to find out whether there are any exceptions for individual situations. Alternatively, if enough other older employees are in the same boat with her, they might try petitioning company management for a policy change.

If this is already a dead issue, you can best help your client by figuring out if she can still live out her dream. If she'll have less pension income in retirement, she may need to modify or postpone her plans. Or perhaps she'll be able to live abroad if she's willing to scale down her living expenses now and save more aggressively for the future. You might do a budget review to help her see where her money is going now, and strategize some creative ways she can cut back without excessive suffering.

To overcome her initial panic, guide her through this planning process slowly and patiently. The more clearly you can help her see that this dramatic change may not be the end of all her dreams, the more easily she'll be able to transform her fears into constructive action.

Measuring Their Options

My new clients, a couple in their late 30s, planned to cash in stock options to fund their kids' college education, pay off the mortgage, and so on. But as the time nears when they can exercise the options, the stock has tanked. They're getting panicky—they've bought a more expensive house than they can afford, have maxed out their credit cards, and own virtually no savings. They seem convinced that their only option is to declare bankruptcy, and this idea scares and depresses them even more. They won't listen to any other alternatives I suggest. How can I get through to them?

I would invite them back ASAP for a strategy session. After giving them a little airtime to play out their worst fears about what might happen, move on to discuss possible courses of action (including some contingency plans if their worst fears do materialize).

Putting on my therapist's hat, I would also suggest that you try to help them look at what life lessons they can learn from this financial challenge—for example, to prepare better for life's unpleasant little surprises, and not to count on windfalls to rescue them in the future. No matter what you may think about their choices, be careful that your tone of voice isn't accusing or judgmental. If they feel attacked or blamed, they'll end up too discouraged to learn from your prompting.

As the next step, encourage them to go home and write down the benefits and risks of the various courses of action you've discussed with them. Each of them should do this separately at first. Then they can share their opinions and decide which strategy makes the most sense. (If this couple tend to be fault-finders and finger-pointers with each other, you may want to invite them back to your office to compare notes more amicably in your presence.)

Through this careful process, you'll be helping them develop a roadmap they can use to navigate from panic to more rational thinking. . . and eventually back to a sound financial position.

Clients Behaving Badly

I've just had my ears pinned back by a recently retired client who's furious at the recent losses in his portfolio. When I reminded him that he's been pushing me to take more risk with his assets, he stormed out, vowing to sue me. I'm pretty rattled, and wonder how to calm him down before he does something we'll both regret. Any ideas?

Market declines can be devastating to people with finite assets, so it's no wonder your client is feeling panicky. If you think this fellow really is upset enough to make a complaint against you, let your firm's legal advisor know at once. For your own sake, I hope you've kept careful records of your interaction with him (and with your other clients).

Legal issues aside, my suggestion would be to try to get him back into your office. If he's still distraught, encourage him to voice his feelings about the money he's lost. Try to empathize with his disorientation and dismay without becoming upset or defensive. By reminding him that thousands of prudent investors are in the same situation as he is, you may be able to take the issue of your professional competence off the table.

Once he simmers down, suggest that the two of you review his goals and his financial situation to determine his best course of action now. By shifting from fantasy ("I'm going to die penniless!") to reality ("Well, I still have $450,000"), you may be able to help him see that his straits are not as dire as he fears. You might mention that when you cautioned him earlier against taking too much risk, it was with precisely this sort of market slump in mind. Make sure he stays closely involved as you refine his financial plan, so he'll feel more confident about taking future market fluctuations in stride.

A Falling Market's Emotional Fallout

After seeing the losses in her latest account statement, a widow who took years to start investing called me up in tears. She accused me of betraying her trust and said she's ready to put everything back in CDs. I strongly feel that this would not be in her best interests, but how can I persuade her otherwise?

Wimpiness isn't applauded in our society, so many inexperienced investors tend to overestimate their risk tolerance. Only when they're hit with a sudden, brutal loss do they find out how much risk they're really comfortable with.

Don't minimize your distressed client's anxiety. Let her voice the pain and betrayal she feels, but try to reassure her that you would never knowingly put her security at risk. Make sure she understands that market slumps are perfectly normal and have happened many times before. Show her time-to-recovery statistics for past bear markets, and review her finances with her to allay any bag-lady fears she may have.

After this review, gently explain why putting all her money in CDs isn't a wise move. Mention, however, that her reaction to her recent losses has clarified for both of you how much volatility she can tolerate. From now on, you'll be able to make recommendations that she should be much more comfortable with. Then help her forge a new plan that calms her anxieties—while avoiding the bigger security risk of investments too conservative to generate the growth she needs.

When Active Investors Lose Their Nerve

My client, a conservative buy-and-hold investor whom I've advised for two years, recently brought her new husband in to see me. An active trader since the mid-'90s, he lost some 60% of his portfolio value in the Nasdaq's tumble. Now he worries that any decision he makes will blow up in his face, and hasn't made a move for months. How can I help him?

Fear caused by his huge loss, combined with a feeling of ineffectiveness that challenges his sense of financial competence, may well have transformed this man's usual decisiveness into shock and paralysis.

To bolster his self-confidence, remind him that not even top financial forecasters can read the market's tea leaves correctly. What's important is to determine where he and his wife now stand in relation to their goals, and see what implications this has for their financial strategy.

If they both agree to this review, be careful not to take sides. When it comes to investing, partners in a relationship are almost guaranteed to be on different ends of the risk spectrum.

One obvious approach would be to compartmentalize their combined investments into long-term holdings and a separate trading portfolio. They might also appreciate more frequent meetings with you to revisit their needs and goals. Whatever the specifics, it's important to find a solution that validates them both.

The Downside of Diversification

I've been asked to "referee" for an older couple, both in their second marriage. He had a substantial real estate portfolio, but when they married she persuaded him that this asset concentration was too risky. At her urging, he transferred most of his wealth into a diversified portfolio of securities—which have almost all gone down! Now he says they'd be fine if he'd kept on doing what he was doing before. She's upset by his bitterness and frustration. Without becoming a marriage counselor, how can I help them through this rocky period?

When people are stressed, they revert to their survival mode. Couples in this situation often attack each other as the cause of their problems. If the husband blames his wife for the way her advice turned out, while she's beating herself up about the same thing, her resentment and defensiveness may lead her to either counterattack or retreat into depression and shame.

If the antagonism is really intense, consider meeting with each party separately to help them vent their feelings about what happened. You can then make use of the strengths and wisdom in their respective viewpoints when they get back together with you as a couple.

Remind them that other investors are feeling equally unnerved by the impossible-to-predict timing of this broad-based market downturn. Help the husband see that hindsight is 20/20, and that things could just as easily have turned out quite differently. Encourage both of them to let go of the past and "forgive" each other for past mistakes (if forgiveness is really necessary).

Your goal should be to find a middle ground where they can go forward, emotionally and financially. However, this can only happen in a climate of mutual respect. If the husband can't stop blaming his wife, you may need to suggest couples therapy to get them back on track together.

Handouts Can Be Harmful

My client's husband was laid off a few months ago, and she's been trying to support him by economizing until he finds a new job. However, her wealthy mother insists on giving her money so their two teenage daughters won't be "deprived." Although these gifts are galling to her husband, my client enjoys being able to afford a better lifestyle with her mother's help. She has asked me whether she should tell her mom to cool it. Help!

Spend some time listening to your client about her conflicted reactions to her husband's layoff. Is she sad for him, angry with him, worried about the kids? Maybe she's feeling financially deprived herself.

After you explore her feelings, ask her about her husband. Does he feel depressed? Angry? Humiliated? Many men (and, increasingly, many women) feel their self-worth is directly tied to the money they make and the work they do. Even if he knows rationally that the layoff was not his fault, he may still be fighting irrational feelings of incompetence and failure.

As the next step, urge your client to find a time when she and her husband are both relatively unstressed and can sit down together to explore their feelings and options. They need to balance several opposing needs: the husband's need to not feel shamed by or dependent on his mother-in-law's financial gifts, and the wife's need to not feel that she and the children are being unduly deprived.

In a compassionate discussion, the couple may be able to reach a compromise that honors both parties' needs and wants. For example, maybe Grandma's financial gifts could be transformed into 529 college savings plan contributions for her. In the final analysis, it may not hurt the girls to learn that they won't always be able to have everything they want.

No matter how this decision plays out, encourage the couple to spend more quality time together while the husband is job-hunting. To help solidify their deep connection, their interactions should be free of talk about money. This can go a long way toward neutralizing stress-related irritability and conflict.

Nouveau Poor

A retired client of mine has always enjoyed the good life, dining lavishly and taking his grandchildren on Caribbean cruises. Unfortunately, he insisted on keeping his portfolio heavily weighted in his former employer's stock, which recently tanked. He's too embarrassed to tell anyone, but some lifestyle changes are clearly necessary. How can I suggest that he handle this?

When people feel ashamed or embarrassed, it's because reality is at odds with their idealized picture of themselves. They fear that others would lose respect for them if they knew. Ironically, the only thing that resolves shame is to risk sharing your failures or imperfections with others, and to see that they accept and embrace you (and may even have similar struggles themselves).

So once you have sympathized with your client's feelings about his financial loss, encourage him to talk openly to family and friends about the new choices he will have to make. By hunting for less expensive alternatives to cruises with the grandchildren, for example, he could open up a valuable avenue of inquiry and discussion with his family. He might even discover that going camping or on nature walks would please the youngsters more. If they are disappointed, he will still serve as a role model in how to rise to the occasion—perhaps a valuable life lesson for his children as well as his grandkids.

For this client and others in his situation, the most problematic response to financial difficulty is to pretend that nothing has changed. By being open with others about his new situation, he could end up with emotional rewards that his lavish spending might never have inspired.

The Road Not Taken

A client couple who worked together have both been laid off by their company. The wife, who seems to welcome the necessity for a simpler life, talks about becoming a photographer and living in a trailer. In contrast, her husband is quite shaken and longs to restore the lifestyle they have enjoyed up to now. At present, their relationship is stressed to the max. How can I get them in sync on their plans?

When they come to see you together, listen patiently to each one's feelings about this major change in their life. You may find that the wife feels excited and liberated, while the husband is traumatized and depressed. See if you can empathize with both partners' world views and life choices.

Once you have heard each one fully and validated his or her feelings and desires, consider asking each spouse to meet with you separately to tell you his or her dreams and fantasies about "the road not taken." For instance, if the husband has ever dreamed of being less encumbered by the need for a lot of money, discuss this possibility with him. Perhaps you can tell him about couples who chose voluntary simplicity and now are happier than they've ever been. When you meet with his wife, help her explore dark corners where her hippie fantasy may not be totally realistic, considering the level of comfort she has enjoyed until recently.

When you bring them together, the exploratory process you've been through will hopefully help them find common ground in the middle. The wife needs to see that her more traditional husband may not be happy with the simple life she envisions, unless it has elements of more traditional stability and comfort. And he needs to consider downsizing their lifestyle in ways that take their new financial situation into account.

This isn't an easy task, but positive results are possible. If their polarization continues unabated, I would suggest counseling to help them resolve their differences.

Taking Layoffs Personally

A single mother who has consulted me seems to be deeply upset about her abrupt job loss. Although it was a result of company-wide layoffs, she told me she feels personally betrayed and keeps reliving the scene where she was let go. She's aware of the need to make financial plans, but her response to my suggestions is either apathy or rage at the unfairness of the CEO's pay raise while she and many others lost their jobs. I'm not sure how to deal with this. Is there a way I can help her get moving?

This client appears to be suffering from a combination of depression and a mild form of post-traumatic stress disorder. You'll need to do a lot of compassionate "hand-holding" while she voices the shock and outrage she is experiencing.

Once she feels you have heard her fully, I'd suggest a combination of approaches. First, help her connect with an affordable job placement service, if her employer hasn't provided assistance in this area. I would also recommend counseling to help her move past her emotional trauma. Reassure her that this doesn't mean there's anything wrong with her; it's simply that someone in her situation needs more emotional support than you can realistically provide.

That said, you may be able to act somewhat in the role of a life planner in helping her overcome her feelings of betrayal and hopelessness. Suggest that she explore sources of hope and healing. More time spent with her child? More walks in the park, or contact with friends? It could help a great deal simply to turn off the constant flow of negativity from TV news and local newspapers. You might suggest that she try a magazine called Hope (www.hopemag.com), whose short inspirational articles focus on people who are working to make the world a better place. Reading this lightens my own spirit and energizes me enormously.

Good luck! Once you soothe your client's spirit and get her some much-needed help and support, she may well thaw enough to take your financial advice in the right spirit.

Entrepreneurial Angst

A client who started her own business with her husband's grudging tolerance has realized that the business is failing and cannot survive. She wants me to help break the news to him, saying, "I can't handle his gloating or telling me 'I told you so' right now." She has also asked me to help her find a way that their lifestyle doesn't have to change. This is a tall order. Any suggestions?

It seems that this couple does not have a good history of open, respectful communication and joint decision-making. This problem certainly goes beyond the situation at hand. However, you can help dissolve the current tensions in several ways. First, listen empathetically to your client's angst about her business failure. Help her explore what she wishes she had done differently and what events were out of her control, so that she can learn from this experience without needless self-recrimination.

As the next step, encourage her to brainstorm bearable ways to downsize her lifestyle. (Fewer grande lattes? Less frequent housecleanings? Shorter vacations in less pricey hotels?) Armed with these suggestions and less defensive about her business's lack of success, she'll be in a better position to level with her husband.

Consider volunteering to talk with him first about what has happened, in order to make the process less emotional. If he can't resist saying, "I knew it!", at least he will be saying it to you and not to his wife. You might take this opportunity to tactfully urge him to be more compassionate with his spouse, who already feels enough like a failure.

If your client ends up being the one to break the news, suggest that she ask her husband to withhold comment until she has laid out the whole story of what happened and why. She can acknowledge that he warned her against the venture, but explain why she felt it was important to try it. If he's still unable to resist gloating over how accurately he predicted her failure, you might suggest that they seek counseling together to decrease the emotional tension in their relationship and heal the wounds of past and present.

Taking Action

In situations like these, helping clients move through panic to calmer emotional states is an important part of your job—and one of its more therapeutic aspects. It's usually a matter of encouraging people to express their anxiety (briefly) and helping them to strategize the actions they can take if their worst-case scenario happens. If your empathetic listening doesn't help reduce the tension significantly, you may need to suggest professional counseling as well. But if you take the necessary time, your patience and sensitivity to their feelings of loss may well do the job.

Once you've lightened your clients' emotional burden, work with them to brainstorm ways they can create a good future without being dependent on rigid perceptions of how things have to happen. Urge them to reflect on the question of "How much is enough?," which most of us don't ask unless circumstances force our hand. Despite their newly limited finances, they may be able to create a rich new life by connecting with their inner resources and hidden dreams. (I'm reminded of the financial planner whose divorce induced him to work less and spend more time with his kids, and who is blissfully happy about his new lifestyle.)

If you do your job well, clients will find they're enjoying more quality time with family, friends, and peers. And over the longer term, I'm confident this coaching will be rewarded with a loyal clientele who stay with you through the ups and downs of their financial fortunes.

STRESS AND TRAUMA
Personal Loss

When a client experiences the death of a loved one, careful, sensitive timing is of the essence. Many planners don't expect a client to make major decisions about his or her money for about a year after a serious emotional loss.

The "normal" length of time will vary with the mourner. But the important thing is to avoid pushing someone to act before their thoughts and feelings, fears and hopes, have been sufficiently aired and explored. If you try to push too hard, you risk the client withdrawing from you and possibly ending the relationship.

Dazed with Grief

My new client lost his wife to a stroke last year, and his parents recently died in an accident. He has inherited substantial wealth from both sources, and I agree with his attorney (who referred him to me) that he needs to invest this money more appropriately. But when I suggested some changes at our first meeting, he made excuses to stay with the status quo. He's obviously still somewhat dazed by his bereavement. When and how should I prompt him to act?

If you feel comfortable expressing your own emotions to him, I would suggest empathizing with his terrible losses and the resulting sense of aloneness and disorientation he must feel.

Don't lose hope if this phase seems to last quite a while. Your unfortunate client was not only widowed but orphaned within the span of a few months. You may want to suggest that he join a grief group (a therapy/counseling group for people experiencing similar losses) and/or see a grief counselor or therapist for support during this very painful and confusing time.

Although you can begin now to discuss where his money is, don't encourage him to take action until he feels more emotionally stable. You can begin this process, however, by exploring with him the legacy his parents and wife would have wanted him to have from them. Then ask him to think about what legacy he would want to have from each source. This may lead you to some ideas about how he can use his money to meet his inner needs and reach deeper goals.

A Frozen Inheritance

A client of mine recently inherited stock in some former blue chip companies from a beloved aunt. I've always considered this client to be quite knowledgeable about investing, but every time I talk with her about moving her inheritance into investments that are more suitable for her own needs, she says she doesn't want to make any changes. I hate to see the value of her holdings slowly drift south. Why won't she follow my advice?

When a close relative dies and leaves an inheritance, very often the beneficiaries are so emotionally affected by their loss that they can't consider making any changes in the nature of that legacy, at least not right away. By keeping the inheritance intact, they honor their loved one and keep her memory alive.

You may be interfering with this process by pushing to sell the aunt's investments right away. Instead, I would recommend that you prompt your client to talk about her aunt's true emotional legacy—her strengths and beloved qualities. The process of letting go can take up to a year, but if you help your client mourn in this way, eventually you should be able to persuade her that her aunt would want the money to serve her in the best way possible. At this point, she will be ready to listen to your advice about investments that are more appropriate for her needs and goals.

Survivor's Risk Aversion

A recently widowed older woman was virtually pushed into my office by a friend. She is paralyzed with fear about making the wrong decisions with the money left by her late husband. Some of his investments were poorly considered, but she won't let me make any changes, fearing she'll lose everything if she makes a mistake. How can I help her through her panic?

You're probably already looking at her portfolio and prioritizing what needs to be done to improve her financial security. But at the same time, be sure to give her some time and space to honor the enormity of the loss she has suffered and the ensuing change in her life.

Let her talk about how adrift and scared she is. It will be normal for her to feel overwhelmed and in shock, almost as if she'd been thrown from her car after a terrible crash.

Assure her that although you're evaluating her situation, you won't pressure her to take action until she's ready. With this reassurance, she should be able to calm down enough to listen to your recommendations, and act on some of them, after the shock of her loss has passed.

The High Cost of Coping with Loss

I'm not sure how to tell a new client that something she gets a lot of comfort from may be endangering her financial security. She's recently widowed and depends on her well-to-do friends for emotional support. However, trying to keep up with them is an expensive proposition, and I'm afraid she'll end up on Social Security unless she radically reduces her spending. What's the most effective way of addressing this ticklish issue with her?

I would start by empathizing with her about her loss. Tell her you know how disoriented she must feel after this painful change in her life. (She probably feels like a survivor of a major earthquake.)

Once she realizes that you understand how this monumental event has shaken her, gently preface your discussion of new life choices by saying something like "I've worked with many widows in your situation, and my experience has shown that you can survive and come out feeling that you're truly financially secure. The key is to find ways to manage your spending carefully, especially in the short term." This lets your client know that she is not alone, and that you don't consider her "bad"; she merely needs to make some new choices to get through this difficult period.

If she agrees with this analysis, explore with her how she spends her money. To make her more conscious of her habits, you might suggest that she keep a spending diary, listing all expenditures and jotting down her thoughts about whether each one was worth the money. With this information in hand, you can help her strategize ways to cut down on her spending without having to part company with her better-off friends. You might also suggest that if her friends are truly supportive, they will accept her need to manage her money more carefully.

If your client is merely spending to fill the newly empty place in her life, or to keep up with her pre-widowhood lifestyle, there's a good chance you can help her devise equally rich and rewarding alternatives that won't be so hard on her pocketbook. It may be a different story, however, if she's a compulsive overspender.

In that case, the suggestion that she needs to cut way back on her spending may cause her to become defensive and even angry at you. When overspenders are forced to deny themselves an immediate-gratification purchase, they have an "internal tantrum" (and sometimes an external one). By telling her that she'll have to say no to herself for the rest of her life, you could make her feel so rebellious that she might close her eyes in denial and jump off the overspending cliff.

On the other hand, even if she's an overspender, she may try your spending-reduction plan if you frame it as a short-term strategy. Then, after you can see that she's willing to cooperate and has started making changes in her behavior, you might suggest other support resources to her, such as Debtors Anonymous or books that focus on helping overspenders curb their addiction (see Additional Resources). But take it slowly. Remember, your newly widowed client is at a precarious emotional stage, and may need to hold your hand a lot until she regains her balance.

Rush to Action

A couple has asked me to help them allocate a large inheritance the wife received after her parents' recent death in a car accident. One of their two sons has a 3.94 GPA at college, while the older boy, who helps out in his dad's business, has a learning disability and a spending problem. I've been trying to elicit a sense of the couple's priorities, but they seem paralyzed by her family tragedy. How can I best help them?

The first thing is to slow the whole process way down. After such a traumatic life change, rapid decision-making is not a good idea and can even be dangerous. It takes time to recover from the shock of loss and get through the mourning process.

So caution your clients that before they make any big financial decisions, they need to sort out their feelings, their values, and their concerns. For example, would they like to use some of their money to help make the world a better place? How do they feel about supporting their sons?

If they do want to share some of the inheritance with the boys, it's important to consider all the options calmly. Should they gift the younger son outright and the older son via a trust, or is it important to avoid the perception of inequitable treatment? If the older brother has a learning disability such as ADD (attention deficit disorder) or ADHD (attention deficit/hyperactivity disorder), this can often contribute to impulsive spending. Part of the parents' money could be used for the tutoring, therapy, and/or medication he may need to make progress in overcoming his disability.

You'll need patience to help this couple assess the challenges of their family situation. Your role in asking questions and reviewing the choices with them will be crucial in helping them put their inheritance to the best possible use.

Taking Action

I often recommend to my grieving clients that they set aside time to "talk to" or write letters to their dead loved one, and to imagine what he or she would say or write in response. If it's a loving relationship, this usually happens organically. One of my clients has regular conversations with a beloved husband whom she lost several years ago. This perfectly sane woman tells me that when she stops communing with him for weeks or months, her life starts feeling out of balance and the mourning feelings build up. If the relationship was painful and unresolved, I encourage clients to imagine what their late spouse or parent or sibling would say if they were speaking from their "best" self, from their soul.

Whether this suggestion appeals to you or not, encourage your clients to take the time they need to grieve properly. If they do, it will eventually free them up to move on, financially and in other ways.

SECTION 2

More Than Money

More Than Money

The longer you're in this business, the more breadth of vision and experience you will acquire about issues that go far beyond portfolio maximization. Spiritual and religious beliefs, moral values, personal integrity, and half-realized yearnings all come into play in the lives of clients who consult you.

This can force you to reexamine the nature of your practice. Do you really want to help clients harmonize their financial behavior with their spiritual beliefs? Whatever the scope of your actual tasks, this is life planning in the purest sense.

If you embrace the challenge of exploring and resolving value conflicts, the next step is to assess your own beliefs, especially regarding money and morality. Once you know where you stand, you'll be clearer about how and where you will feel comfortable guiding your clients.

This internal assessment is rarely as easy as I've made it sound. Often, it means resolving discrepancies between what you believe and the way you actually behave. If you're not walking your talk, it creates an incongruence that can manifest itself in impatience, intolerance, anxiety, or even shame when these issues arise in your work.

As you clean up your act by bringing your behavior into harmony with your beliefs, you'll become more effective at work. Realizing that you live your values, your clients will feel more confident that you can help them succeed on the same journey. And you'll be able to sleep more soundly at night, knowing you've given your best and modeled your true beliefs to those who come in contact with you. Just remember to be patient as you work with clients or colleagues who are still struggling with issues of integrity in their own lives. Try hard to cultivate tolerance and humility. Remember, there are many ways—not just yours—to express deeply held beliefs, values, and ideals.

In working with couples, for example, you may elicit two opposing views that are both valid. For example, I believe in socially responsible investing. My husband believes it's simpler if you just invest for growth, and then give as much money as possible to causes you believe in. I accept this belief as equally valid, though foreign to my own way of thinking. So if you see a couple who represent different points of view, don't take sides on the assumption that one is right and the other wrong. Instead, try to validate both members' views while striving for a compromise that satisfies enough of each person's needs.

New clients may not consciously know whether they are looking for advice that harmonizes with their values. You might explore this early in the getting-acquainted process by asking them such questions as "Is there something you believe is important in life that I can help you strive for?" or "If money were no object, would you change your life from the way it is now?" If they seem uninterested in these questions or super-uncomfortable with them, it may be best to revert to more straightforward financial management.

But if you cultivate tolerance and compassion, I think you can help many willing clients move beyond financial security to true serenity. This, in my opinion, is the wave of the future—the integration of financial advice and money psychology on the deepest level. In this following pages, you'll find ideas that can help you make it happen in your practice.

MORE THAN MONEY
Intrinsic Values

These days, more and more people are looking for deeper meaning in their lives. That may include clients who have been confronted with the unpredictability of life, as well as others facing the spiritual conflicts that money can create.

Your work in this area will be enriched if you have explored your own values, yearnings, and talents. With the insight generated by this self-knowledge, you'll find it easier to help your clients navigate issues of personal integrity and values that go way beyond dollars and cents.

When situations like these arise, here are some ways to help these clients integrate their deeply held values into their personal goals and plans.

Satisfying a Social Conscience

My Gen X client has been driving me crazy with his demand for socially conscious investments. As often as not, he dismisses the stocks I recommend as "not responsible enough." Financial performance, or the lack of it, seems totally immaterial. I'm finding it hard to keep my cool in working with him. Is there any hope for this relationship?

Is there hope? I think it depends on whether you're able to work with a client who seems more interested in doing good than in doing well.

If you can get on board with this goal, the first thing I would do is to make sure your client is clear on the possibility of loss with these investments, no matter how well-motivated they are. You might translate their historical returns into dollars and cents for him, to make sure he's emotionally okay with the risk. Do you as his advisor feel this risk is acceptable, knowing his long-term goals? If you get over this hurdle, consider enlisting his aid in finding stocks that are responsible enough to meet his standards. If you truly want to make the relationship work, encourage his efforts to research candidate companies carefully and comprehensively.

For better diversification, you might also propose some socially neutral investments that are strong performers. Even though these choices per se may not fully meet his criteria, he could earmark a portion of his returns as a donation to charitable organizations. This mixed portfolio of socially neutral and responsible investments might reduce his overall risk and improve returns.

In the event that you and he just can't see eye to eye, perhaps there's a colleague in your firm who's more attuned to this kind of investing and could join you in serving him. As a last resort, you might refer this client to an outside planner who has more experience (and perhaps more patience) in dealing with socially conscious investors.

When a Couple's Values Clash

My client couple are generally in accord on money matters, but there's a Grand Canyon between them when it comes to estate planning. The wife thinks they should "of course" leave everything to their three children. The husband feels strongly about giving the lion's share of their wealth to a local hospice, so more people have an opportunity to end their lives as peacefully as his late father did. How can I help them bridge the gap between their worldviews?

Though difficult to negotiate, this kind of marital conflict is more common than you might expect. Before you can hope to bring this couple together (and I applaud your willingness to try), you need to be sure you understand where they're both coming from.

For example, did a lack of money in the wife's own childhood prompt her desire to make sure their children are well provided for? Was it part of her family tradition that parents automatically left all their assets to their children? If so, has she taken into account her and her husband's net worth, compared to that of earlier generations?

As for the husband, is he solely moved by gratitude toward the hospice and a desire to support their work? Perhaps he also fears that leaving too much money to the children might spoil or weaken them.

Once you know what is driving both partners' viewpoints, you may be able to help them meet in the middle. To make it easier for them to empathize with each other's concerns, ask him, "How would you feel if all the money went to the children?" Then ask her, "How would you feel if most of the money went to the hospice?" Encourage them to listen closely to each other's responses. You could even ask each of them to repeat ("mirror") what the other has said to see if they heard it fully.

Enlist their help in devising a compromise that meets both clients' deeply held values. A possibility that may already have occurred to you is a testamentary charitable remainder trust, which would give the children a long-term stream of income with the hospice receiving the remaining assets.

One further thought: as you try to help this couple find common ground, the husband may feel he should have the primary say in disposing of the money if he earned most of it. If so, encourage him to make room for his wife's needs and feelings in tailoring their estate. Help him understand that only shared power and decision-making leads to fully satisfying intimacy in a marriage—a result that could benefit this couple greatly.

Midlife Crises

A number of my friends and clients seem to be throwing their careers out the window in the throes of spiritual crisis. For example, a lawyer client wants to leave his lucrative prac-

tice to open a free legal clinic, and an entrepreneur has put his business on the market so he can become a minister. A good friend is quitting her job as a corporate comptroller to join the Peace Corps. All these people are in their peak earning years, and it's hard for me to congratulate them on compromising their financial security. Am I wrong to try to discourage them from these choices?

Perhaps you ought to begin with a little self-examination. Do you feel you fully understand the powerful pull of a midlife reassessment? Can you sympathize with wanting to infuse new meaning and energy into life? Have you ever had your own version of this kind of crisis—or are you perhaps due for one? If so, how do you feel about it?

Once you believe you can discuss these life choices with equanimity, meet with your clients (and friends, if you wish) and thoughtfully explore their situation with them. If you have a solid working relationship with them, they won't mind that your bias is helping to make sure they're financially secure. You may find they're open to exploring mid-range options which can reduce their financial vulnerability while still allowing them to live out their dreams.

Of course, many midlife shifts are temporary, so these changes in direction may not last. But to fully exercise your responsibility toward your clients, help them slow down enough to consider all the options (including, of course, the financial cost of living their dream), while validating their desire for a more meaningful life. Be sure to listen respectfully to their longings before offering your cautionary advice, so you are not perceived as raining on their parade. Your role is to show them a balanced way of living out at least part of their dream—if that's what they choose to do after weighing all the options.

Blessed Are the Poor?

My client, who's in his 30s, just had a commitment ritual with his longtime partner. The partner, a part-time carpenter, wants him to sell his investments and give the money away to charity so they can live simply. My client is inclined to go along with this. I think it would be a huge mistake. How far should I go in making my opinion felt?

Don't be surprised if your client doesn't seem like his usually sensible self. Remember that being in love is an altered state, almost a trance in which one's own personality and values may be subsumed for the sake of the relationship.

I think your approach should be to celebrate his happiness, while encouraging him to step back and assess his values and goals. Point out the importance of forging a partnership based on mutual respect, with enough space for both individuals to live out their desire for a meaningful life. Is he really sure that simplicity and poverty are right for him, or is he surrendering her own needs to his partner's?

Try to help him understand the risks of abandoning his nest egg. What if he and his partner find that this lifestyle isn't quite what they expected? Or what if something happens to the partner, leaving your client alone? Show him the impact that giving away all his savings will have on his financial security, now and in the future. I wouldn't play too strongly on the threat of destitution and abandonment, though—you may cause him to panic, back away from this commitment, and blame you for destroying his relationship with his partner.

This will be a delicate balancing act between affirming your client's own goals and values, and supporting a relationship that is making him happy. You might suggest that he set aside his portfolio (perhaps in a revocable trust) while he tries on this new life to see if it works for him. By making it possible for him to return to a more traditional lifestyle if necessary, you could be giving him a gift of incalculable value.

Trust Principles

My clients want to leave a substantial amount in trust for their grandchildren, with the proviso that the kids (now teenagers) must do community service for least two years before receiving the bulk of the funds at age 30. Although this requirement is flexible enough to cover anything from providing rural medical services to running a soup kitchen, the kids' parents are up in arms, insisting that the grandparents have no right to impose their own values on the younger generation. How should I handle this ticklish situation?

It sounds like there's more to this than meets the eye. See if you can find out what underlies the parents' strong reaction to this proviso. Do they feel the grandparents are implying that they've spoiled the kids, or aren't socially conscious enough? Or are they concerned about the children inferring that Gramp and Gram think they're selfish louts who wouldn't consider community service without the bribe of an inheritance?

Once you have more information about the emotional charge attached to this plan, you may have an easier time communicating with all parties. You might even consider bringing in a family therapist to help the parents and grandparents articulate their deeper needs and feelings.

Even though the parents may resent the grandparents' trying to manipulate the kids' behavior from beyond the grave, the fact is that the grandparents have a right to do whatever they wish with their money. If the older folks remain adamant about not softening their terms, I would strongly recommend that they communicate their plan to the grandchildren before making it final. This way everyone knows how everyone else feels, and any hurt or angry feelings can be addressed while the grandparents are still around to deal with the situation.

John Levy, a Mills, California, psychologist who has written a great deal about trusts, observes that putting money in a trust may be perceived as distrust: beneficiaries infer that the grantors were unwilling to trust them outright with the money. While there are often sound financial reasons for establishing a trust, many potential problems can be avoided (or at least minimized) if the parties are upfront with each other about their motivations, fears, and desires.

Risky Business

I'd like to help the young couple who have just consulted me, but I'm afraid they really need a marriage counselor. He puts in 70 to 100 hours a week trading options, and loves it. She hates it. In our first meeting, she begged him to find a more financially secure job that would let him spend more time with her and their infant son. I sympathize with her concern, but I'm reluctant to tell him to change his life. What's the best way to handle this?

Your first step should be to lessen the intensity of this conflict. Meet with each client separately and give each one space to share his or her perspective with you.

Once you've established a good rapport with the husband, ask him whether his life choices really mirror his values (hopefully including closeness with his family). You may have to help him see that if one member of a couple cannot tolerate a financially risky situation and the other revels in it, then both partners need to learn to move toward the middle for the sake of their marriage.

When you subsequently meet with the wife, try to help her understand her husband's way of thinking. For example, his business may feel like his "baby" to him, demanding a great deal of attention and nurturing. Or he may strongly identify success in his work with being a successful provider for his family.

After helping each partner to develop more compassion for the other's position, reconvene with both of them. Encourage them to move toward the middle by "practicing the nonhabitual"—taking some possibly uncomfortable financial action steps for the sake of their love and concern for harmony in the family. For example, the husband might set aside more quality time with his wife and child, while she might learn more about how he manages risk in his job.

Remind them that while they may both feel unsettled by their new compromises, this mutual lack of comfort can be more than repaid with increased intimacy. Once they're more aligned with each other's needs and goals, they'll be better able to move forward financially.

T A K I N G   A C T I O N

When clients come to you with issues like these, proceed with caution. Take care not to lay your own values and judgments on them, and ask enough questions to understand exactly where they're coming from. If you try to honor their values while doing your job as a trusted financial advisor, you'll help create a relationship strong enough to endure midlife crises, spiritual transformations, and other important life changes.

MORE THAN MONEY
Charitable Giving

Other nations that consider Americans to be selfish and greedy often forget that we're also the most generous people in the world to others in need. Indeed, anyone who thought Americans were self-centered would have been quickly disabused of this idea by the outpouring of charitable donations after September 11.

The events that caused millions of people to reexamine the quality of their lives have also raised the question of "How much is enough?" How much money does it take to be secure and provide your family with the essentials? When you have more than you need, what's the best way to share it with the community? And once that decision is made, there's often another hurdle: What will the children think?

More and more planners these days are struggling to help clients balance giving to themselves and their loved ones with giving to worthy causes. It's said that charity begins at home, but as these situations show, it's often finalized in advisors' offices.

Foundation for Conflict

My client, a widow, wants most of her money to go to a local community foundation after her death, but her adult children are pressuring her to leave it all to them instead. She wants my help to restore peace in the family. SOS!

This is never an easy situation. However, I'm glad your client wants to resolve this issue now, rather than surprising her expectant children with a fait accompli after she is gone. Their shock, distress, and disappointment at that point could forever color their memories of their mother.

If you're willing to assist your client, I would meet with her to be sure you know exactly why and how she wishes to pass on her wealth. Get a detailed sense of the family financial history. How well-off is each of her children at present? Are they feeling unloved or unsupported in some way? Perhaps she hasn't made it clear to them that she is not withholding her love, just her money. Can she show them love and support in other ways?

Assuming you are in accord with her preferences, you can then choose to get together with her and the children. Be aware that intense emotions may surface in this meeting. If you feel uncomfortable being put in the position of a bridge between dissenting family members, you might consider asking a trusted therapist or counselor to sit in with you.

If the children are willing to entertain the idea of their mother leaving at least some of her money to a foundation, explore ways for them to take on a role in future foundation decisions and activities. This can add to their professional and community status, while making them feel good about their mother's trust in them.

On the other hand, if their attitude continues to be "If you really love us, you'll leave us your money," you may need to support their mother with a "tough love" stance. Remind them that it is her money, to be spent in the way she feels is most appropriate for her values, her integrity, and the legacy she wants to leave to the world and to her community.

What's It All About, Alfie?

My new client, a young man who started up his own dot-com and took it public, has been accustomed to making money hand over fist and spending it on his own lavish lifestyle. Now investors are turning cool, and he's lost 80% of his former net worth. Though still wealthy, he feels stunned and disheartened by this reversal and no longer wants to throw himself back into the single-minded pursuit of profit. I see philanthropy as a way to give him new meaning and purpose. Any thoughts on how I should present this to him?

I would first talk to this young client about his past spending habits. Explore whether using his wealth to buy a bigger house, a sportier car, etc., really satisfied him in a deeper way. If this is the source of his discontent (as it is for many suddenly wealthy young people), ask him what he would like to accomplish in his life. Depending on his answer, you may want to introduce the idea of supporting a favorite cause or giving back to the community as a way of deriving a different kind of pleasure from his wealth.

By using some of his time or money to benefit others, he'll confer more meaning on his own achievements—past and future—and feel more connected to the world around him. Many community or charitable organizations would welcome his energy and knowhow. Or depending on his financial situation, he might establish a foundation, set up a charitable fund under the umbrella of an existing community foundation, create a charitable remainder trust, or simply make outright gifts to designated charities. Giving in one's own name has become somewhat trendy, but he may prefer to donate anonymously, or to memorialize relatives or friends by giving in their name to some cause they would have valued.

Certainly, being self-centered and impulsive is part of the character of youth. But if you're open to talking to this restless young client without judging his past life choices, he may well hear you about the deep pleasure of volunteering and charitable giving, and eventually choose this path to help make a difference in the world. Then, I think, his recent reversal of fortune will lose much of its sting.

Charitable Plan Makes Children Feel Shortchanged

I'm involved in estate planning for a couple who have been clients for many years. Now elderly, they want to leave a significant portion of their large estate to a favorite charity, with the remainder to be divided equally among their three children. However, the children (now all in their 40s) are complaining bitterly that this philanthropy will leave less for them. They've been pushing for a meeting with me, to their parents' distress. What's the best way to handle this?

As a therapist, I would suggest that your ultimate goal should be deeper reconnection between your clients and their children, if at all possible.

You might start by meeting separately with the children to explain the estate plan to them and solicit their views, provided your older clients feel truly comfortable with this. (You may have to ask several times to see if they're really okay with your meeting with the children in their absence.) If they would prefer to stay involved, consider getting the whole family together to explain the estate plan, see where the most intense disconnections are located, and try to facilitate better communication and empathy. This would be the appropriate time and place to explore whether the children really need more money than their parents had planned to leave them.

If you're willing to take on this task, it would be a wonderful gift to give this family. The children need to understand that this charitable giving is part of who their parents are. In fact, the parents' desire to feel connected in this way to the larger world can be viewed as a valuable part of the legacy they are leaving to their offspring.

However, you may feel as though you're stepping into the domain of family therapists at this point. If the idea makes you uncomfortable, you might invite to your meeting a therapist who is experienced in dealing with family money issues. This professional can help you deal with feelings of deprivation, anger, and hurt, while making sure each family member feels that his or her concerns have been heard and understood.

Even with the support of a family therapist, I know some advisors won't be comfortable stepping into this potential minefield. Instead, you might recommend to your clients that they work independently with one of these therapists to resolve their underlying issues, before returning to you to complete the process.

Keep in mind that your focus is strengthening the family connection. So even if you feel overwhelmed by the tangle of emotions in this group, you may be able to suggest ways your clients can better communicate and connect with each child about the motives behind their estate plan. This will help separate the plan's provisions from the love and support they want to give their children.

Clean Heir Act

My young client considers a pending inheritance from her grandfather to be "dirty money," because his business exploited workers and polluted a nearby river. She is so ashamed of this legacy that she wants to disclaim it. However, her husband insists that they should take the money. How can I help her make the right choice?

Your client is understandably stuck in what George Kinder, author of *The Seven Stages of Money Maturity*, calls the state of innocence: She'd like to bury her head in the sand and stay "pure" and untouched by the family inheritance.

Help her see that a more responsible position would be to take the money and do some real good with it. For example, she might provide grants to the community her grandfather exploited, or repair the environmental damage his business caused. I recommend Christopher Mogil and Anne Slepian's book *We Gave Away a Fortune*, it might inspire this woman to take on the challenge of bettering society, rather than living with painful feelings of contamination and shame from her family legacy.

As for the husband, see if his objectives for the money seem valid to her. If so, you may be able to help work out a compromise that leaves them both feeling satisfied, at least in part.

"And to My Children, I Leave Nothing"

An old friend of mine, a wealthy widower, has become estranged from his children. He intends to leave all his assets to his wife's college, but is adamant about not informing the children of this decision. Knowing the younger family members as I do, I'm convinced they will be devastated to discover after his death that he has left them nothing at all. How can I talk to him about this?

You're right to be concerned about the potential fallout from this cruel choice. No matter what caused your client's rift with his children, this will have the impact on them of being cursed from beyond the tomb. I've heard of children who went into a long-term depression after the shock of such an irreversible rejection.

Knowing the family personally, you may find it easier to set the right tone. With anecdotes of your own or stories provided by your colleagues, try to enlighten this man about the awful effects of withdrawing total financial support from his children with no explanation.

Explore why he is so determined to leave everything to charity. Are his motives at all altruistic? Or is he simply sending a passive-aggressive, hostile message to his children that he's abandoning them to their own devices? ("And good riddance to the lot of you!")

Once you get clearer about his intent, you may be able to soften his resolve. Along with suggesting some combination of a charitable legacy with a bequest to the children, try to open the door to better communication between the father and his offspring. If you're not comfortable facilitating this process yourself, you could suggest a family therapist comfortable with money issues to mediate in this emotionally charged situation.

Keep Cool to Avoid Spoiling

In our preliminary discussions about estate planning, an extremely wealthy couple have indicated that they want to pass all their assets to their two children. I'm afraid this move will only encourage these spoiled, slacker kids to stay idle and dependent for life. I've asked the parents to think about charitable giving instead, but they shrugged it off. How can I get them to reconsider it without angering them?

Your clients want to pass on a legacy that will truly benefit their children for the rest of their lives... and I think that's common ground you can use to broaden their thinking.

First, explore their ideas about helping their children. Once you hear where they're starting from, you may want to caution them tactfully about the dangers of inherited wealth. It's not uncommon for heirs and heiresses to be disempowered by extreme affluence from making anything of themselves.

Ask your clients if they fear that too much money might stunt their children's drive to succeed. Knowing these particular children as you do, you might reinforce parental misgivings with a judicious comment about the kids' apparent lack of ambition to date.

Once your clients have mulled more seriously the risks of showering their children with money, you can suggest specific alternatives: perhaps donating some of their assets to charitable organizations during their lifetimes or creating permanent endowments in their wills, while leaving the remainder to the kids in an incentive or spendthrift trust.

If you succeed in opening the parents' eyes to these possibilities, you'll be performing an invaluable service not only to them (and the charities they endow), but to their children as well.

Leaf Loss on the Giving Tree

Investment losses shrank my client's net worth, so he wants to drastically reduce his commitment to charitable organizations to which he is a major donor. At least one community foundation will be severely affected by the loss of his generous annual contribution. I think he's overreacting, but I'm having a hard time getting through to him. Any suggestions?

Focus on getting him to slow down, breathe deeply, and think out his situation more calmly. This will probably mean taking time to listen to and discuss his fears, so that he can put market fluctuations in better perspective.

Counsel him to realign himself with his deeper long-term goals, which undoubtedly include making a difference in the world. Help him put together a plan that reassures him he will be financially secure, no matter what happens.

Then you can gently remind him of his responsibility to the organizations that are depending on him. Take care, though, to avoid attacking or shaming him with guilt trips, which could cause him to withhold the money even more rigidly. If you can help him get past his panic to think about the big picture, he should be much more open to meeting his philanthropic commitments.

More, More, More

I've been a dedicated community volunteer and charitable donor all my life. Recently, a high-living entrepreneur consulted me about increasing his already considerable wealth through some exotic high-risk investments. I would like to recommend that he consider sharing some of his good fortune with charities instead, but I'm so put off by his greed and self-centered lifestyle that I don't know how to bring up the subject. How can I deal with this?

It won't be easy, because the first thing you need to do is work on your attitude so you can be a better guide to clients like this man.

In my own practice, it helps me to remember that underneath the hunger that may seem to drive this type of client, there are probably old feelings of deprivation and lack of self-worth that impel him to make himself feel important and fulfilled by accumulating objects and experiences.

Try to explore his background with him to find the human being underneath the greedy caricature you perceive. If you can connect to his humanity, you may find a comfortable way of inviting him to give away part of his wealth to further a favorite charity or personal interest.

Maybe you simply need to ask him to consider charitable giving. Many of today's self-made young millionaires did not grow up with a family tradition of philanthropy, and don't have any idea of how to make a difference in the world through charitable donations. In any event, by learning more about him as an individual, you may be able to advise him more respectfully—no matter what he elects to do with his wealth.

Hoarders Keepers

"Midas," my retired client, is convinced that he and his wife will run out of money if they don't hoard it all. Mrs. Midas, however, would like to establish a foundation to help handicapped children (they lost a child some years ago to Down's Syndrome). I believe they are well enough off to fund this program, but so far I haven't been able to persuade him to consider it. How should I proceed?

If you explore how deeply ingrained your client's fears are, you'll have a better idea of what to suggest. Try to find out more about the roots of his hoarding behavior. What is he afraid of? Is there a way to reassure him that his worries are groundless? Only after you've covered this ground will you know whether you can nudge him toward charitable giving (at least in his lifetime).

If he refuses to budge, consider suggesting that he include a foundation endowment in his estate planning. Many hoarders who need to keep the money close to their side in life are willing to part with it after they're gone. Perhaps Mrs. Midas, at least, will still be around to see the benefits of their philanthropy.

Tax Shelter vs. Family Legacy

A wealthy couple I work with are bitterly divided on their estate planning strategy. To save on taxes, she wants to donate most of their assets to charity. He wants to leave the money to their son, despite the tax consequences. A side issue is that the son has been financially irresponsible, and the mother feels that anticipation of a big legacy would keep the boy from learning to stand on his own two feet. What's the best course?

This is a complicated situation to sort out. First of all, it can help you and your clients to figure out what is fueling their divergent desires. Is there something in their respective family histories that has prompted their different choices about passing on a financial legacy?

For example, you could ask the mother what makes her want to give her assets to charity. Was that a custom in her family? Or did she witness some unfortunate result of a young person inheriting a substantial amount of money? I would want to ask the husband if his family gave so much to charity that he perceived the next generation was shortchanged. By understanding their history more fully, you may be able to build a bridge between their very different values and preferences.

It's important to talk to both of them about their son's immaturity with money, too. Does the father agree that there's a risk his son will loaf around in anticipation of his inheritance, and then squander it?

With what you learn, try to find a middle ground that they can both be comfortable with. For instance, perhaps they would agree to put some money in trust for their son, while donating other assets to charities they both support.

You mentioned tax concerns in your question. To advise clients well, I believe a financial planner needs to go beyond dollars and cents. You must also take into account the cost of a given course of action on relationships in the family, and sometimes between friends. Minimizing taxes may be one of your clients' goals, but it's by no means the only one that matters.

In this case, you need to help the couple balance four issues: their concern about their son's financial maturity, their desire to support him now and in the future, their wish to make a difference to society as charitable benefactors, and their reluctance to have their legacy eaten up by taxes. After listening to everyone and making an effort to understand their needs and concerns, you'll be better prepared to advise them wisely.

A Gift of Self-Esteem

My client was just notified of an inheritance from a great-uncle, a biochemist who developed the first treatment for a tropical parasitic disease. He also adopted several children from Third World orphanages, brought them to the U.S., and put them through college. My client feels he can never live up to this impressive legacy, and he's considering giving all the money away. I think he might regret this gesture later. How can I help him get over his feelings of inadequacy?

You need to help this client see that his true legacy is to be the best person he can be, not an Einstein, a Schweitzer, or a replica of his late great-uncle.

Sympathize with how overwhelmed he feels in comparing himself with this icon of a relative. A tough act to follow, to say the least! Then slowly steer the conversation to your client's own hopes and dreams. Has he secretly harbored a passion to create, explore, or make a difference in the world? Does he find joy and achievement in work, hobbies, play? Once you've helped him build on his sense of uniqueness and self-worth by identifying his own special strengths, you may be able to suggest a way to use the inheritance that would do his great-uncle proud.

TAKING ACTION

Most people, I believe would like to feel that they can make a difference in the wider world. If you can suggest the best way for them to leave a legacy while still taking care of their loved ones, you will be helping them immeasurably—and cementing your role as a lifelong resource they can count on for emotional and spiritual as well as material fulfillment.

MORE THAN MONEY
Walking Your Talk

Even if you're doing good work in general with your clients, you may sometimes find yourself recommending important actions or attitudes that don't jibe with your own values. And in your own life, do you always try to act in ways that are in sync with your advice to clients?

Bringing your practice into line with your principles can help you experience more self-acceptance, growth, and fulfillment in every part of your life. Here are some examples.

Family Values

My ex-spouse and I just negotiated joint custody of our two young children. Now I'm trying to decide whether to work fewer hours so I can spend more time with my kids, or to find a caregiver for them so I can continue working full-time. I'd prefer to be with them, but I'm worried about losing my professional edge (not to mention a substantial amount of my income) if I work less. Any ideas?

I empathize with your dilemma. Our society rewards people much more for working long hours than for connecting with their loved ones. Unfortunately, once the children are grown, you may well have tremendous regret about the time and energy you didn't spend with them when they were young.

In a similar situation, one of my clients decided to work less, live on less, and spend more quality time with his child. This decision, he said, transformed his life of work-stress and worry into one of contentment and fulfillment.

I personally think that if you create a harmonious life with your children, any "edge" you lose in your profession will be more than offset by the happiness and serenity you communicate to those around you—both at work and at home. In fact, you're likely to find that clients enjoy being with you even more and will keep seeking you out.

So I would encourage you to live your dream of spending more time with your kids. If you find you need more income, you still have the option of returning to full-time work, or taking a part-time job in a field you enjoy. Remember, you have many choices—not just one—in building a satisfying work life.

About-Face

For a long time I subscribed to the conventional wisdom that investing in equities is the key to long-term asset growth. Having converted most of my clients to this belief, I've now become persuaded that stocks will show no growth over the next ten years or so, and may even decline. How can I explain this about-face to my clients? I'm also wrestling with how to change my compensation (currently pegged to asset growth) to be profitable in a low-growth environment.

If you no longer believe the gospel that investing in the stock market is the best long-term strategy, you'll just have to take a deep breath and assume the role of rule-breaker. I think your only choice is to sit your clients down individually (or perhaps hold a seminar for them all) and explain how you view the market and the potential of stocks during the next decade.

The picture is complicated by your need to make a good living while holding true to your beliefs. When you meet with your clients, you should be prepared to present them with a new model of the kind of financial planning you'd like to do for them. Like many advisors, you may decide you can best serve clients by helping them define their goals and dreams and figure out how to get what they want out of life. By moving beyond investment management into lifelong financial services, you may be able to change from a portfolio-growth-based fee to a value-based compensation plan that rewards you for all your services.

You're certainly not alone in grappling with this issue. But I truly believe that your clients will stick with you if you give them your best efforts (realizing that you may have to reinvent your profession, at least in part, to do this). Hold firm to your beliefs—and good luck in carving out your own path.

Is This All There Is?

It's discouraging how many people have bought into Gordon Gekko's mantra "Greed is good." I'm tired of helping clients to squeeze out another percentage point of return so they can buy a bigger house, a more exotic car, or a go-faster boat. Whatever happened to the idea of sharing one's good fortune with others? I'm so burned out that I'm thinking about quitting my job and going to work for a charitable foundation. Am I overreacting?

You may be in the midst of a spiritual crisis. If so, it's a good idea to sit with these thoughts and feelings for while, and not jump precipitously into a major change of course.

I understand your frustration with the materialistic values you've observed. Ideally, you'd like to change these clients' priorities. But you're their financial advisor, not their priest or rabbi. You may be able to stimulate their thinking about these issues in a way that is not judgmental or evangelistic, but I think you will find it more rewarding to first act on your feelings for your own benefit.

Consider starting out by doing more part-time volunteer work or charitable giving. If your feelings about philanthropy persist and your job seems less and less meaningful, you can feel more confident that joining a charitable organization would be a good move for you.

One reason why so many advisors are gravitating towards coaching and life planning, I suspect, is to make their own worklives more spiritually and emotionally fulfilling. This longing affects many of your clients, too, especially in midlife. Although it's not your responsibility to meet their spiritual needs or fulfill their values, you may find yourself dealing with financial issues that emanate from related concerns or goals. This new alignment can help create the job satisfaction and personal harmony that you are seeking.

Should I Just Hold My Nose?

In discussions with a new client about potential investments, he keeps bringing up tobacco-company stocks, which he believes will profit from price increases. I'm morally opposed to these investments myself, but I can appreciate the practical aspects of his analysis. I'm torn between standing on principle or letting him invest where he wants to. After all, it's his money, not mine. What would you advise?

The answer may seem to be black or white, but I think there are some shades of gray here. How intense is your objection to investing in tobacco companies? Is it merely abstract, or part of the fabric of your being—perhaps because you've lost a loved one to a smoking-related illness? And how wholeheartedly could you work with this client if you agreed to do what he wants?

If you feel your distaste for his choice would leak out (and I suspect you do, since you're asking this question), I would recommend you share with him your moral bias against this investment, and suggest some alternatives that would fit his portfolio strategy.

But you're right—it's his money. So if he insists on going with tobacco-company stock, you have two choices: either to refer him to a colleague who doesn't have the same ethical objections as you, or to continue working with him. That's assuming, of course, you feel you can do so without communicating disapproval or disrespect in the course of your professional relationship. Some soul-searching and honest self-inquiry should help you decide what's right for you, professionally and personally.

Does the End Justify the Means?

A client has asked me to help him distribute his rather substantial assets into trusts for himself, his children, and his grandchildren, so his wife (who has Alzheimer's) can eventually qualify for government-paid nursing-home care. Although I know how painful his decision must have been, this technically legal maneuver feels dishonest and unfair to me. How do I handle this tough situation?

If you truly feel that what you're being asked to do is morally unacceptable, you need to express this view in a way that doesn't make your client feel even worse than he already does.

If he insists that he can see no other course (and you can't come up with one), it would be a mistake to compromise your integrity by taking action that you feel is reprehensible. Consider offering to refer him to other financial planners who may not have the same objection you do about shifting private obligations to the public purse.

It's worth losing this client's business, I think, to keep your sense of values intact. In this stress-filled profession, where clients typically complain when things don't go their way and begrudge you praise when things are going well, you need to live secure in the knowledge that you're doing the right thing for yourself and your conscience.

When the Boss Breaks the Rules

As a relatively young planner, I take discretion seriously. I make a point of assuring our clients that the information they provide us will remain highly confidential. But in a restaurant yesterday, I overheard a senior member of our firm telling a third party about a client's financial and marital problems. My conscience says I should confront this upper-level guy, but I just don't know how to handle it. What do you advise?

For the sake of the firm's clients, I hope you'll talk to your loose-lipped colleague. The fact that he is senior to you makes it a bit touchy, but here's how you might proceed.

First, ask to meet with him in a neutral and private place (not his office or yours) at a non-stressful time. For example, you might get together with him before the workday starts in a small conference room or, better yet, away from the workplace. Screw up your courage and tell him that something's been bothering you. Recount what you overheard in the restaurant. Without attacking him, tell him that you assure your clients of total confidentiality, and that overhearing this distressed you a great deal.

Then give him space to respond. It's possible that the "third party" was someone who needed to know about the client's situation (for example, a tax attorney retained to help in divorce planning). Even so, your senior colleague will probably feel embarrassed that you, and perhaps others, overheard him. He may react defensively to your pointing the finger at his inappropriate behavior, even if you have made an effort to avoid preaching or accusation.

His response will cue you about what you should do next. If he reaffirms that confidentiality is important to him, regrets his indiscretion, and thanks you for being tactful in calling it to his attention, you may be able to continue promising privacy to your clients in good conscience. If not, you may have to begin looking elsewhere for a workplace that reflects your values and your integrity.

Errors and Omissions

As a successful insurance agent, I can't tell you how embarrassed I am to write this letter. Years ago, I told my wife that I was setting up excellent life insurance for her and our children. I fully meant to do it at the time, but never got around to actually buying the coverage. Now my wife wants to borrow against the policies to pay our daughter's college tuition, and I don't know how to tell her that they don't exist. I'm losing sleep over this. What in the world can I do?

To prevent this omission from causing a serious breach of trust in your relationship, you need to address it with your spouse sooner rather than later.

Find some quiet, private time to sit down with her, and with deep humility and sincere regret, level with her about your procrastination. Explain that you truly meant to obtain the coverage, but never managed to get off the treadmill long enough to do it.

At some point, you may want to get together with your own financial advisor and brainstorm alternative ways to fund your child's education. However, your wife will probably be unwilling to discuss this right away and may well need time to deal with her feelings of betrayal.

In situations similar to hers, spouses have told me that what feels irreparable is not the action or omission itself, but the fact that when it is discovered, their mates avoid talking about it. From now on, the most important thing for your marriage is to communicate more fully about actions you take or don't take, so your wife can slowly rebuild her trust in you.

Do As I Say, Not As I Do

When one of my clients recently asked what to do with several stocks he owned, I told him that I still felt they were good long-term investments he should hold onto. He asked then what I'd done with the same stocks in my own portfolio, and I had to admit I'd sold them. Naturally, he wanted to know why I don't practice what I preach! I explained it as a matter of different investment objectives, but it occurred to me later that I enjoy the challenge of market timing (heaven help me!) and have even toyed with day trading. I feel like a fraud. What should I do about this?

If you respect your clients, you'll want to walk your talk in order to be a good model and strengthen your relationships with them. Otherwise, preaching one course of action while pursuing a different one yourself is bound to erode their trust in you. On a deeper, subtler level, it will also affect your own feelings of personal and professional integrity.

As someone who enjoys the thrill of frequent trading, consider the possibility that you may be addicted to peak experiences and high risks. A visit to a local Gamblers Anonymous group may tell you whether the shoe fits. If you're definitely a risk junkie, how about trying hang gliding, rock climbing, or bungee jumping instead? (First, be sure you have a succession plan in place.) Transferring your quest for excitement to some high-intensity sport may leave you free to make less thrilling but more rational choices in your financial life.

In the meantime, don't judge yourself too harshly. I've heard bank officers who deftly handle millions of dollars tell me their personal finances are a mess, and there are many financial planners who have never made time to plan for their own families. So as embarrassing as this situation may be, you're far from alone.

Truth or Consequences

My client is in the midst of divorce proceedings, and I've been helping him figure out how to divide his portfolio for the less-than-generous settlement he proposes to make on his wife. In a phone call the other day, he confided to me that he also has a seven-figure stash in an offshore bank which his wife knows nothing about, and which he has no intention of including in the divorce settlement. As a divorcee who received an inequitable settlement from my own ex-husband, I'm horrified that he has made me an accomplice to this sleazy, underhanded behavior. What should I do?

Although you can't be this man's conscience, your strong reaction suggests that you'll feel polluted by his greed and secrecy if you continue to deal with him. I think you owe it to yourself to tell him politely what you think of his plan, and let him know that if he pursues it, you will be forced to terminate your professional relationship with him.

Being charged with a secret like this is a terrible burden, and I'm sure you've been tempted to alert the wife to her husband's hidden assets. However, I would not encourage this. As unpalatable as your knowledge is, your client shared it with you in the expectation that you would keep it confidential. Also, you don't know what jeopardy you might put yourself or the wife in by disclosing this information to her.

My recommendation is to separate yourself from this man as quickly as possible. His business is far less important than your need to be able to respect yourself.

"No, No—Give Us the Good Stocks!"

Recently, a wealthy couple who are interested in socially responsible investments came to me for advice. Their portfolio has not done well, since many of their previous picks were high-tech companies. They've asked me to select new socially responsible investments that will do better. They also want my words of wisdom on which CEOs and companies have honesty and integrity they can trust. I'd like their business, but how should I handle this?

As you've probably already pointed out to them, any advisor who could infallibly pick winning stocks would long ago have moved to Hawaii and bought her own island.

Nonetheless, you could share with them the criteria you use in determining good investments. For example, an advisor answered this question for me by saying, "I would trust companies that are not merging, buying, selling, or entering new fields where they can create their own rules. I look for solid companies with good track records, where I know something about the corporate leadership." These seem like good guidelines to me.

Be honest with these clients about your view of socially responsible investing. Are you for it? Ambivalent about it? How much experience do you have with it? If you think they might do better investing in more diversified stocks and contributing directly to favored charitable causes, tell them so.

In the event that they're determined to invest solely in socially responsible stocks and you aren't the best person to advise them, consider referring them to someone else who is. Your selfless honesty could lead this couple to refer other clients to you.

Never Too Late

I've always been a proponent of parents communicating their assets honestly and openly to their children. When it comes to my own adult kids, though, I realize that I've never made time to tell them what I'm leaving them and why. What's the best way to repair the omission now?

Before talking with your children, take time to sort out your own feelings. If there are reasons why you've hesitated to tell any of your offspring about your money, write them down. Consider discussing these concerns with a trusted colleague or advisor, and explore ways to minimize or overcome them.

The next step is to get together with your kids. You may want to hold a group meeting first, then if necessary have a tête-à-tête with each child to discuss their reactions. It's okay to start with separate get-togethers, but you'll want to have a group meeting at some point to avoid sibling distrust or jealousy. Try to choose a time when all of you are calm, unstressed, and ready to listen and talk.

To get the ball rolling, apologize for taking so long to have this meeting, and explain what finally motivated you to act. After you explain your plan, allow plenty of time to hear how your children feel about it. In many cases, they will be relieved that you've taken the initiative, sparing them from having to open the emotional Pandora's box of love, approval, trust, dependency, and control after you're gone. The more thoroughly you can work out your thoughts and feelings and communicate with your kids now, the more positive a legacy you'll leave for them.

Who Am I to Say?

Is it appropriate to let my own values influence what I say to clients? Maybe I shouldn't be so positive in recommending it for just about anyone. What do you think?

The issue of whether we should disclose our own values in counseling others is very important to me as a psychotherapist. Unfortunately, it's a question that has no simple answer.

Some therapists work in a very detached, analytic mode and try not to impose their values (or any other part of their persona) on their clients. Others have a more open, involved style, and do at times communicate their personal experiences and values to their clients. I happen to be one of the latter, so this orientation undoubtedly colors my view.

I believe that if you have deeply held beliefs, it's fine to make them known in a way that is not heavy-handed or judgmental. If you're perceived as standing for a certain set of principles and values, you may even attract clients who want to see you for this very reason. In the case of charitable giving, for example, you might be sought out by newly wealthy prospects who want help sorting out such questions as "How much is enough for me and mine?" and "How can I structure a gift to have the most positive impact?" In short, being upfront about your attitude could well be an asset in your practice, not a limitation.

In general, knowing if and when to suggest such a course of action has a lot to do with your clients' past history and their present self-awareness and openness. It's also essential for you to be able to communicate with them free of your own judgments, preachiness, or negativity.

Taking Action

When you become aware of areas where what you do may diverge from what you believe to be right, be gentle but firm with yourself in bringing your actions into alignment with your values. Don't try to make a major change in one fell swoop, but divide the task into small, manageable increments.

When you truly live your values, your personal power will be enhanced as clients sense this congruence of your work and your psyche. And deep inside, you'll find that a more integrated sense of self will do wonders for your serenity and self-respect.

SECTION 3

Your Practice

Your Practice

When you go to work in the morning, are you energized, enthusiastic, and looking forward to a fulfilling day? Or do you dread dealing with clients who drain you of energy, and doing work that bores you or makes you anxious? Do you fantasize about running away from it all, or embarking on a totally different line of work?

The first step in connecting well with clients is to make sure you yourself are in balance as a financial advisor. Whether you're a new graduate or a seasoned veteran, your practice should make you feel good about your contribution to your clients' well-being. If it doesn't, you can often determine where it falls short by following these four guidelines:

1. Think about why you chose this profession in the first place. What excited or intrigued you about it? What skills and talents of yours inclined you toward it? What contributions so far make you feel good about your choice?

2. Consider your most satisfied and satisfying clients. What is it about them that works so well? Do they all share a particular profession or personality trait? If so, think about ways to find and cultivate more clients of the same kind.

3. Review the balance between your work and personal relationships. Does your life feel well-balanced and fulfilling? If not, perhaps you need to reallocate more of your creative energy to your partner, your children, or your parents. What about making more time for exercise, learning, hobbies, worship, friendship, volunteering, or whatever else nurtures your spirit?

4. Assess whether you're getting enough support. This means professional support from co-workers, outside colleagues, and other specialized professionals, as well as personal encouragement from family, friends, and spiritual or community sources.

Answering these questions will force you to step away from the daily grind and gain a larger perspective on your practice. In the variety of situations and issues that follow in this section of the book, you'll find many more ideas that can help revitalize your work.

Once you succeed in creating a practice whose hallmarks are moral integrity, intellectual challenge, and clients whom you care about deeply, you'll find yourself starting the workday with a deep reservoir of enthusiasm and energy. Your clients will respond to this passion, and you'll flourish—not just financially but emotionally, taking full pleasure in all aspects of your worklife.

YOUR PRACTICE
Coping with Change

Changes in your profession can leave you overloaded with dizzying choices. Whether it's online trading, asset management fees, holistic coaching, tax law revisions, or the encroachment of other professionals into financial planning, it seems that never before has there been so much change to cope with.

At some time or other, you're likely to be thrown for a loop by new developments you didn't expect or want. Whether they affect the work you do, the clients you see, or your personal life, these changes may disrupt your plans if you don't take the right attitude toward them. But when you feel caught between a rock and a hard place, take your cue from these examples of how to handle similar dilemmas.

Facing Changes in Leadership

The head of our company passed away recently, a woman we all respected tremendously. The new guy in charge has a radically different personality and is much less of an inspirational team leader. As a result, the atmosphere at work has become quite gloomy. I've been happy working here for more than 10 years, but I'm wondering now whether to stick it out or move on. How can I decide?

My advice is *festina lente*—make haste slowly.

For right now, stay put. It's natural for the unexpected loss of any beloved colleague to throw the entire work group into mourning. When the co-worker you've lost is also an inspirational leader, the intensity of your feelings makes this an especially poor time for radical change.

As you may know, grief tends to come in stages— first shock and denial, then anger, sadness, and mourning (though not necessarily in this order). While you're working through this process, I would suggest getting closer to your co-workers by sharing memories of your former boss and her contributions to the firm.

In addition, look for ways to comfort yourself. Alone or with colleagues, fill yourself up with activities that will help soothe the wounds of loss. If making pesto sauce by hand, playing basketball with the kids, or listening to the Three Tenors does it for you, do it more.

Then, once the initial shock has worn off, take a closer look at your new boss. Try not to compare him to his predecessor—that may be a test no one can pass. But see if you can live with his personality and way of working. If not, waste no time in looking around for a better work climate with an employer who suits you better.

I believe that the feeling of a workplace nearly always starts at the top and ripples down to everyone else. If people respect the boss and feel they're being treated fairly, they usually enjoy coming to work. When they don't like or admire the head honcho, morale suffers.

In such a case, knowing when to leave is an art. If you stay too long, you risk losing energy and self-esteem. But going too soon may make you feel that you surrendered before giving it your best shot—not the best way to cope with change.

A Change in Clientele

It's hard for me to handle the fact that my firm now works primarily with wealthy clients. I miss the good old days when we helped more middle-class folks like me. Unfortunately, this is a poor time to look for another position because my long-time marriage is in the process of breaking up. I'm angry with my colleagues who seem thrilled about our new direction, and my irritability sometimes makes me act like a jerk around them. How can I get over this?

First, forgive yourself for your bad temper. As I tell my therapy clients, whenever you're tired, stressed, or in crisis (and you're probably 3 for 3 right now), you'll revert to your oldest and most dysfunctional mode of behavior—your primitive survival mode. For you, I gather, this mode is cantankerousness and anger.

You need to recognize that the stress in your personal life is complicating a workplace development you otherwise might have taken in stride. Even when divorce comes as a relief, it's always painful. A relationship is being ripped apart, and it's normal to feel that part of you is being flayed open too. If you expect this, you can give yourself time and space to heal. Try to surround yourself with nurturing friends, and (if you can tolerate it) talk about your pain with them. Also, seek out things that raise your spirits: movies that make you laugh (or cry), music and books that please and console you, meditation that calms your soul.

As for your disappointment about the changes at work, talk to your boss about the possibility of continuing to specialize in less affluent clients. Even if this door is shut, I would agree with you that now is not the time to quit. Leaving a marriage and work simultaneously is too much loss and change for anyone to have to bear all at once.

So focus on what you do enjoy about your job (and your private life) till things begin to stabilize. In the meantime, it might help to discuss the change in clientele with trusted colleagues—people you think might sympathize with the feelings of loss you're experiencing. Eventually, if your company doesn't offer any avenue for you to do the kind of work you love, start looking around for another place that will value your unique gifts and your commitment to clients who aren't super-wealthy.

Regarding this last point, I've heard many planners and other investment professionals complain about the universal focus on clients who can "show me the money." This is probably inevitable, since it's much easier to keep a house from falling down than it is to build one. But it may comfort you to know you're not alone in your commitment to folks who don't have a fortune.

Selective Beliefs

I've begun signing new clients to fee agreements, and I truly believe this is the wave of the future. However, I hesitate to ask my existing clients to convert from commission-based compensation, since they seem to be happy with it. Trouble is, I sometimes feel like I'm talking out of both sides of my mouth. How can I overcome this?

I think it's okay to have a mixed practice if that sits well with you—but not because you're too chicken to broach the subject with your current clients. If you truly feel that fee arrangements are more advantageous, you owe it to these clients to confront the subject head-on with them.

That said, it's perfectly natural to fear that a change in compensation might upset some of them enough to leave. To reduce this risk and alleviate your anxiety, I would suggest that you address the issue in small increments.

Starting with one or two clients with whom you have a solid history, explain the pros and cons of a fee conversion and ask for their feelings about it. Though scary at first, this kind of exploration can also provide an opportunity to clarify and clean up old, messy aspects of the relationship.

Slowly but surely, you will find out whether your client connections are strong enough to weather the change. And by discussing the matter personally with each client instead of simply announcing a change in your compensation policy, you will make them feel respected and valued. Little by little, you'll have the satisfaction of aligning this important aspect of your practice with your own beliefs.

The Risk of Following a Dream

Lately, I've considered directing my practice toward financial coaching and helping parents educate their children about money—two areas I think I'd be good at and would really enjoy. My spouse has encouraged me to go ahead, but turning away traditional clients is a risky move in today's economy. Should I sit tight for a while? I'm not hurting financially, and am okay with what I'm doing now.

By all means, move toward the kind of work where your "juice" is. But remember, you don't need to take excessive risks to get there. For example, I would suggest putting a toe in the water by giving talks and writing articles on these two topics. See if this low-commitment method of expressing your interest elicits inquiries and referrals you can pursue.

You may discover that you're still on a learning curve and don't feel quite comfortable yet in charging clients your full rate. I myself have gone through periods of working for free in a new area before it feels organically right to begin charging for my expertise. As your own confidence increases, you may choose to move gradually from a reduced fee to a full fee. In any event, I firmly believe that exploring new territory will lead to greater satisfaction in your work, and eventually to appropriate levels of compensation.

Incidentally, you don't have to quit your current clientele cold turkey and plunge off into the unknown. Just replace clients lost through attrition with new money-making activities, as your practice evolves toward new areas of interest and commitment.

When Not to Go with the Flow

Nowadays, the conventional wisdom in my planner group seems to be that after the initial phase of developing a financial plan, we should move into asset management. I can understand the economic motivation for this, but my own intuition and strengths tell me that I should stay primarily in the role of a planner. What do you think about this?

Naturally, I'm biased in favor of your instinct. It makes sense for you to stay in a field in which you feel better equipped to make a valuable contribution.

I believe that changes in the marketplace will never invalidate the vital role financial planners play as therapeutic educators, advising individuals and couples on their financial lives. There are plenty of planners who want to do asset management; you don't have to be one of them. Instead, I'd encourage you to develop and promote unique aspects of your planning process (ideally, aspects you really enjoy), so you can create a niche in the kind of work you love. Who knows, perhaps you'll create a financial planning practice of the future that will meet needs neglected up to now—your own as well as your clients'.

Going against the crowd like this is never easy. You can feel very lonely and out of sync with whatever group is espousing some new "truth" or dogma of conventional wisdom. But if you remain true to your own beliefs, perceptions, and intuitions, and have the courage to stand up for them, I believe you'll find much more satisfaction in your worklife. What's more, I suspect you'll run into kindred spirits along the way who will confirm your views—and make your own wisdom seem much less unconventional.

Letting Go of a Work Partner

My partner and I have built a successful business over the past eight years. Now that his wife has been offered a great job opportunity on the other side of the country, he's decided to try setting up as a sole practitioner in their new location. As a feminist, I applaud his willingness to support her career, but I find myself feeling angry and resentful of his decision to break up our good working relationship. Should I tell him how upset I am?

First of all, accept the fact that even if your mind (and your feminist consciousness) totally approve of your partner's and his wife's decision to move for the sake of her career, your inner feelings will be several steps behind this rational acceptance. After all, you've had a successful "work marriage" for years, and it's totally natural for the child in all of us to feel abandoned and even somewhat rejected in this situation.

Even if you know in your heart of hearts that your partner is not rejecting you, you do need to talk to him about why your "irrational" anger and negativity toward his big move may bubble up from time to time. If you ask him to understand this and overlook any occasional coolness or short-temperedness on your part, you'll put safe boundaries around these (hopefully) minor eruptions if they recur, and will be able to wish him well more wholeheartedly.

Don't try to minimize the fact that this is a big change for both of you. By letting out your inmost feelings about this parting of the ways, you will lighten the load and make your negotiations go much more smoothly. And who knows? When your partner gets out there, he may change his mind and decide he'd like to rejoin forces with you in a bicoastal practice. You can sow the seeds of this possibility in your discussions now, but leave space for him to decide to go it on his own. He may have a need to prove himself in this way that says nothing negative about your past partnership, but only reflects his own longing for a new kind of autonomy.

In any case, by allowing yourself to process the current situation emotionally, and leaving the door open for the future, you'll be better prepared for whatever may happen.

New Kid on the Block

I'm a newcomer to a successful firm whose associates have been working together for a long time as a tight-knit group. I assumed they would appreciate new ideas and a fresh perspective, but they seem so unfriendly to my suggestions that I'm beginning to wonder why they hired me in the first place. What should I do about this?

The longer these people have been together, the more their relationships will have evolved toward a closed family circle. As an "outsider," you're like a new kid suddenly plunked into their midst, disrupting long-established patterns.

No matter how great a track record you had before you joined the firm, you'll have to work to earn your colleagues' trust. So instead of trying to jump right in and change things, take time to learn as much as you can about the firm's way of operating, its history, and its own unwritten rules. Build rapport first, then support, and finally alliances.

Only then should you offer your own suggestions about new ways to run things. Provide your creative input gently and diplomatically, so people don't think you're implying that you're smarter or cleverer than they are, or that the old way of doing things was wrong. Even in a healthy "family," no one likes being openly criticized. But if you're patient and tactful, they may come to value your unique position as someone who can look freshly at their situation.

Giving Up Independence

I've been approached by a CPA who's interested in affiliating with me. My first inclination is to say yes since the arrangement would have financial and marketing advantages, but I'm reluctant to give up my autonomy. How can I resolve this dilemma?

Practical advantages aside, it's important to be sure of blending well, temperamentally as well as intellectually, when you collaborate with someone. If you don't mesh effectively with this accounting professional, it can affect not just your worklife but the quality of the work itself.

For example, my creativity dries up completely when I try to collaborate on a book or article with someone whose chemistry is wrong for me. By contrast, the fit is so perfect with my longtime co-author and editor that the work flows out more effortlessly than if I were doing it alone.

To find out whether you could work productively with this CPA, take time to explore each other's personal and professional outlook. I would suggest meeting several times, informally as well as in a formal office setting. Voice any concerns or hesitations up front, and try to work out boundaries that will protect your professional independence. If the chemistry seems right, interview some accounting clients to see if you're comfortable with the way your prospective partner works with them.

The next step might be to try out this "work marriage" in small increments. A test with one or two clients should give you a good feel for how well your collaborative relationship will work. Don't hesitate to bow out if it doesn't feel like a real plus to you. But if the fit seems right, you might find that affiliating with this CPA will help both of you broaden your professional understanding, insight, and expertise. Just remember to take it slow.

Too Much of a Good Thing

My practice has gotten so busy lately that it may take two or three months before people can get in to see my partner or me. I'm concerned word will get around that we're too busy, and we'll lose clients as well as credibility. It also bothers me that I'm beginning to feel overloaded and disconnected from the aspects of my work that I used to enjoy most. I never thought I'd regret our success, but it's getting so I hate to go to the office. What would you advise?

Congratulations on your business's growth—and don't beat yourself up for having a hard time with it. As I often point out to my clients, it's often easier to deal with adversity than with success, since we're usually more comfortable with the old familiar problems than with new pleasures which threaten to sweep us away to places we've never been before.

Let's address first your loss of "juice" due to overwork. My suggestion would be to declare a timeout from work for one weekend, and spend that time identifying what kind(s) of clients or which aspects of financial planning give you the most satisfaction and fulfillment. Then strategize ways to attract these clients or this kind of work.

Colleagues and friends may be able to help you brainstorm innovative ways to bring in more of the sort of business that turns you on. Once you put this plan into action, you can start referring the clients and tasks you least like to others who will be more committed to dealing with them.

To help with your other concern about your "waiting list" potentially discouraging new clients: start by making sure you have a warm, welcoming message on your voice mail (or pre-program your secretary) to communicate the upturn in your practice and the ensuing wait for an appointment. Assure those who call that if they aren't comfortable waiting for their initial visit with you, you will be happy to refer them to a qualified colleague who may be able to meet with them sooner.

If you've begun to focus on attracting the kind of clients you really want to work with, you might adopt a sort of professional triage system, finding time for those you want to see and putting the others on a waiting/referral list. For those who don't make your "A" list, I believe a polite fib about your busyness is totally permissible, since you don't want people who call to feel rejected and you do want them to persist in getting the help they need. To increase the proportion of prospects who meet your desired profile, you might consider a new community-wide communication program that positions you as an advisor specializing in this segment's needs. . . if, that is, you don't mind having more success to contend with.

A Voice in the Wilderness

My successful practice combines financial planning with speaking and writing about financial matters for consumers. I recently joined a new firm where virtually all the other principals come from brokerage backgrounds. I like these people and hope to establish a good relationship with them despite our different viewpoints, so that I don't feel like a lone voice crying in the wilderness. Any ideas?

It sounds like you're off to a good start if there's already a climate of mutual respect and friendliness. To build on this and diminish the prospect of your ending up lonely and ostracized, I'd recommend making a point of having a one-to-one business lunch, tea, or dinner with everyone in the firm (or at least with the other principals, if it's a large organization) so you'll feel more connected to each other personally.

At these half-professional, half-personal meetings, share your work passions. Talk about the aspects of planning that matter to you, and invite your workmates to tell you what they like or love about the brokerage side of the business. After establishing these personal contacts, I'd suggest organizing an internal meeting around your area of expertise, where you can discuss your approach to financial planning and relationship-building and everyone else will have the opportunity to contribute.

In these discussions, you'll probably find you can learn a great deal that is valuable in your own work. And with good will on your new colleagues' side, your initiative in opening a dialogue may lead to creative brainstorming about how your expertise can help the business as a whole.

The Big Cheese

Our three-person practice has grown so well lately that we've had to bring five more people on board. We find it's most efficient to have one person do an initial interview, and then direct the prospective client to the advisor or assistant who can best serve them. However, this upsets some prospects who call expecting to speak directly to the "big cheese." Is there a way to handle these concerns without losing the benefit of our new structure?

Since the problem here is one of unmet expectations, better communication could help you head off more instances of client disappointment or resentment.

I would recommend sending out two letters as soon as possible. The first, to your current clients, should tell them about your new intake procedure, and how it will (or won't) change your way of working with them. The second letter (or announcement) should inform potential clients about the way your newly expanded business works. Reassure them that you're deeply committed to seeing that all your clients receive quality financial services, and stress that at your firm, the "big cheeses" work together with the junior or more specialized staffers to make sure every client's needs are met as cost-effectively as possible.

The more you can communicate your new structure and new screening procedure before people call and are surprised by it, the better the chances of avoiding offense to those who hate change, or who want to feel catered to and important.

You may have to invest in advertising to get the word out—but if this effort helps keep just one client or prospect from badmouthing your inaccessibility, it will be money well spent.

TAKING ACTION

Human beings are relatively adaptable, but sometimes you can accommodate change only by compromising things you treasure. If the cost of coping would be high enough to make your situation unbearable, start looking around for more attractive options. (Sometimes just exploring other choices can make your present situation feel better than before.)

In general, my recommendation for handling change is to communicate openly, first with yourself (an honest internal dialogue about what's going on), and then with people around you, so everyone knows what's happening and how best to deal with it. Take stock of what you can proactively do to improve the situation. Visualize how things could get better, and determine whether your own fear of changing might be standing in the way.

Most of us are creatures of habit, and change—no matter how wonderful it seems in the abstract—may feel a little scary when it descends on us. So be gentle with yourself in adapting to changes in your practice, and don't be afraid to seek help and support from colleagues and other professionals whom you like and trust.

YOUR PRACTICE
Preventing Burnout

The business of financial advice can be immensely stressful. Clients often blame you for things you can't control, but are less vocal in their appreciation when you make it possible for things to go well. So it's up to you (and the colleagues who support you) to shore yourself up when you know you're doing your best, regardless of the ups and downs of the market.

If stress is persistent and uncontrollable, it can cause even the most dedicated advisor to burn out. Those of us in "helping professions" are particularly vulnerable. After years of trying to solve other people's problems, we find we're running on empty, drained of energy, empathy, and resilience. If you're under a lot of stress at work, or even fear you're burning out, read on for some ideas.

Getting to the Heart of Stress

There's been a fair amount of personal stress in my life, but I always figured life was full of ups and downs. Lately, though, I find I'm resenting every new client demand and snapping at people I work with. I feel tired all the time, even on weekends. A good friend told me she thought I was suffering from burnout. How can I tell? And is there anything I can do about it, short of quitting my job?

Your first task is to get clearer on what is stressing you out. Don't try to talk yourself out of your feelings by saying things like "everyone has pressures in life, and I'm no different." Your stresses are your own, and they need to be examined and attended to in order to reduce their harmful effect on your life.

If your personal problems have affected you deeply, you could be suffering from depression that goes beyond occupational burnout. In this case, consider talking to a therapist or counselor. But if you believe your work situation is creating (or contributing in a major way) to the symptoms you describe, burnout could well be the cause of your blues.

Some common signs of burnout are fatigue or exhaustion, insomnia, feelings of depression (or in some cases, free-floating anxiety), lack of interest in work and perhaps in other aspects of life, and changes in eating or sleeping patterns.

If you're a sensitive and empathetic person by nature, you may be all the more susceptible to burnout. To help insulate yourself from being sucked dry by the negativity of client problems, consider trying a powerful visualization technique sometimes recommended to therapists. It's simply to start the day by imagining a large golden energy-filled membrane around you which filters out negative influences and lets in the positive ones. This may sound weird or airy-fairy—but anything you can do to remind yourself of your own protective boundaries is a good idea.

If you find you still can't shake your blues, don't let the situation drag on. Whether burnout is the source of your problems or a byproduct, a counselor may be able to help you find ways to relieve the stress causing your symptoms.

"Back to One"

I know this will sound like I've lost my mind, but a weird thing has happened. I just got back from vacation expecting to feel rested and refreshed, but I'm not. I keep having to ask myself, "Now what is it I'm supposed to do next?" just so I won't forget some of the routine things that ought to be second nature. I'm worried about feeling so disoriented and unmotivated. What can I do to get back on track?

I would recommend a principle called "Back to One," which was outlined in a book of the same title by the late Sheldon Kopp, a much-loved and well-respected therapist.

To practice Kopp's principle, just ask yourself what's the first step you need to take to get back in the saddle. The beauty of this concept is that you don't face the overwhelming task of charting an entire multifaceted strategy—just identify the one thing you need to do first. (In fact, the "back to one" approach is universal enough to benefit just about any financial advisor, burned out or not.)

The step you decide to take may be work-related. For example, you may decide that you need to focus better on getting a full, clear idea of why clients have come to see you, and of their strengths and weaknesses regarding money. Alternatively, you might choose a stress-relieving step such as setting limits on your workweek, getting more exercise, exploring a talent or interest, or making more quality time for a relationship with your mate, children, and/or friends.

Whatever you decide to do, going "back to one" will relieve that feeling of "what am I doing here?" disorientation in your work, and help you get back in the groove.

Viva Variety

I followed your advice some time ago to identify the kind of clients I'd prefer to work with. Now most of my practice centers on medical professionals, but the problem is that I keep dealing with the same issues over and over. What can I do to spice up my uninspiring worklife? One of my married clients has sent me signals of romantic interest, and I'm having fantasies of actually taking her up on it. Is this a sign that I've gone off the deep end?

Unfortunately, we humans aren't wired to handle boring, predictable routine very well. In fact, many of us are somewhat addicted to the thrill of peak experiences. If we don't have some level of stress and risk in our lives, we'll often create it for ourselves—as you're contemplating doing. (Don't even think about it!)

As far as your disappointing venture into specialization is concerned, I know where you're coming from. In my own therapy practice, I decided I loved working with couples. Before long, I had too many couples to see—and it dawned on me that despite the satisfaction of couples work, it's also quite exhausting and demanding. I then decided to do more "business therapy," another specialty which excited me a lot; but before I knew it, I had too many business clients coming in for help.

With the benefit of this experience, my further advice to you is "Moderation in all things." If you're seeing too many doctors, take a breather and look for a whole new audience. Artists? Musicians? Golfers? Or if you're bored with the problems of affluent professionals, what about business owners, retirees, or people with inherited wealth?

To sort out where you want to go from here, it may help to talk to colleagues who know you well. In the meantime, stop judging yourself for not being happy with too much of a good thing. It's perfectly normal to feel this way. Or at least perfectly human.

Live to Work, or Work to Live?

Although I want to do right by my clients, I also have a wife and kids, as well as hobbies I enjoy. But my co-workers are so competitive that I know they'll consider me a slacker if I say I don't want to take on extra work. What are your thoughts on this?

Whenever I'm asked this question, it makes me feel sad. What began as the sensible Puritan precept of "sow and ye shall reap" has grown way out of control, like a sort of cultural kudzu. As a result, we've lost the idea of life balance, which I feel is a tragic shame and a major cause of individual burnout.

These days, many people like your colleagues have no other way to define their value than by their work. Therefore, they assume that the harder they work, the more valuable they must be. Some workaholics, I suspect, even believe they'll win points in heaven for laboring through 80-hour workweeks. I'm not one of these martyrs, and I'm happy to hear that you're not in this group either.

I strongly recommend that you take the initiative in countering this pernicious belief. Find colleagues in other firms and friends in other professions who share your commitment to family, relationships, hobbies, and life balance in general. You might put together an A.W.A. (Anti-Workaholics Anonymous) lunch group to periodically share extracurricular enthusiasms. Back at the office, consider nudging the status quo by starting a company softball team, or putting together a family picnic. Become an icon for co-workers who want a more balanced life. By mentoring those who realize that your firm isn't the be-all and end-all, you could be instrumental in helping them move in a healthier direction.

Last, be sure to share with your workaholic colleagues all the good things you're achieving in your job. That should dispel any suspicions they may have that anyone with a balanced life just can't be working hard enough.

Making Time for Yourself

I'm a dedicated life planner who advises clients to slow down and smell the flowers, especially after 9/11. But in looking at my hours for the first half of the year, I realize I'm working harder than ever and taking no time for myself. How can I rectify this when people need me more than ever to help create security in their lives?

Slowing down, relaxing, and living in the present are an ongoing challenge for me, too. In fact, that's why the phrase "Healer, heal thyself" is so common among therapists.

You've already taken the first step by sharing this concern with me. The second step is to confront your own rational-sounding self-talk about why you can't take time to do this right now. (e.g., "people need me more than ever.")

Unless you walk your talk, your clients will intuitively sense that something is amiss in your advice about slowing down and enjoying life. They'll wonder whether you really believe in what you're telling them to do. Meanwhile, you'll be burning out with increasing speed and intensity.

Paradoxically, taking more time for yourself can help make you more efficient at work. And even if some tasks must be postponed for a while, you'll find it's not cataclysmically important to clean off your entire desk every day.

A good way to begin taking better care of yourself is with simple new rituals of self-care that can become habits, then traditions. Make these personal commitments as binding as a promise to a client. Twenty minutes of walking every weekday? An hour every Sunday to call or e-mail old friends? Meditation early in the morning or before going to bed? Whatever self-nurturing activity you choose, starting it and keeping it up may not just lower your blood pressure, but allow you to feel greater harmony with the clients you are helping to heal.

Staff Burnout

Since the death of our practice's beloved founding partner, the productivity of the financial planners on my staff is way down. They seem listless and unable to concentrate. I've thought about having a strategy session to discuss new ideas and get them more excited about the future. What do you think?

This may not be the time to push for new strategic concepts or organizational change. Routine and structure can help the healing process by allowing people to build on what feels normal and familiar.

Start by letting your staff know that you believe in the importance of coming to grips with sadness, fear, apathy, and other feelings. I'd suggest establishing a weekly or biweekly get-together—perhaps a breakfast or dinner—expressly for emotional sharing and healing.

In addition, consider hiring an outside facilitator for a staff retreat. By taking your colleagues out of their normal work environment to a peaceful, healing place, you'll make it possible for them to dedicate more time and space to bond with and support each other. Even a day away from office stresses may help them calm and heal in more ways than you (or they) can imagine.

Setting Emotions Aside

My widowed father recently died after a long illness, and it devastates me to realize that both my parents are gone. I find myself dragging around the office without any interest or ambition in my work. I've been telling my colleagues that I feel fine, mostly because I'm afraid I'll break down if I try to explain. How long will this go on? Is there any way to put my emotions aside so I can function better?

The loss of a parent is one of the most traumatic life events that any of us ever experience. When we lose our last parent, as in your case, the sense of aloneness and grief cannot be expressed in words. Whether the relationship was strong, distant, or dysfunctional, we feel abandoned and cheated of the love we never got, or longing for more of the good things we did receive.

For the sake of your own emotional health, I believe you should stop trying to bottle up these feelings inside. Instead, share your sorrow and loneliness on appropriate occasions with close friends or co-workers. To paraphrase Elizabeth Kübler-Ross, the renowned authority on grief and dying: any emotions you let yourself feel or express about the death of a loved one will pass relatively quickly; it's the ones you don't acknowledge that hang on for years.

If you're thinking, "I could never talk to people I work with—I might lose control of myself," don't let this fear stop you. Caring people are usually not put off by tears. On the contrary, they feel closer to those who can risk being so vulnerable with them.

If you feel your heartache is interfering with doing your job, I would also recommend that you consider joining a grief group or seeing a grief counselor. By surrendering to the mourning process, albeit in small installments, your healing may proceed more quickly. But it will still take a long time to lighten your burden of loss and sadness. Give yourself that time, and be loving and compassionate toward yourself in as many ways as you can.

Unscrupulous Competition

Several of my clients are being cold-called by brokers who have set up on their own after being laid off by their firms. These guys are promising the sun, the moon, and the stars to my impressed clients, who are now requesting that I match the brokers' lower fees and prom-

ise the same pie-in-the-sky portfolio results. I want to shake these clients and ask how they can be so gullible, and so disloyal, after all we've been through together. Obviously that's not the ideal way to handle this situation. What do you suggest?

You need to take these clients' annoying demands much less personally before you respond to their requests and challenges. Face it: you could be the most dazzling planner in the world with the most wonderful client relationships, but you still live in a society where many people are always hoping and trying to get something for nothing. To get over the intensity of your hurt feelings and anger towards these clients, I would talk the matter over with colleagues who are understanding and supportive.

It may also help to write down your thoughts and perceptions about what your clients want, and why their expectations are unrealistic. You can develop this solely for your own edification, or turn it into a document you send these clients before inviting them to get together with you.

Then, follow up with a face-to-face meeting with each client. In discussing their concerns, you might mention some cautionary tales about fly-by-night tipsters and "advisors" who have cost their customers a great deal of money. Tactfully bring up instances when you have gone above and beyond the call of duty for your clients over the years, and ask what they know about the brokers' reputations, ethics, areas of expertise, and resources.

But while building a bridge back to reality for your clients, take care to empathize with their desire for excitement and magic in their portfolios. When people are "flying" in an altered state, contemplating glorious new possibilities, it's no fun to be brought down to earth. So be gentle and sympathetic as you communicate what they can realistically expect.

When Personal Problems Affect Your Work

I'm in the midst of a very painful divorce, which has had an unfortunate effect on my work. The other day a longtime client called to ask about a quarterly meeting I should have scheduled with him and his wife almost two months ago. If we had met when we should have, I would have recommended portfolio changes that would have left them better off that they are now. As it is, I'm horrified to realize that my oversight has cost them money. What should I do?

If you haven't actually blurted out, "Good Lord, I forgot," you might simply explain that unforeseen pressures caused you to postpone the meeting. Apologize for not having let them know, and try to schedule the consultation as quickly as you can. At this point, you can present your recommendations. To bolster client satisfaction, I would try hard to point out some recent trend or event that makes your advice today better than it would have been a couple of months ago.

While I don't think any good purpose is served by volunteering how much money the delay in meeting cost them, be sure to tell the truth if it comes out, or if they ask you directly about it. Though they will certainly understand that the strain of a dissolving marriage may have preoccupied you, they'll also realize that you dropped the ball by not having a good support system in place—a datebook, tickler file, computerized follow-up calendar, efficient personal assistant... you get the idea. You'll have to reassure them about steps you are taking to make sure that this kind of omission doesn't happen again.

Even so, it's hard to predict how they may react to discovering the cost of your mistake. Less accommodating clients may walk out the door if you feel unable to compensate them for losses due to your oversight. On the other hand, if you've built up a good relationship with this couple, they may forgive you and agree to keep working together. In this case, it would be a positive step to schedule the next quarterly meeting before they leave your office. Alternatively, you may want to set up an intermediate meeting at no extra charge, to make sure their concerns continue to be answered.

I'm a Believer

I'm passionate about long-term care insurance, and have become an expert in this field. However, the demand so far has been much lower than I had hoped. I don't know whether to abandon this specialty and find another niche, broaden my focus, or try to hang on until market demand catches up with me. Right now I'm so frustrated and discouraged, I can hardly think straight. Can you help?

Take heart—you may not be at the market's mercy as much as you think. From a professional standpoint, have you really tried every avenue to bring the public your message about LTC insurance and your expertise in it?

When you're feeling calm and refreshed, I would take some time to brainstorm about this with a supportive colleague who's good at marketing. What kind of person would you truly enjoy selling long-term care insurance to? Explore creative new ways to get out the word to this target audience. At the same time, work on Plan B: another possible niche you could develop to broaden your skill set and help more clients. This planning process will give you a greater sense of taking charge of your future, instead of simply waiting for the dice to fall.

On a personal level, nurture your spirit to combat the fear and depression you're feeling. Spend more time doing whatever restores you and gives you energy. This combination of personal and professional "recharging" will help stave off worry as you continue offering services you believe in.

Will My Practice Survive?

Whenever I read about a big financial company swallowing up another independent advisor, I feel like a deer in the headlights. It's getting harder and harder to summon the energy to keep my own small business growing. I could try to find work in one of these huge firms, but my heart isn't in that, either. How can I snap out of this feeling of dread?

Doomsayers seem to be everywhere lately. But it's important not to succumb to them—after all, no one can predict the future for sure. If you want to stay in a small firm and do the work your way, keep at it with as much passion and commitment as you can muster.

To escape your "trapped in the headlights" despair, think about what you love most about your work, and what you could do to make it more exciting and enjoyable. If you draw a blank on this, try writing a fantasy obituary for yourself. What would you like this obituary to say about your abilities and accomplishments between now and your demise? Bizarre as it may sound, this exercise has helped many of my own clients awaken dormant dreams and re-energize their lives.

If nothing you can think of sounds enjoyable or fulfilling, you may have allowed the naysayers to stop you from believing in yourself. Other factors may also be involved, such as personal stress, too much work, unhealthy living patterns, or lack of friendship, community, or spiritual connection. Once you identify what unmet needs may be slowing you down, you can make time to address them.

Last, consider the work options that will be available to you if your practice for some reason does not survive. (If you go through this revitalizing process, though, the odds are good that it will succeed.)

Even in this worst case, you'll have the satisfaction of knowing you gave your business 100%, and didn't succumb prematurely to the gloom-and-doom predictions around you. And having already thought about alternatives that interest you, you will be well positioned to pursue a new path to success .

Taking Action

The key to managing stress is to recommit yourself to moderation and balance. Remember not to judge yourself harshly if you feel exhausted, depressed, anxious, or unproductive. Take time to identify the sources of these feelings, and devise innovative ways to tackle and change them. Consult supportive friends and colleagues to help brainstorm solutions.

By making work a part of your life, not its all-consuming nucleus, you can keep excessive stress from leading to burnout and sending your creative energy up in smoke.

YOUR PRACTICE

Relationships with Colleagues

Your practice may not actually be full of family members, but it can sometimes feel that way. When one person has a problem, a worry, or an unresolved issue, it affects everyone who deals with him (or her).

How well do you get along with the other "family members" at work—your partners and/or support staff? Which ones feel supportive and nurturing? Which are aggressive to the point of undermining your self-confidence? How can you work more productively with them, and with the outside colleagues you deal with on a regular basis?

By understanding more about the dynamics that may operate under the surface of your relationships, you can learn to manage sticky situations like these.

Teaching Without Preaching

A talented young planner in my firm was completely gung-ho on a particular market sector, and many of our clients bought into his rationale. Now the sector has imploded, and several of them have griped to me about getting burned. Without cramping this young man's enthusiasm, which I find an asset, I need to remind him of the importance of diversification. What's the best way to go about it?

The sensitive way you asked this question shows that you're already aware of the risks of coming across as a know-it-all judgmental authority.

Sometimes the excitement and idealism of the young is a tremendous asset... and sometimes the excitement of pursuing a hot lead can become both blinding and addictive. By talking to your colleague, you'll get a better idea of where he's coming from and how best to proceed.

The classic way to broach this kind of conversation is with a "warm start"—for example, a sincere compliment on his energy and enthusiasm. Then you can move to the area of concern. Without positioning yourself as an infallible authority on market behavior, tell him of your long-term success with diversified portfolios. Impress upon him that you want your firm to have a well-defined investment policy, so that clients know when they sign on what they can expect.

If he's still convinced that sector stocks are the only way to go, you have two choices. Either position him as your "aggressive growth" planner for those clients who can accept the risks, or tell him he needs to find another firm that's more comfortable with his outlook on the market.

A Shoulder to Cry On

A planner in my firm is terribly distraught about an impending divorce. She cries at the drop of a hat, loses her temper often, and wants to talk to me endlessly about her rotten husband, a two-timing spendthrift who is fighting her for custody of the children. I feel for her, but I'm getting burnt out listening. I'm also worried about how her behavior may be affecting our clients. How should I bring this up with her?

Timing is important. Don't risk lashing out at her at a time when you feel exasperated or unable to cope any longer with her neediness.

I would suggest getting together with her in some neutral location, perhaps over lunch. Ask how this misfortune has affected her work in recent weeks. Tell her that you feel for her in her distressing situation, and offer some helpful ideas if you can.

If she responds to your questions and your sympathy, you'll be in a better situation to offer assistance. If possible, you might share anecdotes about how friends or associates in similar situations managed to heal while continuing to function. It may also be appropriate to suggest a support group or professional therapeutic help.

If your colleague persists in deluging you with her grievances (which may well be the case), simply tell her as gently and caringly as you can, "I'm sorry, but can we change the subject and talk about something pleasant for a few minutes? That would help me come back and listen some more." This feedback should alert her to the probability that she's been overwhelming friends, family, and colleagues everywhere with her pain, and that everyone needs a break from so much intense suffering.

If intervening this actively makes you feel uncomfortable, you always can just back off and make excuses about being too busy to talk with her. However, this won't alleviate your concerns about her effect on clients, or give her any support to improve her behavior. Eventually, it may even result in a blowup by you or by her. For my money, gentle, constructive confrontation is better than avoidance and neglect.

Holding on to a Good Associate

A young associate in my planning firm just confided to me that she's never been comfortable with the high stock allocations we typically recommend. The thought of all the value our clients have lost makes her want to switch into a field like career counseling. I think she's a great asset to our firm. How can I persuade her to stay with us?

Before you can begin to change her mind, she has to feel that someone in the firm understands and appreciates her viewpoint. So when you get together with her (ideally in some unstressful location), the first thing is to listen nonjudgmentally to her frustrations about having endorsed an asset allocation she didn't feel comfortable with.

After she's aired these feelings, tell her what you truly value about her contribution to your business. See if she's open to reassessing her role in a way that better suits her values and strengths. For example, you might suggest that she consider expanding her skills to become a life planning coach, creating balanced plans to help your firm's clients realize their dreams and goals. If she's willing to step up to the plate, this "crisis" can become a real opportunity for personal and professional growth.

Here's another possibility: why not ask her to become your in-house risk counselor? She might, for instance, put together seminars about the many faces of risk, educating clients about the scale of gains and losses in past years, and reinforcing such risk management techniques as diversification and dollar-cost averaging. When markets are particularly volatile or overpriced, hers could be the calm voice of reason reminding clients to brace themselves for a rough road ahead. (When Money Plans, a planning firm in Silver Spring, Maryland, warned clients just before a downturn, they responded with gratitude for the alert instead of panicking when the markets plummeted.) By taking on this vital educational role, your colleague would contribute to strengthening client relationships without having to endorse a specific asset allocation.

Leaky Boundaries

I'm concerned about one of the advisors in my financial planning firm. Although he's been with us barely a year, everyone in the office is intimately familiar with all his problems, anxieties, and traumas. I've cautioned him about keeping these personal issues out of conversations with clients, but he says openness is important in building relationships. What do you think?

A difference in personalities may be responsible for at least part of your quandary. If you're an introvert who gets energy from being alone, you may have difficulty empathizing with an extrovert who re-energizes from sharing thoughts and feelings with others.

That said, it sounds as though this advisor may be at an unusually needy place in his life. Have you asked him lately how his work and his life are going?

If he is not overwhelmingly stressed at the moment, he may simply have what I call "leaky boundaries," which means he needs to discriminate more carefully in what he says and to whom. People in this category often just blurt out whatever they're thinking and feeling, regardless of whom they're talking to or what situation they're in.

So when you meet with this fellow, try to start with an understanding of his personality and temperament. If you're gentle and sensitive to his needs, he may more readily accept your advice to choose a few friends or trusted colleagues to confide his troubles to, at times when personal sharing is the order of the day (e.g.

not right before a big client meeting). You might also suggest that sharing one's woes and worries with others can backfire. Inundating a client or colleague with personal information may be a turn-off that results in less professional respect, not in a better relationship.

In general, try to be as constructive as possible in talking with this "leaky" advisor. It's a good idea to start and finish by saying something positive about him (either professionally or personally), so he doesn't feel you're landing on him like a ton of bricks. The message you're delivering is a touchy one, but it's vital for the good of the firm and his future in it.

Missing: One Mentor

My first job is proving to be a big disappointment. I was recruited before graduation by the head of the firm, a wonderful older gentleman who reminded me so much of my grandfather that I liked him at once. But now that I'm actually on board, he always seems too busy to answer questions, give me pointers, or comment on what I'm doing. I thought bosses were supposed to encourage and mentor newcomers, and I'm bewildered by his lack of support. Am I just naive?

Hmm. Let me ask first whether your grandfather was one of your primary authority figures when you were growing up. If so, there's a good chance that your expectations of a boss—the main authority figure at work—may have been modeled on his behavior. If your grandfather was warm, encouraging, and supportive, you may have been expecting your new boss to behave in a very similar way.

If this is the case, your best course of action is to lay those hopes and expectations aside and try to see your new boss in his own light. No matter how earnestly he may have recruited you (and keep in mind that his persuasive powers were probably enhanced by your delight in his apparent resemblance to your grandfather), it sounds as though he is at heart not a warm, mentoring sort of person.

So if you want support, take the initiative. Ask other staff members for their suggestions. Perhaps another senior associate would be willing to serve as a mentor for you, providing the sort of help and support you found at home and expected to have on the job.

However, part of your task should be to "parent yourself" by giving yourself encouragement and reinforcement. Instead of focusing on your feelings of need and deprivation, take time to let in the positive things you do on your job by keeping a list of your good qualities and achievements. This practice can help you rely less on others to keep pumping you up, while making it easier to profit from whatever guidance or help your boss or other mentors do have to offer.

Old Guard vs. New Guard

I've recently joined a planning firm headed by a father and son who couldn't be more different in their approaches. The father is obsessed with staying abreast of all the latest tech-

nology, while the son says the future belongs to planners who are empathetic and responsive to human needs. Who's right? I feel pulled in both directions.

It could be that they're both right. As long as practitioners are honest with themselves (and with their clients) about what services they can provide, I believe there is plenty of room in this business for both sides of the brain.

In the meantime, I would caution you against trying to get on board with someone else's program unless it suits your own capabilities, interests, and appetite for learning. Otherwise you'll feel like a square peg in a round hole, and wind up with doubts about your own calling.

Instead, step back from these two strong influences to look at your own strengths, weaknesses, and preferences. How would you really like to contribute to your clients' financial well-being? Does it delight you to adopt the latest technological advances in your work? Or does your true gift lie in tuning into your clients' needs with sensitivity and insight?

Let your mind run free to imagine what cutting-edge contributions you might be able to make to the future of your profession. Then put these creative ideas to work in your own practice. You'll win, your clients will win—and your father/son team just may expand their worldview.

All in the Family

Our eight-person planning firm ought to be a big happy family, since we've had no turnover in the past 10 years. But it seems to be just the opposite: the longer we work together, the more we squabble and disagree. Is this a case of familiarity breeding contempt, or am I just in the wrong company?

In the therapy work I've done with business owners and associates, I've observed that the more devoted people are to their work and the longer they stay together, the more the business eventually begins to look and feel like a family—in bad ways as well as good. Grudges, hurts, and resentments (both large and small) tend to accumulate. Habitual relationships begin to feel like family dynamics, with interactions among "parents," "siblings," "grandparents," "children," and so on.

You're on the right track with your comment about familiarity. I believe that negative communication habits set in at almost any organization that gets too closed. As Samuel Beckett said in *Waiting for Godot*, "Habit is a great deadener." To further complicate the problem, no one can take accurate stock of their own blind spots when it comes to relationships.

The solution is to breathe some fresh air into the system. I would suggest instituting periodic staff retreats or regular on-site meetings facilitated by an outside expert.

Look for someone who's good at getting people to think differently, perhaps leading off with some outside-the-box exercises to limber up. No matter what topic you go on to address in the meeting (client needs? the future of the business? trends in the industry?), your facilitator can help open up new avenues of communication and creative brainstorming, and bring new life to a system that may have gotten stale. If everyone participates with good will, I think you can expect your firm to begin feeling less like a dysfunctional family and more like an enjoyable place to work.

Father Figure

About six months ago, I joined a practice headed by an authoritarian financial advisor who's old enough to be my father. In fact, he reminds me so much of my dad, a retired Army colonel, that I find I have a hard time standing up to his judgments and voicing my own opinion. My timidity seems to make him even more critical of me. Even while I'm commanding myself to be more assertive, it's sometimes all I can do not to burst into tears. What can I do about this terrible situation?

Take heart: this revival of old family dynamics in the workplace is not as unusual as you may think. Unfortunately, that doesn't make it any less painful.

The first thing you need to do is focus on ways this man is different from your father. Is he taller? Shorter? Thinner? Stouter? Mustached? Balding? Bow-tied? Identify at least one visual cue, and hopefully one or two emotional cues, that will remind you he is not your dad.

Then, to reassert your professionalism with him, consider sending him a crisp, well-written memo outlining the good ideas you were too "regressed" to voice when your old feelings took control of you. (Don't allude to your regression, of course.) To further distance yourself from echoes of the past, why not act boldly? Invite him to lunch and try to find out more about him and his own family.

Although you may still find yourself "getting small" now and then in reaction to his authoritarian style, you'll be building a bridge that allows you to return to your competent-adult self more and more quickly each time. (Good emotional health is when your demons occur less and less often, with less and less intensity—not when they disappear.) As you work on forgiving yourself for your childlike behavior, and keep reminding yourself of your own strengths and your boss's vulnerabilities, you'll find new and better ways to relate to him. As a side benefit, you may find yourself able to enjoy a healthier adult interaction with your father, too.

Dealing with Doomsayers

A colleague in my small financial planning office is a real worrywart. Almost every day he broadcasts doom and gloom about radical changes that may put us out of business (wirehouses taking over the world, the Internet replacing human interaction, insanely complex regulations crippling us all, etc.). It's driving me nuts. How can I help him calm down and buy myself some peace?

To help your colleague learn to relax and stop obsessing about possible dangers, you might try these tactics:

First, find a time to approach him when you're not overly stressed or impatient with his one-note blues. Suggest that the concerns he has been voicing lately are certainly valid, at least in part. But instead of merely bemoaning an unknown future, you think it might be more productive for the two of you to come up with some ideas to help your firm survive whatever storms may come your way. You might make this important get-together a long business lunch, or even an afternoon retreat.

You could also advise your friend to try a centering technique which often works well for worriers: to write down his worries (at the time of day he worries most, if possible), then brainstorm how he would respond if the worst happens. As the last step, he should put this list away and try focusing on the good stuff—his blessings and sources of gratitude, both in work and in life in general.

Consider finding him a copy of the Serenity Prayer that so many 12-step programs rely on. It goes like this: God, grant me the serenity to accept the things I cannot change, courage to change the things I can, and the wisdom to know the difference.

By taking these positive steps, you can help your worrier colleague turn his mind to thoughts and feelings that will nurture his health and well-being... and indirectly yours as well.

The Personal Lives of Bosses

Our firm is headed by a married couple who seem headed for an especially bitter divorce. I'm so upset about this, I'm having trouble sleeping at night. How can I keep this development from affecting me so much?

Did bitter discord between your parents worry and frighten you as a youngster? Or are you, perhaps, in an intimate relationship that's feeling rather shaky these days? In either of these cases, your upset now may be a reflection of that more personal trauma, making you anxiously fear the worst.

If you have a good rapport with either the husband or the wife, you might consider approaching him or her in a relaxed setting, perhaps over lunch or a drink after work. Try to discreetly express your concerns about maintaining a positive atmosphere at work in the midst of the personal emotional pain and trauma the two spouses must be undergoing.

If what you know about both bosses' personalities tells you that this approach won't work, shore up your defenses by getting support from your work "siblings"—especially those whom you find are emotionally sensitive and compassionate, but not as gripped by this marital trauma as you are. If worse comes to worst, you may be in for a difficult period at your workplace. But remember, the situation will eventually resolve itself one way or another, and you'll then be able to resume your productive work life.

When the Heir Apparent Is Junior

After working at the same firm for many years, I'd assumed that I would take over the practice eventually. But now that the boss's retirement is looming, it seems he's planning to pass the business on to his son, who doesn't even have CFP certification. I feel mad enough to quit on the spot. Should I?

I wouldn't advise making any decision of this importance in a state of rage. Instead, I would suggest that you meet with your boss privately (preferably away from work, in a neutral environment where it will be easier to level with him), and tell him exactly how you feel and what you think. Find out what prompted his decision. If you can't imagine working for someone else with less experience and expertise than you have, tell him so.

You might also consider getting together with the son. See if he's willing to carve out a new role in the company for you with a level of authority and financial rewards that would satisfy you.

However, I wouldn't wait for these meetings to take place before beginning to look around for other options. There must be places to work where you would feel more validated and respected—or perhaps this is the push you've needed to start your own business.

Whichever avenue you pursue, try to set aside any feelings of self-pity or vengefulness. Instead, do whatever it takes to shore yourself up with self-respect and self-affirmation. Reach out for the support of friends and colleagues who love and respect you, and who can remind you of your talents and the value you give to them and your clients. Proceed to explore your other work choices, not in panic but slowly and surely, until you have one or two really good alternatives. Then have that meeting (or a second meeting) with your boss to discuss where you are with each another.

If he still insists that his son will take his place and the son won't create an acceptable role for you, be prepared to hand in your resignation and disconnect from this firm. Family loyalties go deep, and sometimes it's impossible to overcome them—even with years of faithful service.

Stealth Mentoring

My firm recently took on a young man fresh out of school. He's bright and very knowledgeable in some areas (perhaps even more so than I am), but in terms of life experience and client skills, he's totally green. I'm willing to share some of the things I've learned in 20 years of advising clients, but he acts like he doesn't need any help or guidance. I hate to see this kid make mistakes that will reflect badly on our firm. How can I get him to accept some coaching?

Arrogance is often a shield for insecurity, you know. To complicate matters further, I suspect that your young colleague feels patronized instead of befriended. If you're secure enough in yourself, start by being big enough to publicly validate this young man's expertise where it does exist. Ask for his opinion now and then in those areas where you believe he excels. Once he feels that you appreciate his strengths, he may be willing to learn from you in a more open-hearted fashion.

A subtle but effective way to coach him could be to work on putting together a team presentation, where he addresses some of the technical issues and you focus on how they'll impact the client's life and goals. This will give him an opportunity to pick up tips from you on client skills, while showcasing his own expertise and, perhaps, giving you the chance to learn something new.

Also, consider asking him whether he has any questions or concerns about his new profession. This may open him up to consciously considering what he could learn from you.

Remember that in our culture, it's common for many men to view human relationships as competitive rather than cooperative. I applaud you for trying to get beyond the traditional one-up, one-down mindset so you can develop a collegial relationship based on trust and respect. If you assume that despite this young man's inexperience, you both have something to learn from one another, you'll lay the groundwork for the best kind of communication and mutual benefit.

Whether Your Skin Is Thick or Thin...

I recently made a client recommendation that I later began to have questions about. To get another viewpoint, I approached a colleague who has been an advisor much longer than I have. But instead of mentoring me in a helpful, positive way, she lit into me with a blowtorch, telling me how off-target my proposal was and what I should have done differently. Maybe she's right, but I came away feeling about two inches tall. I know this woman has a lot to teach younger colleagues like me. Should I tell her how her attitude affected me, or not? And how can I ask other people for support if this is the response I get?

One of the main ways to reduce stress in your worklife is to get good at choosing the colleagues you can trust enough to ask for support, sympathy, constructive criticism, and learning. You don't want someone who will always say "yes," no matter what.

But I think you should ask yourself first if you're so sensitive to any feedback or criticism that almost no one could do it right. If this is the case, you need to do some personal work on strengthening your self-esteem.

If not, try to find colleagues who will help you review your actions and recommendations without making you feel bad about yourself. You might begin by telling your highly critical associate how her comments affected you. If she isn't normally so scathing, your feedback may make a difference in her attitude. If it doesn't, leave her out of the loop when you seek help and support, and look around for other associates to share your worklife with.

Of course, if you decide you should revise the recommendation you made, have the courage to go back to your client and correct your mistake. No one needs to be perfect all the time. In fact, if you like yourself well enough, you know you don't need to be perfect. But it's important for all of us to reflect on our strengths and weaknesses, and work on our defects while building on our strong points. A strong, supportive collegial network can be extremely helpful in this ongoing process of self-improvement.

Money Disagreements

My partners and I are debating how to charge for our services. Several of them have taken the view that commissions are "bad," which I don't necessarily subscribe to. We need a solution which makes sense for us, and which our clients will accept as a fair trade for the value we provide. Any ideas to help us out of this dilemma?

You shouldn't feel you have to follow any sort of party line on compensation. What's important is what works best for your own skills and type of practice.

For example, when I started my own practice many years ago, a great many therapists didn't charge for the first session unless a continuing relationship developed with the client. This never made much sense to me, because one of my greatest assets is the ability to get clients comfortable with the therapy process. Knowing that a first session with me typically had great value (even if the client chose to see someone else or decided to wait a while before entering therapy), I decided to charge more for my intake session than for subsequent appointments. Since I felt comfortable explaining this to clients who asked, it never became an issue.

So if you prefer commissions, or a combination of fees and commissions, stick to your guns. After formulating your position, you might write a brief explanation for your clients and colleagues, outlining why you've chosen to work this way and inviting them to discuss it with you if they wish. You'll clarify your rationale as you put it down on paper, which will help you develop an easy way to explain it face-to-face. It would also be a good idea for your firm to send a letter to all of its clients explaining fee structures for the different partners.

By getting clear on how you're compensated, and comfortable about the services you provide in exchange, you can avoid some of the moralizing around this emotionally charged "fees vs. commissions" issue.

Biting the Hand That Fed You

After working in my uncle's financial planning practice for three years, I left six months ago to join another firm. Although I'm very grateful that he gave me my start in the business (and even asked me to be his baby daughter's godfather), the job change has proved to be as good for me professionally as I had hoped. But whenever I see my uncle now, he either ignores me or reproaches me angrily for leaving him. I'm not sure what I did wrong, but is there a way to patch up this important relationship?

Many people take it personally when someone else severs a relationship with them. These feelings of abandonment and rejection are intensified when a family member is involved, especially if the relationship was fairly close. Since your uncle mentored you (and probably derived great satisfaction from doing it), he must feel a sense of loss. Somewhat irrationally, he believes you bit the hand that fed you.

I don't know how much time you gave him to become adjusted to the idea before you actually left, but your departure obviously still hurts him deeply. At this juncture, it might help salve his wounds about your exit if you write him a long letter expressing your gratitude (in detail!) for everything he shared with you professionally and personally. Praise his care and skill in mentoring you. Point out that just as children of even the best parents need to break away from home to establish their own identity and claim their healthy independence, you felt it was time for you to strike out on your own professionally.

Apologize for any pain he may feel at the suddenness or untimeliness of your leaving. Tell him it was hard for you, too, to leave that comfortable professional "womb" to deal with strangers on your own.

Finally, stress how much the personal connection means to you. Remind him how much you love his child, your godchild, and how deeply you want to be there for her and to be close to him and his family. I would end the letter by asking if he will go to lunch or dinner with you to help restore a relationship you value tremendously.

If this heartfelt communication encourages your uncle to meet you halfway, you'll have made great strides in helping heal the wounds caused by your departure.

Letting Someone Go Gently

In a hurry to handle a surge of business, my partner and I added a third planner to our practice—the worst mistake we've ever made. We seem to argue all the time with the new partner. She's a good planner, but her personality, philosophy, and style just don't fit ours. We've decided we want her to leave, but she's pretty insecure and we don't want to devastate her. What's the best approach?

I think one of you should sit down with the new partner and discuss with her, carefully and gently, the change you want to make. In this case, the difficult message might be best delivered by a woman; but if you and your original partner are both male, the one with stronger people skills should handle the matter.

Be sure to communicate that this is a difference of orientation and temperament, and that no one is "bad" or "wrong." In fact, it's a good idea to mention some of her strengths and the good things you value in working with her. Ask if there is anything the two of you can do to support her as she makes the transition to leave your firm. If you feel her personality is better suited to working on her own, you might ask whether she has thought about running her own business instead of trying to adjust her style and skills to those of an existing partnership.

Emphasize that you want to give her plenty of time to make this transition—at least 60 to 90 days, I would suggest. Only after you've fully communicated the necessity of the change as compassionately as possible, and given her time to react to it, should you meet as a threesome to iron out the details.

If this whole situation feels too emotionally loaded to handle on your own, consider hiring a trained mediator to help you sort out your three-way "business marriage" and move toward an amicable divorce. Bringing outside air into your closed system may help enormously in cooling overheated emotions that can be generated in this kind of split.

But even with this help, expect the rejected partner to feel hurt and angry. It won't be easy for her to deal with being kicked out, especially if she's insecure and has a shaky support system (or none) outside of work. That's why I emphasize the need for gentleness and empathy, no matter how difficult you've found her to work with. Once you've made peace with your decision to ask her to leave, you'll probably feel much less anger and irritation in dealing with her from day to day, and will find it easier to help her get ready to move on.

Knowing When to Leave

Lately, the networking group I've worked with just isn't meeting my needs any more. But when any of the planners in the group try to leave, the others take it personally and do their best to guilt-trip them into staying on. How can I get out of this arrangement with my relationships intact? I still like most of the people in the group and don't want to cut my professional and personal ties with them.

Knowing when to leave, and how to leave well, are important life skills well worth developing. The problem is that many groups function like close-knit families who can't stand to see anyone leave, and whose members take the leaving as a personal betrayal or rejection.

I would try communicating one-to-one over lunch or dinner with the members you feel closest to. Help them understand how your personal priorities are motivating you to want to spend your time doing other things. If you're the kind of person who prefers working alone or in a smaller group, you could explain that this is one reason prompting you to leave. If not, you could share other things happening in your life that are making it feel less right to stay.

A caveat: if something's going on in the group that makes you want to flee, you can choose to stay and fight to turn things around—provided you have the energy and think you'd be supported by other members. But if you don't have the stamina for this struggle, I'd advise you to leave without stirring up the whole group any more than necessary. As you walk out the door, don't fire any parting shots about what's wrong with the setup unless you're willing to risk alienating the entire group as you go.

TAKING ACTION

Once you identify the specific colleagues (and kinds of people) who make you feel energized and accepted, brainstorm ways to increase your contact with them. For example, you might try to benefit more from their expertise by forming a peer group (as therapists often do) to discuss difficult clients in a supportive and creative atmosphere. Or have monthly golf, lunch, or dinner meetings with this small group of valued colleagues to keep your work fresh and less lonely. Think creatively—and let the strengths of others help make you stronger.

YOUR PRACTICE
Getting Support

In these trying times, connecting with family, friends, colleagues, and counselors can be a true source of healing and support—when done at the right time, in the right context, and in the right ways. For ideas to help fine-tune your networking skills, consider the following situations.

Who Will Help the Helper?

Lately, my clients seem to be bringing me more and more of their emotional problems. They expect me to help them find solutions, but I feel overwhelmed trying to handle these sticky situations and charged feelings. What should I do?

You don't have to take this on alone. Get help!

For example, I know a financial planner in Atlanta who has a mental health counselor sit in regularly on client meetings. His clients feel tremendously supported by this collaboration. If you'd rather move emotional issues out of your office, look for a therapist who will meet separately with your more challenging clients.

Planners and therapists/counselors are starting to work together more and more. Sometimes the planner takes the initiative, referring clients with money conflicts for counseling. After some therapeutic help, they return to the planner. In other cases, a financially savvy therapist may take the lead in referring clients to a planner. For instance, I have made referrals to therapeutically-oriented planners whom I trust to help my clients.

Personally, I think these collaborations are the wave of the future. In fact, I'd like to see financial planners' training incorporate more money psychology and investment psychology, to make them more comfortable and skilled in dealing with the "soft side" of their clients' money issues.

The Courage to Confide in Others

My wife is making me write this! As a financial advisor for over 15 years, I'm a take-charge person who has learned to handle just about anything. Lately, though, I find I'm doing a lot of my work on automatic pilot. I'm tired most of the time, yet can't seem to catch up on my sleep at night. I hate to burden you with my problems, but should I be concerned about this? Or am I just getting burned out?

I think it may be time to try sharing your burden, instead of keeping your problems to yourself.

First of all, it's normal to feel somewhat embarrassed, ashamed, or helpless in circumstances like these. The behavior you describe—an inability to control your focus at work—probably doesn't conform to your idealized image of yourself as someone who is in charge of things. You may even be concerned that if others knew of this "failing," they would think less of you or even shun you. The irony is that the only way to resolve the situation is to risk sharing your anxieties with other people and, contrary to your fear, find that you are accepted for who you are.

In the process, you'll learn more about what has really been bothering you. Are you stressed out by your clients' demands since 9/11? (If so, see the chapter on this topic in "Stress and Trauma.") Are you pushing yourself to work long hours when you'd prefer to devote more time to your family or your own creative nourishment? Or does your work itself no longer feel as meaningful to you? These can all be reasons to feel burned out.

Whatever is troubling you, I urge you to take the calculated risk of discussing it in depth with your wife, a good friend, or a discreet colleague. If you don't know anyone suitable to be a confidant, consider visiting a counselor or therapist, where whatever you share will be kept confidential. I can almost guarantee you'll feel a significant lightening of the burden you've been carrying by yourself.

When Spouses Won't Listen

My "therapeutic education" skills seem to work well in the office, but they've been a flop at home. Whenever I try to talk to my husband about his obsessive online trading, my low-key, sensitive approach meets only anger, resistance, and denial from him. What should I do about this?

It's a universal truth that spouses do not want to hear their imperfections pointed out, however sensitively, by their mates. In couples therapy, I can't count the number of times one partner has responded with thoughtful agreement to an observation I've made, only to have the other partner explode in frustration: "I've been telling you that for years! How come you never paid attention when it was me saying it?"

I think the answer is that all of us have intimacy fears and dependency issues. Marriage (or a long-term relationship) is so close that we feel tremendously vulnerable having to admit mistakes or shortcomings to our mate, especially when he or she exposes them.

So by all means, share with your spouse your concern about how his trading is affecting your financial security or your marriage. But despite all your expertise with your clients, don't consider it a personal failure if he won't listen to you. It's unfortunately true that many men find it humiliating to be criticized, gently or not, by a wife, so the fact that you are the one commenting on his potentially addictive behavior may only raise his hackles.

In this case, a third party may be able to help you break the logjam. Suggest that the two of you meet with a couples counselor or a financial professional to discuss your differences. If your husband says he doesn't need counseling, you could always say, "But I do! Please do this for me" (or "for our relationship").

Proceed with caution—but don't give up on resolving this serious issue.

No Man Is an Island

Although I've tried hard to manage my stress levels lately, none of the usual remedies seem to be working. Walking and jogging leave me as tense as ever. When I try to talk things over with my spouse, it just stresses us both. Do I need professional help?

At the best of times, most of us struggle to cope with our worries about health, children, spouses, ex-spouses, jobs, finances, and so on. This everyday tension has been increased exponentially by the stress our nation has experienced lately.

So even though all your tried-and-true methods are good, don't expect them to have an effect overnight. It will take time to stoke the fires of your formerly centered self.

In the meanwhile, don't make the mistake of isolating yourself. Continue to talk about the way you feel. In fact, you should reach out even more to loved ones and friends around you—perhaps even to a spiritual advisor. Consider joining community volunteers who are helping in some way to improve the situation.

There truly is strength in numbers. Whether you connect in person or via the Internet (warm hugs are great, but emails can soothe, too), keep trying to return to reassuring routines, worthwhile work, and meaningful relationships on all levels.

If your stress still doesn't improve, professional counseling may help. But don't jump to the conclusion that this is necessary before patiently exploring alternatives in your own backyard. Getting used to a more tense environment and figuring out ways to heal, connect, and calm yourself will take more time than you may think.

Bridging Generation Gaps

In dealing with inherited wealth in families, I find the intergenerational issues are sometimes so emotionally charged and shrouded in secrecy that I feel way out of my depth. Would it help these clients to open up if I had a therapist sitting in with me? Or should I refer them separately to a therapist before I see them? Or refer them first, then invite the same (or a different) therapist to join us when I get together with them? And by the way, how can I suggest that they need to see a therapist in the first place?

Let's first address how to broach the subject that counseling might help them. I suggest that you think of a gentle way to advise your clients that many families in their position find it difficult to create an open, objective climate where the best decisions can be made. Tell them you know other clients have benefited from working with an expert to resolve their differences and establish more candid communication.

When it comes to coordinating with the therapist, my experience is that you may want to ask your clients for their preferences. Financial planners often send conflicted couples, individuals, and families to me first. After we've worked together for a while, these clients are then ready to return to financial decision-making with their advisor. But if your clients are more comfortable having their psychological expert join them when they meet with you (assuming you can take this level of emotional intensity), it may work very well to do it in tandem.

As you may have already sensed, I believe it's impossible to lead clients to change before their thoughts and feelings are aired and at least somewhat resolved. If you try to push them into action prematurely, you run the risk that they'll bolt, disregard your recommendations, and/or blame you later for goodness knows what perceived errors in judgment or timing. So be patient in giving your clients time to get on the same page with each other—or at least in the same chapter. You'll then be able to guide them in making better decisions about their money.

If you're searching for the right therapist partner, be sure to give yourself a choice by interviewing more than one candidate. You may find one therapist you want to refer to, and another you'd prefer to work with in person. There's no "right" or "wrong" way to establish this collaboration—just trust your instincts and be flexible.

Referring Clients with Addictions

I'm not getting anywhere in helping a client solve his severe spending problem. I think he needs counseling to find out why he can't seem to change his behavior, but how do I find the right therapist to send him to? If I find someone he's willing to see, will the therapist expect to consult me on the phone about him?

You're right that overspending can be a serious addiction calling for professional help. In fact, some psychiatrists are treating difficult cases with the same medication used for obsessive-compulsive disorder.

To begin with, tell your client frankly that you think he should seek support to change his deeply ingrained spending behavior. You might refer him to Debtors Anonymous, a free 12-step program for chronic overspenders with chapters in most U.S. towns and cities (www.debtorsanonymous.org).

I'd also suggest that you check with friends and colleagues (or even look in the Yellow Pages) to find therapists who specialize in treating addictions such as drinking, smoking, overeating, or gambling. Interview them, ideally in person, to see if they're comfortable dealing with money issues (many therapists aren't). If the answer is yes, consider referring your client to this expert.

How the two of you interact once your client has begun counseling depends mostly on the therapist's preferred approach. Some will gladly talk with you; others won't. If they do, most therapists feel it's both ethical and respectful to get the client's written permission before you agree to confer.

Offering Your Clients New Insight

I read everything I can find about the "psychology of money," and would like to educate my clients about some of the emotional questions you address. What's the best way to introduce these psychological issues?

One way to show your interest in keeping your clients informed is to invite a money psychology expert (we're a small group, but we're active) to speak to them during a seminar or client appreciation dinner. These meetings tend to be entertaining, informative, and productive. Your clients will feel well taken care of and will probably appreciate your gentle nudging to consider their own blind spots, fears, and irrationalities, so they can be more receptive to rational financial decision-making.

You might also considering sponsoring a community-wide financial workshop with yourself and a money psychology expert as co-presenters. This would allow you to communicate to a broader audience your special interest in integrating the psychological and practical aspects of money management.

Another possibility is to send your clients a good book, audiocassette, or video on money psychology. (See Additional Resources for some suggestions.) A gift like this could be tied in with the holidays, as a way to help start the new year on a better financial footing.

By the way, it's great that you're tuned to the underlying issues many clients must grapple with before they can take charge of their money in a healthy, balanced way. That's what "money harmony" is all about!

When "Therapy" Is a Four-Letter Word

If I had a dollar for every time I've wanted to have a therapist with me in the office, or to refer a client to one, I could probably afford to quit my practice! My problem is that so many people get nervous about the idea of "therapy." Is there a way to deal with this?

Instead of therapy, call it counseling (which it is). Or you might say you know an expert who is skilled in helping individuals—or couples or families, whatever the case may be—deal with the kinds of issues or problems your clients are facing. Tell them stories about others this expert has helped.

If and when you need to spell out that this consultant is a therapist, consider sharing an anecdote or two about similar situations where therapists have been helpful. Reassure your clients that seeking counseling simply means they're looking for expert help to be able to make more rational life decisions. If necessary, be willing to discuss the stigma our self-starter culture attaches to the word "therapy," and point out that it's high time people felt free to get the help they need from trained professionals without feeling ashamed or inadequate. In fact, you might even say you think it's a sign of courage and intelligence to get help when it's needed. The point is, your willingness to talk clients through their resistance to counseling can work well, as long as you yourself don't think it's a sign of weakness for someone to need therapy in resolving their problems.

Rare is the financial advisor who can't benefit from finding new and effective ways to harness the tools of therapy and money psychology. Knowing you can rely on a therapy professional to help your clients work through their fears and blocks, you'll feel much less overwhelmed when clients with problems enter your practice. Moreover, I believe you'll find yourself able to respond much more effectively to meet these clients' deeper needs.

When You're Parting Company

My five-year-old partnership is about to come to an ugly halt. My colleague and I disagree more and more about everything—the direction our business should be taking, what kind of clients we want, how we should charge. We've decided to split up, but we can't even agree on how to divide our business. Is there such a thing as a business divorce counselor who could help us break up more amicably?

When people don't see eye to eye and don't have a good way to work out their differences, long-standing business relationships often take on the same characteristics as unhappy marriages or dysfunctional families. In fact, I would view your partnership as a kind of work marriage.

Many couples therapists are beginning to counsel unhappy work couples like you and your partner. It's sometimes impossible to give a relationship respectful closure without a little help. Support from a therapist or mediator can make it much easier to reach decisions about ending your partnership that both of you will be able to live with.

You're certainly not the only one who's ever needed help with a situation like this, so don't feel bad about it. Instead, give yourself some credit for being open to professional assistance that will help your partnership dissolve with less recrimination, wounding, and ongoing tension. Seeking a therapist's support is also sensible preventive care. If taking on a partner ever seems to make sense in the future, you don't want to be so terribly scarred by this breakup that you're too traumatized to ever again work with someone else.

To find the right "business divorce counselor," ask friends and trusted colleagues if they know of anyone. Some business coaches specialize in couples or dyads in business together. (See Additional Resources if you need referral info.) Perhaps both of you should interview recommended candidates. If you can't agree, you may have to draw lots to see which of you will choose the therapist—although I hope it won't come to that.

Having been through a divorce of my own (personal, not professional), I can testify to the benefit of working with a couples therapist first, and then a mediator. In my case, the collaboration bore fruit in the form of a long-lasting friendship between my former partner and me, who still work together to raise our wonderful son.

Help for a Troubled Friend

I've been friends with a certain colleague for a long time. His home life has been rocky in the past year or so, and he's developed a drinking problem which is beginning to seriously affect his job performance. I'm afraid that if I don't keep covering for him he'll get fired, but I'm becoming more and more frustrated and resentful because he doesn't seem interested in cleaning up his act. Is there a solution to this apparently hopeless situation?

Your loyalty to this co-worker certainly goes above and beyond the call of duty. In fact, I wonder if you're replaying a long-ago drama in which you rescued (or tried to rescue) a similarly dysfunctional member of your family—a sibling, perhaps, or a parent you tried to cover for and protect? If so, you're particularly susceptible to this kind of "enabling" behavior.

That's all the more reason to sit down with your friend and level with him. If he doesn't stop drinking and get help, tell him that you won't keep protecting him. This allows you to set healthier limits for yourself without walking away from your desire to help your friend. Even if he's furious with you at first, try to get him to start on the road to recovery through Alcoholics Anonymous or a therapist specializing in addictive behavior. Otherwise, you'll only exhaust yourself if you keep trying to protect him. Worse yet, you run the risk that his deteriorating behavior may drag you and the whole firm down with him.

I hope your friend is courageous enough to admit he has a problem and get help with it. If not, as painful as it may feel, you need to stop covering for him. You—and the others in your firm—don't deserve to drown with him.

Will a Referral Leave You Liable?

After trying in vain to make progress with a very difficult couple, I've finally recommended that they seek therapy together. I referred them to several counselors who were highly recommended to me, but now I fear that if the therapy fails, they might come back and hit me with a lawsuit. Is this a reasonable concern? And if so, how can I protect myself?

In this litigious world, one can be sued about almost anything by almost anybody. So my first suggestion is to consult your insurance expert (if you haven't already) to see if errors and omissions insurance will protect you.

However, be sure to balance healthy self-defense with your desire to serve your clients well. You don't want to become so terrified that you'll freeze up instead of giving them well-thought-out advice. If you get too uptight about the risks, you'll end up not being much help at all.

On the specific issue of referrals, I would recommend giving clients a written list of specialists, with a disclaimer on the same page absolving you from responsibility if they're unhappy with the outcome.

Though the goodwill you've established can't shield you from an ungrateful, unbalanced individual, it should encourage you to continue putting your clients' needs first in the planning and advisory process. But check with your insurance professional too, to see if you can make yourself safer financially.

Taking Action

These days, the process of reaching out, connecting, and sharing can be a tremendously important source of reassurance and self-renewal for yourself, and for your clients as well. This kind of contact helps make it possible to move from a place of fear and anxiety toward trust and serenity—a shift that can make your worklife more productive and your personal life more fulfilling.

Afterword

Thanks for taking this journey toward what I call "money harmony." Now that you've deepened your understanding of this varied and interesting terrain, you have many of the tools you need to forge more solid relationships with even the most difficult clients. With your knowledge of money psychology, you will be a better listener, a more compassionate and patient partner in financial decision-making, and (if you so choose) a better and more creative life planner.

If you want to hone your skills and insights further, don't hesitate to let me know. I make it a priority to respond quickly to advisors' emails and phone calls, and I welcome invitations to help you educate your clients about money psychology and conflict resolution at seminars or appreciation events.

Even if our paths don't cross directly, consider re-reading sections of this book that are relevant to your individual needs. A deeper understanding of money psychology will lead to more fulfillment in your work and better lines of support between you and your colleagues, while serving as an antidote to burnout. In particular, the chapter on "Walking Your Talk" will help you align the way you live your life with your values and the wisdom you impart to your clients. This, in turn, will bring you more serenity and satisfaction in every part of your life.

I hope you and your clients enjoy the journey toward money harmony – and other kinds of harmony as well. If you have any questions or concerns, please feel free to e-mail me at om@moneyharmony.com, or, for more resources, visit my Web site, www.moneyharmony.com.

Additional Resources

WOMEN AND MONEY

- Many women can benefit from communications tailored specifically to their needs. *Money Shy to Money Sure* (Olivia Mellan and Sherry Christie, Walker & Co., 2001) is organized around the seven myths women often need to debunk to take charge of their money, and offers concrete steps to financial empowerment to women of all ages.

- Barbara Stanny's *Prince Charming Isn't Coming: How Women Get Smart About Money* (Penguin USA, 1999) shares her own journey, from losing all her money in a disastrous marriage to learning about personal finance, and then helping other women take charge of their money.

- In *Secrets of Six-Figure Women: Surprising Strategies to Up Your Earnings and Change Your Life* (HarperCollins, 2002), Barbara Stanny helps outline the defining characteristics connected to self esteem and self-confidence and other qualities that help create financial success.

- *The Money Mystique: A Woman's Guide to Achieving Lifetime Financial Confidence* (New Harbinger Publications, 2001) is a great resource from Karen Sheridan, a money manager and consultant who is wonderfully attuned to money psychology.

OVERSPENDING

- In *Slash Your Debt: Save Money and Secure Your Future* (Financial Literacy Center, 1999), authors Gerri Detweiler, Marc Eisenson, and Nancy Castleman show how to develop a personalized money plan that will free up more money for savings.

- *Maxing Out: Why Women Sabotage Their Financial Security* (Little Brown & Co., 1998), by Colette Dowling, is a recovering overspender's vulnerable account of her recovery with the help of Debtors Anonymous and other resources.

- Mary Hunt's *Debt-Proof Living* (Broadman & Holman, 1999), along with her newsletter, The Cheapskate Monthly, offer useful information for spenders who want to embrace creative frugality.

- For insights into the world of excessive spenders, consider *Overcoming Overspending: A Winning Plan for Spenders and their Partners* (Olivia Mellan with Sherry Christie, Walker & Co., 1997). It offers valuable tools for "recovering overspenders" in couples relationships, as well as individuals.

COUPLES AND MONEY

- "In the Prime: Couples and Money, with Olivia Mellan" (available via www.moneyharmony.com or 202-483-2660, ext. 4, is a 43-minute video presentation to a financial planner audience about money personalities, couples polarization patterns, and ways to resolve money conflicts.

- Money personalities and other keys to understanding financial behavior are introduced in *Money Harmony: Resolving Money Conflicts In Your Life and Your Relationships*, by Olivia Mellan, available in paperback (Walker & Co., 1995) or in hardcover as *Your Money Style: The Nine Attitudes to Money and How They Affect Happiness, Love, Work and Family* (MFS Communications, 2000).

- You'll find excellent emotional and practical solutions for partners in *Couples and Money: A Couples' Guide Updated for the New Millennium* (Gabriel Books, 1998) by Victoria Collins, CFP, who is also a psychologist.

DIVORCE AND MONEY

- *Financial Custody: You, Your Money, and Divorce* (Alpha Books, 2001), by Joan Coullahan, CDP, CFP, and Sue van der Linden, CFP, offers practical and psychological tips for dealing with divorce issues.

- One of the best references on this topic is *Divorce and Money: How to Make the Best Financial Decisions During Divorce* (Nolo Press, 2002) by Victoria Collins and Violet Woodhouse.

- For another good resource that focuses specifically on women's needs and concerns, I would suggest Patricia Phillips' *Divorce: A Woman's Guide to Getting a Fair Share* (Arco Press, 1995).

MONEY AND VALUES

- George Kinder's *The Seven Stages of Money Maturity: Understanding the Spirit and Value of Money In Your Life* (Dell Books, 2000) offers an excellent exploration of the psychological and spiritual stages of evolution from "innocence" to "aloha."

- *Everything You Know About Money Is Wrong: Overcome the Financial Myths Keeping You from the Life You Want* (Regan Books, 1999) is a fine resource from Karen Ramsey, CFP, who brings a spiritual and psychological dimension to her advice.

- Richard E. Vodra's *Enough Money* (Xlibris, 2001) is a superbly common sense guide from a Certified Financial Planner who knows how to get to the heart of financial serenity.

- In March 2003, look for a new video series titled "*Living with Money,*" sponsored by the Episcopal Media Center in Atlanta. The purpose of these videos is to explore and define the role and meaning of money in society and in their personal and spiritual lives, and assists participants in achieving a healthy, balanced money life. It features discussions with financial planners, clergymen, Vicki Robin (*Your Money or Your Life* co-author), and me, among others. They will be available through www.episcopalmedia.org, or 800-229-3788.

CHILDREN AND MONEY

- *Dollars & Sense for Kids* (Kiplinger Books, 1999) by Janet Bodnar (*Kiplinger's* "Dr. Tightwad") is great, and great fun.

- *Simple Ways to Help Your Kids Become Dollar-Smart* (Walker & Co., 1994), by Elizabeth Lewin and Bernard Ryan, Jr., suggests age-appropriate ways to help children learn the value of money and how to use it wisely.

- The National Council on Economic Education (www.ncee.net) has published an interesting series of workbooks, including these three in the Financial Fitness for Life series: *Steps to Financial Fitness: Student Workouts Grades 3-5*; *Shaping Up your Financial Future, Student Workouts, Grades 6-8*; and *Talking to Your Kids about Personal Finance, Grades 6-12: An Activity-Based Guide for Parents*.

- If you're looking for a good resource to help new graduates launch themselves into the world of work and money, consider *Life After Graduation: Financial Advice & Money Saving Tips*, by Terry Arndt and John Ricchini. For info call 877-569-9816, or email info@LifeAfterGraduation.com.

WEALTH ISSUES

- More Than Money is a nationwide network of more than a thousand people exploring the intelligent and compassionate use of personal wealth. They offer a subscription to a quarterly journal, individual coaching, an annually updated resource guide, conferences, and workshops. Topics

- include: money and relationships, family, investing, philanthropy, work, and more. More Than Money, 226 Massachusetts Ave., #4, Arlington, MA 02474: www.morethanmoney.org or 781-648-0776.

- The Inheritance Project has published three books and seven booklets (including *Working with Inherited Wealth Clients: A Guide for Professional Advisors*) about the emotional and social challenges and opportunities of inherited wealth. These publications can be ordered via www.inheritance-project.com. Estate planning is a topic that often makes clients feel anxious or intimidated. For a book on this topic that does a fine job of incorporating the psychology of money issues, I would refer you to *Best Intentions: Ensuring Your Estate Plan Delivers Both Wealth and Wisdom* (Dearborn, 2002), by Colleen Barney, Esq., and Victoria Collins, Ph.D, CFP.

BEHAVIORAL FINANCE

- If you're not already familiar with it, definitely put on your reading list *Why Smart People Make Big Money Mistakes--and How to Correct Them: Lessons from the New Science of Behavioral Economics* (Simon & Schuster, 1999) by Gary Belsky and Thomas Gilovich.

STRESS AND TRAUMA

- For working with children of all ages (and many adults as well), I highly recommend "Remembering September 11, 2001: A Manual for Caregivers," prepared by the Christian Children's Fund (www.ChristianChildrensFund.org or 800-776-6767).

THERAPY AND COUNSELING RESOURCES

I would begin the search for good therapists in your area by seeking word-of-mouth recommendations. If you don't have any luck, here are other places to find help:

- American Academy of Experts in Traumatic Stress (www.aaets.org). A multidisciplinary network of professionals committed to the advancement of intervention for survivors of trauma. AAETS has members in every state and over 40 foreign countries.

- American Association for Geriatric Psychiatry (www.aagpgpa.org). A national organization dedicated to promoting the mental health and well-being of older people and improving the care of those with late-life mental disorders.

- American Association for Marriage and Family Therapy (www.aamft.org). For a list of marriage and family therapy practitioners in your area, call 202-452-0109.

- American Counseling Association (www.counseling.org). Has general information that may help you locate a counselor in your area.

- American Mental Health Counselors Association (www.amhca.org). This national organization can help you find a mental health counselor in your area.

- American Psychiatric Association (www.psych.org). Has 38,000 U.S. and international member physicians with the goal of ensuring humane care and effective treatment for all persons with mental disorders, including mental retardation and substance-related disorders. If you need a psychiatrist who can prescribe medication as well as do therapy, and you can't find personal referrals, this may be the place to start.

- American Psychological Association (www.apa.org). Promotes research and represents the professional interests of psychologists in the U.S. Includes a "find-a-psychologist" referral feature.

- Eye Movement Desensitization and Reprocessing International Association (www.emdria.org). EMDR treatment works with emotional distress arising from difficult childhood experiences, or recovery from the effects of traumatic incidents, such as auto accidents, assault, natural disasters, or combat trauma. A very effective short-term treatment for many kinds of stress and trauma.

- National Association of Social Workers (www.naswdc.org). Among the members of this organization are clinical social workers, who do therapy and counseling. To find a social worker in your community, e-mail bprather@naswdc.org.

- National Counseling Intervention Services (www.interventioninfo.org). To help a family member who is in denial or resistant to getting help with a serious addiction, call 800-279-3321 for a list of qualified interventionists, or check the Intervention Resource Center Web site shown above.

"TWELVE-STEP" PROGRAMS

These free programs help people recover from addictions of various kinds. They include:
- Debtors Anonymous (www.debtorsanonymous.org): 781-453-2743.
- Alcoholics Anonymous (www.alcoholics-anonymous.org): check your Yellow Pages for local phone numbers.
- Gamblers Anonymous (www.gamblersanonymous.org): 213-386-8789.

- Overeaters Anonymous (www.overeatersanonymous.org): 505-891-4320.

- Sexaholics Anonymous (www.sa.org), a fellowship of men and women who share their experience, strength, and hope that they may solve their common problem and help others to recover.

- Sex and Love Addicts Anonymous (www.slaafws.org), a self-help fellowship open to adults who suffer from a compulsive need for sex or have a desperate attachment to one person.

- ACOA (www.adultchildren.org): 310-534-1815. ACOA stands for Adult Children of Alcoholics, but many members' spouses or parents are other kinds of addicts.

MONEY THERAPISTS AND MONEY COACHES

This is a very partial list of mental health counselors who work with financial planners:

- Margo Geller, 2987 Clairmont Road, Suite 400, Atlanta, Georgia 30329. Email: margo.geller@gvfinancial.com, or 404-601-5711. Geller is a money therapist who works directly with financial planners and their clients.

- Lynne Hornyak, 1301 20th St. NW, Washington, DC 20036. Email: Lynne@WealthHealthy.com, or 202-387-5923. Hornyak is primarily a money coach and often is a "virtual coach," communicating online with her clients.

- Olivia Mellan, Olivia Mellan & Associates, Inc., 2607 Connecticut Avenue, NW, Washington, DC 20008-1522. Email:om@moneyharmony.com, or 202 483 2660, ext. 4. Mellan is a money coach and money therapist, these days doing more and more coaching and less and less therapy.

FAMILY BUSINESS EXPERTS

- Judy G. Barber, Family Business Consultant and Mediator, One Embarcadero Center, Suite 4100, San Francisco, CA 94111. Email: judgb@aol.com, or 415-673-0689

- Marty Carter, Charles D. Haines LLC, 600 University Park Place, Suite 501, Birmingham, AL 35209. Email:marty.carter@charlesdhaines.com, or 205-871-3334.